Wishing you all the best!

With warmest regards,

Steve Shallabarger

Get your FREE motivational poster!

Follow these simple instructions:

1. Visit www.BecomingYourBest.com and click on "store."
2. There are different motivational posters for each Guiding Constant. Choose the one you want.
3. Send an email to Support@BecomingYourBest.com with your Name and Shipping Address and poster choice.
4. We'll ship the 11 x 14 size poster for free within 1 - 3 business days. Enjoy your free gift!

Steven R. Shallenberger

www.BecomingYourBest.com

Praise for *Becoming Your Best*

"I can say with confidence that the principles taught in this groundbreaking book, *Becoming Your Best,* will provide you a fool proof roadmap on how to excel in life. Whether you're interested in becoming the best coach, athlete, spouse, parent or the best in your career, you need look no further than applying what is taught in *Becoming Your Best.*"

— Dallin Larsen, Founder and Chairman, MonaVie

"*Becoming your Best* is a very special book indeed. Steve masterfully teaches how to blend all of the variables that you control, with eternal principles of success. He also helps people to see that they can control vastly more variables than they would ever believe. I believe this book will positively change who you become. It will make you more successful in any pursuit but more importantly, it will help turn you into the person you might otherwise only dream of becoming. I think that anyone who reads this and incorporates the teachings, will like themselves better and deservedly so because, they will become their best. Steve is a walking success story of his teachings. He is one of the most impressive people I have ever met. What a treasure to be able to learn from him."

— Blake Roney, Founder and Chairman, Nu Skin

"I have a few books on my shelves that have deepened my appreciation of profound principles of life. I have many that articulate strategies and tools that lead to greater results in many domains. But I own precious few that excel at both. Shallenberger not only invites careful thought about first principles, but offers generous wisdom from a lifetime of experience to make them live in your life. This is not a book to *read.* It is a book to *live.*"

— Joseph Grenny, co-author of *Influencer: The New Science of Leading Change and Crucial Conversations: Tools for Talking When Stakes are High.*

"Steve Shallenberger has been an inspiring leader in several companies and three different industries, while at the same time being highly sought after as a guide to others through their own business and personal development. *Becoming Your Best* is the distillation of that lifetime of experience into a set of clear, timeless principles from which all of us can learn how to develop and sustain excellence. *It's the most valuable time you will spend with a book this year!*"

— Randal Quarles, Managing Director, The Carlyle Group and
former Under Secretary of the U.S. Treasury

"If you're motivated to improve, don't put down this book until you've read every page. Whatever your profession or background, *Becoming Your Best* provides a masterful approach. It's filled with real-life, inspirational stories as well as powerful tools that an individual, family, or organization can immediately implement."

— Jack Canfield, Co-Author of *The Success Principles*
and *Chicken Soup for the Soul*®

"A fascinating book on understanding and improving one's personal balance, one's relationships and one's leadership and management success. I wish I could have had this book when I started my Air Force career in 1970! Steve Shallenberger's research, timeless stories and delightful writing style, make this a book you'll want to refer to for the rest of your life—I know I will! Enjoy."

— Gregory "Speedy" Martin, General, USAF (Retired)

"A must read for anyone looking to lead themselves and others through a transformation of success in life, family, and business. This is one of those books that I will pass down to my son in hopes that he will adapt Steve's 13 Guiding Constants to becoming your best! Required reading for anyone who strives for excellence."

— James D. Murphy, Author of *Flawless Execution* and
Founder/CEO Afterburner, Inc.

“Our greatest friend Steve Shallenberger is a positive influence on everyone he meets. He’s distilled the principles which have steered his own life into *Becoming Your Best.*”

— Richard and Linda Eyre,
New York Times #1 Bestselling Authors

“*Becoming Your Best* is a fun and inspiring book to read. It provides simple, yet compelling, strategies to dramatically improve your effectiveness, level of accomplishment and personal satisfaction in the way you go about doing it. I highly recommend *Becoming Your Best* for corporate leaders!”

— Bob Marquardt, President, Management & Training Corporation

I’ve worked with thousands of speakers who have amazing ideas. Steve and his team have developed something powerful in *Becoming Your Best.* Every person, family, or organization needs to attend a live *Becoming Your Best* event and read this book. It’s a game changer!”

— James Malinchak, Featured on ABCs Hit TV Show
“Secret Millionaire”, Founder, www.BigMoneySpeaker.com

“Performing a leading role in The Phantom of the Opera demanded my best every single night, so I’ve been committed to personal and professional development for many years. Becoming Your Best offers a unique step-bys-tep process that will teach you how to give a Broadway-caliber performance in your life and business!”

— Sandra Joseph, Broadway star of “The Phantom of the Opera” and
co-author of *Your Creative Soul: Expressing Your Authentic Voice*

"As an author and leading authority of motivation and positive self-talk, I can attest that *Becoming Your Best* teaches something powerful. It can benefit any individual or organization! Many people talk about ways to improve, but the team at *Becoming Your Best* is unique because they actually provide an organized blueprint to help anyone achieve their best. *Becoming Your Best* is not only motivational and inspirational, but they give you the specifics on how to take action!"

— Michal Y. Noah, PhD and author of renowned children's book: *A - Z The Universe in Me*

"I've What is offered in *Becoming Your Best* is a powerful and simple approach. It's obvious Steve has taken years of research and effort and provided a one-stop solution. The unique approach taught in Becoming Your Best can be used by an individual, family, or an organization. I invite you to feel the power of *Becoming Your Best!*"

— Anson Dorrance, Women's Soccer Coach, North Carolina, 22 Time Collegiate National Champion

"*Becoming Your Best* has made such an amazing difference in my life and the lives of all the associates I work with. It is a system that is invaluable and has such a profound impact in so many areas in my professional and personal life. I use this system with my office staff continously and they are always amazed at the results. The 13 Guiding Cosntants are a way of life for me and by using them on a daily basis, they have brought me a life of happiness and joy!"

— Julie Richardson, CEO, Energy Efficiency Inc.

Becoming Your Best

Published by
Eagle Systems International

Manufactured in the United States of America, or in the United Kingdom when distributed elsewhere.

Second Printing: 2013

Shallenberger, Steven
Becoming Your Best: The Competitive Edge
ISBN: 978-0-9888459-1-6

www.BecomingYourBest.com

To my extraordinary wife Roxanne

ACKNOWLEDGEMENTS

I AM FOREVER INDEBTED to remarkable mentors and advisors who have deeply touched my life: Cal Clark, David Conger, Stephen R. Covey, Robert K. Dellenbach, William N. Jones, Thomas S. Monson, Gardner H. Russell, Lael J. Woodbury, and all of those who have had a powerful influence for good. May I pass it along!

David C. Clark, my business partner, who has been ever encouraging and supportive. To my extraordinary friends at Synergy Companies. YOU are among the best! I appreciate the years of experience with my friends at Eagle Systems International and Covey Leadership. You continue to change the world for good.

To my Harvard CAN Group, and Young President's-World President's Organization forum members, friends and associates. The Inkling's Groups—Rick and Linda Eyre, Kathy Clayton, Jerry Johnson, and Barry Rellaford. Thank you for invaluable perspectives and recommendations.

To my friends and associates at the Utility companies, and in the Energy Services Industry, who continue to work on world class services.

I am grateful for my family and extended family members (Humpherys, Quarles, and Shallenbergers), including my ancestors, grandparents, and parents. Thanks Mom!

I will be forever grateful for the encouragement, brain trust, and writing ideas of my friend, John Wilkinson. Without John's help, I may not have been able to launch my thoughts into a book.

To Rob, Dave, Steven, Tom, Daniel, Anne and their spouses! Rob, thanks for your wise counsel and tireless drive. To each of the children, and Roxanne—you have had such a huge impact on my life.

I appreciate the creative talent and dedicated efforts of Barbara Quittner. Also, to the scores of individuals who reviewed the manuscript and offered such valuable recommendations and encouragement, including but not limited to: Natalie Anderson, Erin Bakke, Karilyn Carreon, Stephen M.R. Covey, Winn Egan, Angela Eschler, Andrew Gibbons, Wynn Hemmert, Kathy Jenkins, Greg Link, Steven McCarty, Dave Wayt, and Ben Welch.

To Joseph Grenny and Kevin Small, for their seasoned advice and Rebecca Merrill for sharing her years of experience.

CONTENTS

FOREWORD
by Stephen R. Covey

Some books stand out like a beacon in a storm. Such books help you realize that as you focus on the things you can control, you can be a stronger and more capable individual, you can have stronger and healthier relationships, and you can create excellence in your organization. Such books can also be powerful catalysts for helping you make major breakthroughs in effectiveness and in reaching your potential.

Becoming Your Best is just such a book.

Have you ever felt you could improve in certain areas of your life—and that such improvement could have a significant impact on your personal effectiveness and happiness? Have you ever felt you could do better in your relationships? *Becoming Your Best* is about helping to build strong individuals, strong relationships, and strong leadership and management. It contains powerful principles and tools that can help anyone become the best they can be. The world needs strong, principle-centered individuals with strong relationships and strong leadership and management skills, and *Becoming Your Best* will help you become one of these people!

I believe this for two reasons.

First, I have known and watched Steve Shallenberger for more than thirty-five years. I know him to be a principle-centered individual who has touched tens of thousands of lives for good.

I have often felt that I teach the principles of "highly effective people" and that Steve puts them into practice. He knows what it is like to begin with the end in mind and to put first things first. He understands that a highly effective person has to achieve a private victory before he or she can achieve a public victory. He knows firsthand how to reach "third alternatives" through listening empathically and working toward win-win solutions. Most of all, he cares for other people and is dedicated to lifting and building. I admire these attributes and want to read and listen to an author who actually lives these principles through both adversity and success in his personal life.

Steve has led numerous organizations and companies, both public and private. These entities have achieved a sustained excellence for decades, employing thousands of people in the printing industry, energy services industry, and leadership and self-improvement industries. Steve has been active in the Young Presidents and World Presidents organizations, both of which are dedicated to the education and success of chief executive officers. These extraordinary organizations have given Steve exposure to some of the best leadership and management practices around the world.

Second, *Becoming Your Best* is not a flavor-of-the-month type of book. It contains time-proven principles on how to achieve your fullest potential, how to create innovative and imaginative solutions, and how to find peace and balance in a chaotic and turbulent world.

This is a practical book that deals with threats, opportunities, and challenges at the street level. It is not a hypothetical book; it is a book full of inspirational stories and examples of how to work through real-life challenges as you make the good better and the better best.

I am deeply impressed with this book because it reminds us that the best still lies in front of us and that we can each achieve the best within us. *Becoming Your Best* teaches how to recognize and think through the obstacles that prevent us from realizing our dreams, hopes, and desires. It clearly shows us how to turn those obstacles into a proactive plan to achieve a sustainable positive result. Simply, the principles in this book lead to the realization of hopes and dreams.

Becoming Your Best is a way of thinking that can change lives and organizations for good. It is a book of possibilities and hope for all, regardless of age, nationality, or circumstances. It is a book of encouragement, vision, and solutions.

Regardless of your title or position—whether you are a president, parent, coach, leader-manager, administrator, technician, mechanic, professional, farmer-rancher, civil servant, soldier, teacher, team member, employee, or the leader of a country—*Becoming Your Best* will inspire and lead you to greater heights.

With its deep inside-out approach, *Becoming Your Best* will help you *do* what I teach. It will help develop and strengthen the foundation of the best that "can be" in your life and in your associations with others. I highly commend this book, and I wish you a grand experience on the journey of becoming your best.

Stephen R. Covey

Introduction

The 13 Guiding Constants and the Becoming Your Best Blueprint

YEARS AGO, when I was fresh out of college, I managed 300 employees and wanted to find a way to inspire and lead them. I started searching for a common denominator of success that might be found in all successful people and organizations. I thought to myself, *If there was a common denominator of success and if I could teach it to our employees, what would that do for our company?* This question started a journey of research to identify the factors of success or traits that set apart peak-performing people and organizations.

After 40 years of intensive research, my team and I have indeed identified a common denominator of success. In other words, a set of traits and factors of success that are found over and over in successful people and organizations. I've narrowed that list down to 13 of the most critical factors and I call those "Guiding Constants".

In the process of identifying the 13 Guiding Constants and looking for the common denominator of success, I came across many types of people, especially people who appeared to be successful from an outward appearance. These same people oftentimes found themselves struggling with an inner desire to achieve a greater sense of personal peace, effectiveness and meaning, and maintain happy and productive relationships.

Years ago, I was initially surprised by some of the comments I would hear from "successful people", until it became apparent that every person has their own set of challenges and struggles. I began to realize that our challenges come in every shape and size and oftentimes there are similarities to many of our challenges. Do any of these "real comments" sound familiar?

I feel like I am on an endless treadmill! Emails, telephone calls, messages, high pressure projects with deadlines now, and absolutely no end in sight. How can I get better organized and be a more effective time manager to get control of this situation?

I supervise many people within my organization. How can I bring out the best in each person? I realize that as each member of our team or family grows and is at the top of their game, our organization has a better chance of being at the top of its game.

A CEO shared, *I just had the best year ever in our company, but I got divorced during the year. Was my best year ever in business really worth the cost in terms of what happened in my personal life?*

Our company has been #1 in our industry for years, how do we avoid complacency and stay #1?

I feel like I can contribute more at work--I feel under-employed. How can I become one of the most valued employees and feel like I am giving my best, regardless of the circumstances I feel like I am in?

I have a strained relationship with my children--I don't even talk with one of my sons anymore. How can I restore these important relationships?

My relationship with my wife is on the rocks. She informed me that she wants a divorce and doesn't really love me anymore. I am so discouraged.

I am an entrepreneur having a difficult time making payment every Friday. On Monday, all that I can think about is how do I get the money for Friday again. I am getting worn out. How do I get things on track or get out of this mess?

I have been trying to quit smoking for 30 years. I have tried at least 10 different times. How do I stop smoking?

I am so busy with everything and everyone else in my life--I'm not taking care of myself. I feel like I give, give, give and I have nothing left for me. I have let myself get out of shape and it is starting to affect me physically and emotionally. How can I find balance in life?

I am concerned about who my teenage children are hanging out with. They look like total flakes. I realize how crucial this time in life is to help keep them on a solid pathway for a productive and happy life. How do I handle this without taking control of their lives?

I've lost everything! My job, my husband, and my home. Where do I go from here?

I am addicted to prescription drugs. I am buying prescriptive drugs under the table illegally. Nobody really knows. I am not the person I used to be. My family suspects drugs and has called a family meeting to talk about it. I fell down the stairs the other day and my children had to help me to my room. The spark has gone out of life. What do I do? Help!

I have had a wonderful career as a senior partner in a large multi-national accounting firm. I retire in 10 months from now. I haven't really thought about what to do when I retire? What is the best use of the rest of my life?

I am the executive of a large multi-national company. My annual income has been in the range of seven figures. I have five children and a wonderful wife. I am addicted to pornography. The addiction has affected everything. I was fired from my position because there were concerns about possible sexual harassment issue by me. I fear I will lose my family and children? How can I break this habit and get back on track in life, without this horrible distraction?

I just received the news that I have a serious health condition that will have a significant impact on my life? How can I stay positive, continue to do my best in life?

I am a full-time mother with four young children. Sometimes I feel like I will go crazy with all of the demands that come from a growing family. How can I maintain my health, happiness, stay in shape, be a good mother and have a happy marriage?

We just discovered a major flaw in the service that we provide to a major customer. It could be a minor problem or a major one. We aren't entirely sure right now. This is a big deal. What is the best way to approach this issue?

I have an anger issue! I have especially noticed that this anger can turn into road rage. It has put me and others at risk. I have also noticed this anger is starting to affect my patience levels at home and at work. I am afraid that this anger will cause a serious problem someday. This isn't the person I wanted to be! How do I subdue this beast?

Maybe you can relate to one or two of these circumstances or have someone close to you that is dealing with one of these situations.

The promise of this book is that it will give you light, hope, encouragement and a clear positive pathway of how to attack these types of issues in life. We've designed a blueprint to help you and those around you find an exciting pathway that results in greater effectiveness, happiness, health and prosperity. This isn't another flavor of the month, this blueprint is designed so that it can be used for the rest of your life and provide a sustainable difference.

Becoming Your Best is not about comparing yourself to another person. It is about Becoming YOUR Best! We may learn from others and be inspired by others, but resist comparing yourself to another. We are all different. You have unique talents, gifts, skills and abilities. There is NOBODY like you. The crown jewel of life is becoming the best that you possibly can. In the process of Becoming Your Best you will also create a legacy that will touch others for good.

Even though it's not a comparison, we've found that those who live the 13 Guiding Constants do have a competitive edge, especially in the business world. Later in the introduction, I'll briefly illustrate a couple examples of how the Guiding Constants have given companies the competitive edge and made a significant difference in their long-term success. But first, let me briefly explain the background of the Guiding Constants.

The 13 Guiding Constants

For centuries, mariners and explorers have relied on the heavens for navigation because the stars never change position. For thousands of years, the North Star has been available, unmoving and constant, to any who looked to it. Those who know how can still use it to find their way. Each time I see the North Star, I'm reminded of the principles and laws that govern the universe and assure its constant order.

Just as countless people throughout history have understood key principles and used the appropriate tools to achieve extraordinary results—in flight, medicine, communication, electricity, engineering, and sports, to name a few—so each of us can come to understand key principles that bring about success in life. The laws that affect your success in life are just as timeless, universal, and dependable as the North Star. This is why I chose the term *Guiding Constants*, because they are as constant as the stars in the heavens. When you understand and master these constants and effectively use the

associated processes and tools, you will achieve significant results on your journey to become your best.

History teaches much. One of the things you'll notice is that over time there have been many individuals, teams, relationships, organizations, communities, and even countries that have faltered and failed. During the same period, other individuals, teams, relationships, organizations, communities, and even countries have prospered and succeeded.

What makes the difference? What leads some to high levels of performance while others struggle at the opposite end?

Based on my research, I believe the 13 Guiding Constants make the difference! Sustainable health, happiness, and prosperity stem from these Guiding Constants.

The flow of materials in this book is designed to help you master each of the 13 Guiding Constants, individually and in your organization.

This book is divided into three parts that build on what I consider to be some of the most important areas of our lives.

In Part One, we'll discuss the keys to strong personal success—the Guiding Constants of character, imagination, knowledge, persistence, and peace and balance.

In Part Two, we'll review the keys to strong relationships—the Guiding Constants of respect, trust, listening, and choice.

And Part Three, culminates to help us understand the Guiding Constants of strong leadership and management—vision, plan, priorities, and accountability.

It's worth taking a few minutes to review what is meant by *strong*. A *strong* person is dependable and predictable. He or she can handle stress and pressure with grace, can be counted on, doesn't collapse when needed, can contribute to positive solutions, and can make a difference for good. Being *strong* is a positive and desirable quality.

It's important to realize that *strong* does not mean overbearing! It *does* mean being true to character, building and using a vibrant imagination, and hanging in there when others quit or give up in the middle of the battle. A strong person can make a positive difference in his or her world.

While being strong is essential, it's only part of the power you'll find in the *Guiding Constants*. The unknown author of a compelling parable illustrates the real value of these constants in our lives:

> *A wise woman who is traveling through the mountains finds a precious stone beneath the babbling waters of a stream. She tucks the stone into her bag and continues on her way.*
>
> *The next day the woman encounters another traveler who is suffering from hunger. When she opens her bag to share her food, the hungry traveler sees the precious stone. Knowing it could provide him security for a lifetime, he asks the woman to give him the stone. She does so without hesitation.*
>
> *The hungry traveler goes on his way, rejoicing in his good fortune. A few days later the woman is surprised to encounter him again on the path. He had sought her so he could return the stone.*
>
> *"I've been thinking," he says. "I know how valuable the stone is, but I give it back in the hope that you can give me something even more precious. I want that quality within that enabled you to give me the stone."*

This learning and application process is the polishing of the precious gem that resides within you and every one of us. It's a result of *Guiding Constants*—qualities within us, like those of the woman in the parable, that bless you and everyone you encounter. If you are to make the *Guiding Constants* game-changers in your life, you have to cultivate and polish them.

Every individual, strong or weak, starts out at the same place. As you learn to apply the *Guiding Constants* you will become increasingly stronger and more capable. Polishing, in fact, appears to make all the difference.

In his book, *The Outliers*, Malcolm Gladwell described studying people who were exceptional, good, or fair at what they did; his quest led him to analyze everyone from pianists and violinists to athletes, doctors, politicians, and business leaders. Regardless of their area of focus, the one characteristic that most contributed to their level of success was how much time and effort they spent polishing their skills.

At the Juilliard School of Music, for example, Gladwell found that the "elite" musicians had practiced 10,000 hours, the "good" musicians had practiced 8,000 hours, and those who might become music teachers had practiced 4,000 hours. The principle didn't apply just to musicians—it was the same for hockey players, mechanics, writers, and every other person. Those who put in 10,000 hours of practice were among the top at what they did. As a matter of fact, they are in the process of becoming their best.

The Becoming Your Best Blueprint.

I've been asked repeatedly by leaders , "how can I make this sustainable for my company so that it's not just a flavor of the month? In other words, a lot of training companies leave good material, but it's tough to implement. How do we implement this?" Let me answer that question now.

Benjamin Franklin was one of the most influential statesmen in history. Yet when he was just twenty-one, his employer called him one of the most obnoxious, ignorant, know-it-all people he had ever met.

Many would have been defeated by such a stinging rebuke, but Franklin decided to do better. He developed thirteen virtues—no direct relation to the 13 Guiding Constants—that he believed would make him a better person.

His plan was simple. He worked on each virtue for one week at a time. After thirteen weeks, he started over with the first virtue. His was an ongoing plan: thirteen weeks times four cycles equaled fifty-two weeks—the number of weeks in a full year. That meant he could work on his virtues continuously throughout the rest of his life.

His was a lifelong process that helped Benjamin Franklin become one of the most important figures in world history. In his autobiography, he credits much of his success to this process of working on one virtue a week.

Inspired by Benjamin Franklin, we've created the **Becoming Your Best Blueprint.** The blueprint is results-based and is designed to help you or your organization implement these Guiding Constants. The blueprint is to simply focus on one Guiding Constant a week, personally and as an organization. Repeat this for 13 weeks and then start over and repeat the process (13 x 4 = 52 weeks). Over time, the Guiding Constants will seamlessly become part of you as you work to master each one. It's like trying to eat an elephant in one setting...impossible. But, if we take a bite at a time, eventually we finish the elephant. The blueprint is designed to help you and I refine these factors of success over time and it will have a great impact. Business leaders love this because of its simplicity to implement and yet the power and results that it has in their organizations!

There are numerous organizations that have incorporated the blueprint. As I mentioned, those organizations that follow this blueprint have experienced tremendous results. One company we've recently worked with experienced a 70% increase in revenue in just one year. The employees in this organization use to be unhappy and disgruntled, now they look sharp and each one is innovating in their respective areas. The leaders of this company cite the blueprint as the reason for their success and transformation. This particular company has their teams spend about five to ten minutes together at the beginning of the week to discuss a Guiding Constant and then they focus on that Guiding Constant throughout the week. Over time, it's had a significant influence on everyone who's associated with that organization.

We want to help in the process, so as a company, we send out a weekly motivational message for each Guiding Constant. The message shares a story and a new tool to implement it. Some organizations simply take this email and review it weekly with their employees. What's nice is that you can do whatever works well for you personally or your organization.

It is my desire that people and organizations reach principled goals. It is my desire that relationships, regardless of where they are today, can be happier and stronger and can enjoy a higher level of trust. And it is my desire that all people—including you—will experience the satisfaction and thrill of becoming the best that they can.

Get ready to experience the extraordinary thrill and satisfaction of achieving a new best. The overall process is exciting and liberating; it's like being in a spacecraft as it breaks free from gravity, enabling you to see the earth from a totally different perspective. Remember, your best is yet to be and ONE person can make a difference!

To this end, I dedicate this book.

Steven R. Shallenberger

How to Gain the Most Out of *Becoming Your Best*

1. Consider using the **Becoming Your Best Blueprint** and focus on one Guiding Constant each week and repeat this four times during the year (13 X 4 = 52 weeks). Visit www.BecomingYourBest.com and enter your name and email to receive the weekly motivational email.

2. Quickly read through the entire book, using the columns to note your impressions and how you apply what you're reading. Underline or bookmark key concepts as you go along.

3. Review the "In a Nutshell" section at the end of each chapter to remind yourself of the key principles and ideas in each chapter. Feel free to add to the "In a Nutshell" section when you review the book again.

4. Get a notebook you can use to record your thoughts and ideas. As you think about the different concepts, start writing your ideas about how to apply them in your life.

5. Look at the application section in the back of each chapter. Take time to reflect on some of the individual and group exercises; they'll provide powerful learning and growth experiences.

6. Teach others about the concepts you are studying, especially the ones that stand out for you. As you prepare to teach others, the depth of your understanding will increase. Invite those you teach to teach others.

PART ONE
STRONG INDIVIDUALS

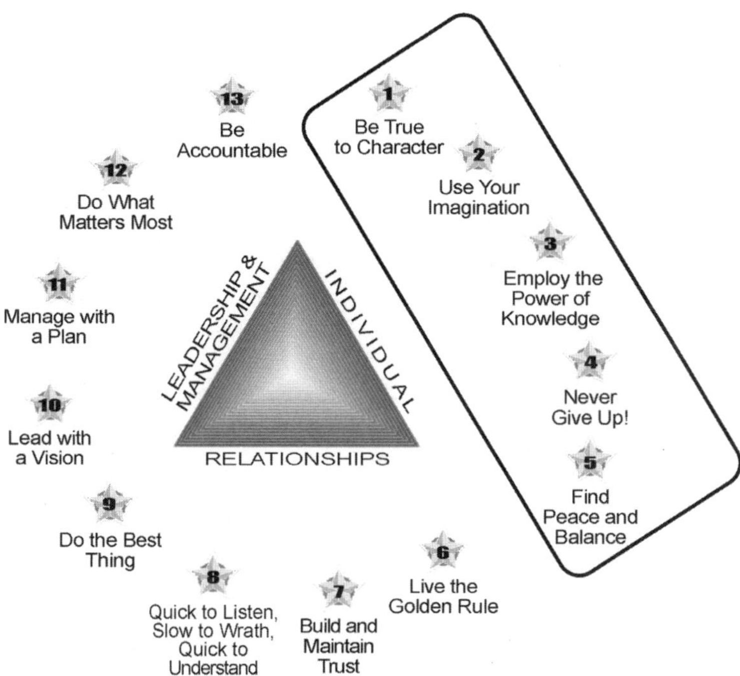

Guiding Constant 1

Be True to Character

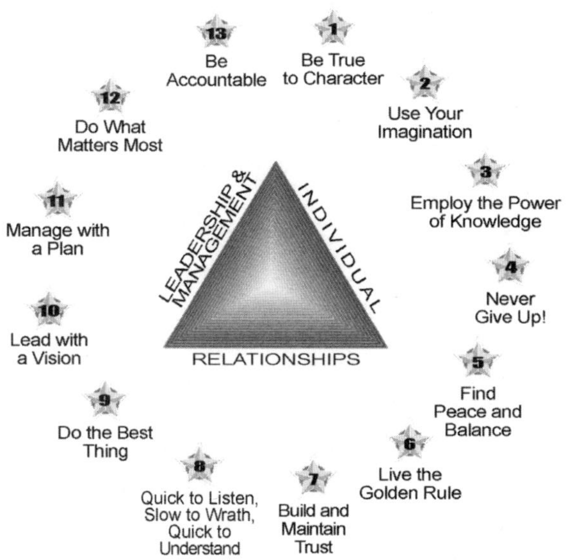

Integrity, Honesty, Respect, and Correct Principles

A MOTHER ONCE BROUGHT HER CHILD TO GANDHI and asked him to tell the young boy to stop eating sugar because it was not good for his diet or his developing teeth.

Gandhi replied, "I cannot tell him that. But you may bring him back in a month."

The mother was angry as Gandhi moved on, brushing her aside. She had traveled some distance and had expected the mighty leader to support her parenting. But having little recourse, she left for her home. One month later she returned, not knowing what to expect.

The great Gandhi took the small child's hands into his own, knelt before him, and tenderly said, "Do not eat sugar, my child. It is not good for you." Then Gandhi embraced the boy and returned him to his mother.

Grateful but perplexed, the mother queried, "Why didn't you say that a month ago?"

"Well," said Gandhi, "a month ago, I was still eating sugar."

How does Gandhi's example exemplify character?

What if all were true to themselves in this way? How would the world be different? How would your community be different? Your company? Your family? You?

What Does It Mean to Be True to Character?

Being true to character means your actions reflect your beliefs, and your beliefs are based on correct guiding principles. At the very bedrock of character is integrity, honesty, respect for others, and alignment with correct principles.

What Is the Feeling and Impact of Being True to Character?

When you are true to character, the feeling is good, solid, and confident. The impact is remarkable in the sense of added confidence, increased opportunities, stronger relationships, expanded influence, and an enviable reputation.

Each of us is endowed with a conscience; you know right from wrong. If you're not tuned in to this feeling of right or wrong, you can get off course. The impact of violating character—integrity, honesty, and respect for others—is devastating. It can result in broken lives and relationships, shattered trust, destroyed organizations, prison time, disappointment, diminished opportunities, reduced influence, and a tarnished reputation.

Being True to Character Is a Choice—Will I or Won't I? It Is Your Choice

Being true to character is a choice. Most often, you make that choice in the quiet recesses of your heart as you look in the mirror.

As you determine whether you will be true to character, you experience a defining moment—the moment of truth. Once you make that decision, it gets easier to either be true to character or to violate character. Your repeated actions make it a habit.

Developing character is an ongoing learning process of making choices; over time, you become finely tuned "within" to make the right choices. You may make mistakes, but at those times you can catch yourself and get back on the right track until one day, you are beyond reproach. You have mastered being true to character. What others see without is the exact same within. This is at the very heart of character.

What Is the Impact?

The impact of being true to character is enormous. Consider Gandhi. An entire nation sought his wisdom. People lined up for hours for the chance to meet with him for just a moment. And his impact involved much more than sugar.

Gandhi's authority came from a power within; he established a moral authority by his actions. He aligned and centered his life with powerful, correct principles, and his leadership ultimately led to the independence of an entire nation of 300 million people through peaceful means.

By having integrity, honesty, respect for others, and by centering his beliefs on correct principles, Gandhi found internal strength, peace, clarity, and direction. As a result, he led effectively despite an often confusing and troubled environment.

Einstein said, "Setting an example is not the main means of influencing another—it is the only means."

As you learn and internalize the Thirteen Guiding Constants, you will develop a moral authority within that will have a powerful influence without in your life and in the lives of others.

Developing Character: Fifty Miles in Twenty Hours

When our oldest son Rob was fourteen, he announced that he was going to participate in the 50/20 event with the Scouting organization—a challenge that involved walking fifty miles in twenty hours. I told Rob that this sounded like a serious challenge. I then reminded him that when Shallenbergers start something, we finish it. Rob said, "I understand, Dad. I will finish."

Unfortunately, I wasn't nearly as plugged in as I should have been in understanding what he was up against. I didn't realize that of the thousands of Scouts and leaders who participated, only 15 to 20 percent finished the entire fifty miles.

Yikes.

With the group, Rob started the walk from a city fifty miles away around 4 or 5 p.m. I figured I would go to the finish line the next day and cheer him on. Some father!

At 4 a.m. the next morning, I heard a noise; as I got up to check things out, I found Rob in bed. I sat down next to him and asked what happened. He said he had walked as far as the city of American Fork—about thirty miles from the starting point—when one of the parents of a boy in his troop drove by and asked if he wanted to go home. He said, "I decided to jump in the van. After all, I had walked thirty miles. I was so tired. That's what happened."

"Rob, do you remember what I said? We agreed that if you start something, you must finish?" He nodded. "How about if we go back to where you were picked up and I will walk in with you?"

Rob agreed. He got dressed, and my wife dropped us both off in American Fork. There was still time to complete the fifty miles in twenty hours.

It started getting light, and with another person to talk with and provide encouragement, it got easier. Rob actually ran the final mile to cross the finish line. It was a grand accomplishment. But far more important than anything else that happened that day, Rob learned that when you make a commitment to yourself to do something, you do it. And I learned to be a more attentive father.

Rob went on to complete the 50/20 twice in two years. The next year, his two younger brothers David and Steven also finished the event. It wasn't easy. In fact, it was painful. But Rob's example and influence on the others was significant.

The Strength of Character Is Developed Over Time

Strength of character is built over time as it is tested, refined, and becomes tempered, similar to what happens to steel or a diamond. At first, the raw materials of these substances are brittle or soft. But when heated white hot and compacted, the molecules change; the end result is a material that is among the strongest known to man.

As your integrity, honesty, and respect for others is tested, tried, and refined, you learn—the molecules are changed, or your moral fabric is developed. The end result is character you can count on. This character establishes a moral authority *within* that gives you great power and credibility *without.*

You are taught and reminded of this every day—through personal experience, by watching others, and by examining history and literature. You can plainly see the consequences of being true to character or of violating it.

Mandela: Courage to Stand Up for What is Right!

A classic example is Nelson Mandela. As the newly elected president of South Africa, and after spending twenty-seven years in prison for opposing apartheid, he was completely preoccupied with uniting his country. He was not interested in a country of white or black, but a country of equals.

Then Mandela learned that the Black National Caucus had voted to eliminate the leading South African national rugby team—a team whose players were white.

Such an act would have been deeply offensive to the white population and would have driven a huge wedge into his goal of unifying the country. Against the counsel of his advisors, he immediately left his office and headed to the meeting of the caucus, which was still in session.

With great respect, he addressed the group and asked them to reconsider their decision. He explained his future vision of South Africa and asked *who stood with him.* The vote was retaken and the decision was rescinded by one vote.

With the vote from the Black National Caucus in hand, Mandela enlisted the help of Francois Pienaar—the "big blonde son of apartheid," a symbol of all that the blacks hated about white political control of South Africa. Pienaar was the star and captain of the national rugby team. When he met with Mandela, they agreed to a partnership that would establish them both as men of the deepest character—men who would forever impact the civility and unity of South Africa, influencing millions of people, even those outside South Africa. Pineaar said, "I left that first meeting with the feeling that we were in good hands in South Africa. I felt safe with him."

Two years later this same rugby team won the world rugby championship, a victory that united the country of South Africa.

Have the courage to be true to character. Exercise integrity, honesty, respect, and correct principles. Be determined you will not sit idly on the sidelines of life when issues of character come up. Your character will be evident in how you conduct yourself with all people, and you will become a beacon in the world.

To Thine Own Self Be True

In William Shakespeare's timeless classic *Hamlet*, Polonius gives his son a "blessing," or "father's advice," as he ventures out into the world. Polonius's advice is priceless and lives across the centuries. Especially notice how he starts out:

"And these few precepts in thy memory. *See thou character*. Give thy thoughts no tongue, Nor any unproportioned thought his act. . . . The friends thou hast, and their adoption tried, Grapple them to thy soul with hoops of steel. . . . Give every man thine ear, but few thy voice: Take each man's censure, but reserve thy judgment. . . . Costly thy habit as thy purse can buy. . . . Neither a borrower nor a lender be: For loan oft loses both itself and friend; And borrowing dulls the edge of husbandry. *This above all—to thine own self be true: and it must follow, as the night the day, thou canst not then be false to any man.*"

As they departed, the father said to his son, "Farewell. And remember well what I have said to you."

Being true to yourself is a hallmark of character—one that Shakespeare's fictional father committed to his son. This is extraordinary advice for any parent to a son or daughter.

As you think of a person that you greatly admire, being true to character is likely one of the master qualities of his or her life, whether manifest in a private way or observed in public life.

What Could Challenge You and Test Your Character?

As you move through life, you'll likely have daily reasons to be reminded of the advice "To thine own self be true." And you're just as likely to have daily opportunities to answer the critical question, *Will I be trues to character?*

When the waters are calm, it's easier to respond, *I will*! But what about those times when things heat up and you're under blistering stress? Those moments put your character to the test.

- How will you respond when you are mistreated, accused, bad-mouthed, hurt, or misunderstood?

- How will you respond when there is the opportunity to take advantage of another, especially if no one would ever know?

- How will you respond if you have the chance to take something that isn't yours and you'll likely never be caught?

- How will you respond in situations when you have power or position over others? Will you maintain your character, or will you violate integrity and honesty, abandon respect for others, and fail to align with correct principles?

As you think of instances in your own life or in the lives of others, it's not difficult to see examples of when you or others were true to character. In those cases, you did the right thing and the consequences were positive. But when you or others violated character, the consequences were disappointing and often devastating.

A study of history provides us with the perspective of thousands of years as we consider character. Think of the leaders of nations who were true to character; in those cases, it's easy to see how the people in those nations were greatly blessed. The opposite is also true: When leaders violated character, it's easy to see the great misery that followed.

The same principle holds true in science, education, medicine, business, athletics, and virtually every key area of life. You can probably think of many examples.

As you think of those who have stood tall throughout history—in both the short and long terms—they are typically those who have been true to character.

Now consider those who are thought of in disgrace; they're likely the ones who violated character and abused leadership. While the good generally wins out over the bad, it generally takes a long time to make things right and to reestablish trust. It requires consistently being true to character.

Like everyone else, you'll face tests every day. You'll have lots of chances to determine whether you'll be true to character. The great thing about these tests—and your victories over them—is that deepening your character is possible. And it's worth it. Your victories will become your "sugar" story—and, as with Gandhi, will exemplify your character.

Some of the best tests of character come in the midst of fierce competition—a situation in which it can be difficult to practice respect and civility. It may be difficult, but it's absolutely possible to be a ferocious competitor and still be civil. You can be strong on the issues while being strong in character; the evidence is kindness and sincere respect for others.

President Ronald Reagan provided a great example through his political differences with Speaker of the House Thomas Phillip "Tip" O'Neill Jr. O'Neill's public treatment of Reagan was disgraceful. O'Neill called Reagan the most ignorant man who had ever occupied the White House. O'Neill also said that Reagan was "Herbert Hoover with a smile," "a cheerleader for selfishness," and "an amiable dunce." Privately, O'Neill and Reagan were always on cordial terms—or, as Reagan himself put it in his memoirs, they were friends "after 6 P.M." It was even said that the two could enjoy a drink and tell Irish jokes. Reagan was a realist; he understood the nature of politics and knew he'd never get all he put on the table. Nonetheless, he had the ability to stay true to his core principles while maneuvering with others who saw things differently—and, importantly, the ability to respect them as fellow travelers.

Establish Character in the Home and in Your Private Life

As Roxanne and I were raising our five sons and a daughter, we set family rules and kept them posted in our kitchen. Some of those rules were:

- We don't cheat.
- We don't lie.
- We don't spit on one another.
- We don't scare each other (by hiding behind doorways, etc.).
- If we hurt someone's feelings, we say, "I'm sorry."
- We don't punch or pinch each other.

Although simple, these were our "character" rules, and they became a way of living for our family. As our children are starting to raise families of their own, it is fun to see them teaching these same basic principles to their own children. It is also inspiring to see them lead with character in their various professions and avocations.

Your inner core of character is reflected in your integrity, honesty, respect, and ethics. It creates the foundation of success in your personal, interpersonal, and organizational relationships.

When your life is based on the bedrock of correct principles, it is much easier to be strong on principle while being respectful and considerate of others. When you are deeply committed to being true to character, the principles will guide your response to every test of your integrity, honesty, and civility.

Let's start by looking at the hallmark trait of honesty.

Be Honest in Small Things

Some years ago, one of our employees was caught punching time cards for other employees. Later, the same employee was caught taking $11.02 from our petty cash box. It would seem that these were small, forgivable acts.

When I brought this employee in, she admitted taking the money and falsifying other employees' time cards.

As I carefully considered the situation, I ultimately decided to terminate the employee. She was beside herself with anger and felt she had been unjustly treated because she had stolen so little. I responded by telling her that it wasn't the amount, it was the principle. Eighteen months later, I saw a newspaper article detailing her conviction for embezzling thirty-four thousand dollars from the next company she worked for. She was sentenced to one year in prison—a tragedy heightened by the fact that she was the mother of two young children.

Your character cannot be limited to the size or the amount. The principle is constant whether it involves a penny or millions of dollars. How much would it take to test *your* character?

If You Aren't Telling the Whole Truth, You Aren't Telling the Truth

Born just a few years after America's Revolutionary War, Abraham Lincoln grew up in what is now the midwestern United States, in a time of horses, wagons, and hand plows.

The back country where he grew up had no neighborhood schools and few teachers, so Abe never did get much of an education. He and his older sister, Sarah, had to walk nearly two miles to the one-room school they were able to attend for a couple of years.

It wasn't long before Abe's family moved even farther west to the small settlement of Pigeon Creek, Indiana. Here Abe helped his father build a log cabin against the side of a hill.

When Abe was only nine years old, his mother died. Abe's father soon married another woman who brought with her a stepbrother and two stepsisters for young Abe and his sister. The new family was a happy one, and they all pitched in to accomplish the necessary work.

That summer Abe had to clear some land that was covered with trees so the family could plant corn. Abe's younger stepsister Matilda always wanted to go with him to the woods, but her mother forbade it because she was so young. One day Matilda decided she was going to sneak out to the woods anyway. When she finally arrived at the area Abe was clearing, she could barely see his tall, lanky body and the long-handled ax bobbing up and down among the thick trees.

I know, Matilda thought. *I'll sneak up behind Abe and surprise him!*

She quietly crept closer, hiding behind trees and stumps so that Abe wouldn't see her. Just as she finally caught up to him she slipped and fell against the ax, cutting her foot.

Abe wrapped his handkerchief tightly around her foot to stop the bleeding and held her until she stopped crying. Then he asked the obvious: "What are you going to tell mother when she asks how you cut your foot?"

Matilda gave it some thought. "I don't know. I guess I'll tell her I cut it on the ax. She doesn't need to know it happened in the woods."

Abe pondered her response for a minute, then said, "Well, that's the truth—you *did* cut your foot on the ax. But that's not the whole truth."

As they continued to talk, Matilda finally understood that telling part of the truth wasn't enough—and that getting scolded was a small price to pay for being honest.

Abraham Lincoln was committed to living an honest life from a young age. He told the whole truth, even if it meant he'd get in trouble, and he encouraged others to do the same.

Bobby Polacio and the Rope-Climb Record

Another important aspect of honesty is to tell the truth *even though there is no chance anyone will ever find out whether you are lying.* That's what happened to a young man by the name of Bobby Polacio, who had only three tries to break the school record in the rope climb. Bobby was keenly aware of the existing record: a mere 2.1 seconds. He had thought of little else all weekend.

As the boys lined up in the gym for warm-up exercises, Coach Roberts told them, "Today we'll be doing the rope climb. As you know, the school record of 2.1 seconds has never been broken. But I have a feeling that Bobby Polacio may break the record today."

Everyone turned to Bobby with a thumbs-up gesture. *They all think I can do it,* Bobby thought. *Even Coach Roberts thinks I can do it. I have to break the record—I can't let all those people down.*

Each boy would get three tries to break the record. Bobby was so nervous that he went to the end of the line. All the other boys went first, and some got close to breaking the record. Then it was Bobby's turn.

With everyone shouting encouragement, Bobby jumped to the rope and climbed as fast as he could, left hand over right, right hand over left, all the while lifting his knees as high as he could. He touched the wood at the top and slid down the rope, looking at Coach Roberts in anticipation.

His time was 2.1 seconds. He tied but did not break the record. Disappointed, he walked to the end of the line and waited for his next try.

His second turn came and he made it in two seconds flat. But the celebration was cut short when the coach, acting on a hunch, asked Bobby if he had actually touched the wooden support at the top of the rope.

Lowering his head, Bobby replied, "No, Coach . . . I didn't touch the top. I missed it by a fraction of an inch."

Tears in his eyes, the coach blew his whistle to get everyone's attention.

"Gentlemen, I have something to tell you. Bobby has not set a new record today, but he has done something far greater—he has told the truth. Bobby is the only one who knew that he did not touch the wood at the top. We should all look up to him for his example."

For a moment no one said a word. Then one of the boys yelled, "You still have another try, Bobby. Go for it!"

At the signal Bobby jumped higher than before and used every muscle he could to pull himself higher. Bobby touched the top and came down—tired, out of breath, and hopeful.

Coach Roberts looked at his stop watch. "You did it, Bobby—1.9 seconds!"

It was a great accomplishment to break the school record, but it was a far greater accomplishment to tell the truth. Bobby was honest, and no one would ever forget it.

You build the fabric of your character by the things you repeatedly do. Over time, your repeated acts become habits—and honesty becomes part of who you are.

Choose to Respond with the Strength of Character When Unfairly Accused

Still another part of character is manifest in the way you respond to injustices. Not long ago, our firm was being interviewed for a large services bid. At the conclusion of the successful interview, the individual in charge pulled me aside and said, "By the way, I was talking to a consultant the other day, and he said that your HVAC firm does poor quality work." His comment took me totally by surprise.

I immediately felt angry and defensive but determined to listen and try to understand the context and source of the feedback. As I weighed out how I would respond, I realized I had the opportunity to provide a principled response—one based on integrity, honesty, and respect for others. Focusing on this course of action provided a much clearer perspective and way to respond.

The next day, I wrote to the individual in charge and expressed my appreciation for his candor and courage. I pointed out that his comment was simply not correct—that our customer satisfaction and quality levels were extremely high, consistently in the ninety-seventh to ninety-eighth percentiles. In other words, our quality, workmanship, and customer satisfaction were in the upper 3 percent.

I indicated that we were grateful for feedback and that we would continue to work to have a 100 percent quality and customer satisfaction. I also mentioned that we would welcome the opportunity to meet with the person who provided the feedback, listen carefully to what he had to say, and look for ways to improve our operations.

Regardless of whether we won the bid, I wanted to provide this person with the other side of the story and let him decide for himself what was correct.

The firm that interviewed us appreciated this principled response. Over time we've had many positive experiences together involving millions of dollars of work with top-notch quality and high customer satisfaction.

Character When Others Are Vulnerable

Still another display of character is made in how you treat those who are vulnerable. William N. Jones, a mentor and friend, introduced me to N. Eldon Tanner, a former speaker of the Alberta, Canada, legislature and the Alberta Minister of Lands and Mines. Mr. Tanner had also become one of the leaders of a worldwide religious and humanitarian organization.

I later learned that Mr. Tanner had demonstrated his character in an unforgettable way. A man who had fallen on hard times came to Mr. Tanner's office one day. This man and his family owned a piece of property that Mr. Tanner's organization had long been interested in. Mr. Tanner knew this man and his family were desperate to raise whatever cash they could—and that he had an opportunity to obtain this property at a bargain price if he took advantage of the situation.

What did Mr. Tanner do?

Mr. Tanner, who had a sterling reputation for honesty and integrity, asked the man if he had had an appraisal done. He then indicated that his organization would pay him the fair market value of the property as confirmed by the appraisal. The property owner was stunned that Mr. Tanner would not try to take advantage of his vulnerable situation. He left with gratitude and admiration for this noble and fair businessman and the organization he represented.

You Can Learn by Making a Mistake and Correcting It

Sometimes you learn integrity and honesty when you make a mistake—a situation in which your true character is put to the test. This happened to one of our excellent summer salesman. Based on his fabulous first summer with us, Jim (not his real name) was invited back to manage a team of sales reps; he would manage the team and also work as a sales rep himself on the East Coast.

One morning I received a call from Jim, who said, "I have embarrassed you, embarrassed the company, and embarrassed myself. I must resign." With that somber statement, I thought he must have molested a child or killed someone and was calling from the police station. I asked, "What did you do?"

Jim was sober as he admitted, "I lied to a customer, telling him that his neighbors said they should buy our products. The guy called his neighbors and confirmed that my story was not true. I am so sorry. Now you can see why I must resign."

I told Jim that I appreciated his call—and that sometimes the best way to *really* learn to live a principle is when you have violated it and feel the painful consequences.

What I told him next was important: "I would like you to go back out, apologize one more time to the customer, tell him that you were wrong, and tell him you are committed to never doing this again. Then determine in your own heart that you will live honesty to a T."

Jim agreed to do exactly that. He worked for another eight years as an outstanding contributor to our organization and went on to become the CEO of a very successful firm—a firm that has a reputation not only of industry leadership but of unquestioned business integrity.

Measuring Character

In our company, we hold an annual retreat for organizational and planning purposes. Among the things we do during this two- to three-day day retreat is review the company's operating values and principles: in other words, the company's character. We have done this for more than twenty-five years. Included in our assessment are these values:

- We treat people right.
- We don't lie, cheat, steal, or tolerate any among us that do. (This is taken from the honor code of the United States Air Force Academy.)

We also distribute a list of questions on ethics to help us evaluate our decisions based upon integrity, honesty, and respect for others:

1. Is it legal? Will I be violating either civil law or company policy?
2. Is it balanced? Is it fair to all concerned in the short term as well as the long term? Does it promote win-win relationships?
3. How will it make me feel about myself?
4. Will it make me proud?
5. Would I feel good if my decision were published in the newspaper?
6. Would I feel good if my family knew about it?

Good Men and Women Do Finish First

You've heard the old adage, "Cheaters never prosper." The principle of being true to character would have us know that *winners never cheat.*

Jon Huntsman, chairman of the internationally respected Huntsman Chemical Corporation and founder of the world-class Huntsman Cancer Center, wrote an incredible book, *Winners Never Cheat!* In it he discusses what it means to be true to character:

> *Good men and women can and do finish* first. *And millions of wonderful people live noble and successful lives. And they can live with a clean conscience. No regrets.*
>
> *Leaders should not worry greatly about occasional mistakes, but they must vigilantly guard against these things that will make them feel ashamed.*
>
> *When we make an agreement or negotiate to buy or sell a company or product, we work to take care to outline clearly, with benchmarks and accountability, the desired outcomes of that agreement. This allows both parties to carry out the spirit and intent of the agreement.*

Years ago, United States president Ronald Reagan, and Russian president Mikhail Gorbachev concluded a landmark agreement to significantly reduce tactical nuclear warheads by 30 percent—leaving approximately six thousand warheads on each side. The agreement was based first and foremost on the *character* of these two presidents who signed the START Agreement. They provided a moral authority that bridged decades of mistrust. At the same time, they built in checks and balances (benchmarks and accountability) to verify their agreement. From this settlement came a statement from Presidents Reagan and Gorbachev that gave comfort to all. "Trust and Verify" became the guiding principle on both sides of the disarmament agreement.

The fact is that those who violate integrity, honesty, and respect of others will be caught and punished, either by the law or by the power of natural consequences. The prisons of the world and the trash heaps of broken lives attest to the truth that cheaters do get caught. Violation of the principle of character will catch up with you sooner or later.

Life is simply of greater importance than money, power, status, and possession. So you might as well decide to *be honest.*

George Washington: True to Character and a Man of the Ages

George Washington has many titles: father, husband, uncle, student, soldier, patriot, colonel, general, president, commander in chief, founding father, land owner, public servant, defender of liberty, peacemaker, and man of character, to name just a few.

To fully appreciate the depth, power, and influence of his character, which is perhaps his greatest asset, it helps to understand some of the things he experienced.

He presided over the writing of the Constitution and was unanimously chosen to serve as the first president of the United States (1789–97) because he consistently demonstrated a conscientious effort and moral obligation to serve his fellow citizens.

The model that he established for the executive branch has been used ever since—among other things using a cabinet system, defining separation of powers, delivering an inaugural address, and returning to life as a private citizen after two four-year terms as president.

President Washington's leadership helped to establish a strong, well-financed national government that avoided war, suppressed rebellion, and won acceptance among Americans of all types. He has been recognized ever since as the "father of his country."

The most recognized military and political leader of the new United States of America, he led America to victory over Britain in the Revolutionary War as commander in chief of the Continental Army. Historians give the commander in chief high marks for his selection and supervision of his generals, his encouragement of morale, his coordination with the state governors and state militia units, his relations with Congress, and his attention to supplies, logistics, and training.

One of the great distinguishing events in American history is that after victory was finalized in 1783, he resigned his commission as commander of the armies and returned to his plantation at Mount Vernon. This prompted his enemy, King George III, to call him "the greatest character of the age." His act of retirement from public service caused the people to want him to serve even more. Two years later, he became president of the United States.

Once again, his character and mastery of powerful guiding principles positioned him to uniquely orchestrate solutions to difficult issues that others were simply not able to solve. The impact of his remarkably effective leadership provided an inspiring model for others to follow.

He returned to his beloved Mount Vernon as a private citizen in 1798. In Robert Frost's words, George Washington was "one of the few, in the whole history of the world, who was not carried away by power."

In addition to his incredible contribution to the establishment of the nation, his concern for others gives a deep and revealing glimpse into his character.

Kindness and Consideration to a Servant

During one particularly difficult situation, General Washington was engaged in earnest consultation with Colonel Pickering until after nightfall. Washington prepared to stay with Pickering overnight. When asked if there was straw and a blanket, Primus, a Black servant responded, "Oh yes, plenty of straw and blankets—plenty."

Two humble beds were spread side by side in the tent, and the officers lay down while Primus seemed to be busy with his required duties before he himself could sleep. He worked—or appeared to work—until the steady breathing of the two officers indicated that they were sleeping. Seating himself on a box, he leaned his head on his hands to obtain as much rest as he could.

Washington suddenly awakened in the middle of the night. Looking around the tent, he saw Primus.

Washington rose up in his bed. "Primus, what did you mean by saying you had straw and blankets enough? Here you have given up your blankets and straw to me that I may sleep comfortably, while you are obliged to sit through the night."

"It's nothing, General," said Primus. "It's nothing! I'm well enough! Go to sleep again. No matter about me!"

"But it *does* matter," said Washington, who insisted that the servant share his bed, throwing open the blanket and moving to one side of the straw as he spoke. Shocked at the idea of sharing a covering with the commander in chief, Primus nonetheless couldn't refuse the resolute and determined Washington—and there they both slept until morning.

He Died as He Lived

Death was unlikely to have been on George Washington's mind as he went out to check on his farms, as was his habit, on Thursday, December 12, 1799. His recent health had never been better. He had been making various plans for an active future. That day he remained outside for approximately five hours, despite the fact that—as he recorded in his journal, which he kept faithfully—the weather was very disagreeable. He described a constant fall of rain, snow, and hail with a high wind. Wet and chilled, with snow still clinging to his hair and coat, Washington decided not to change his clothes before dinner.

Even though he had the signs of a cold and sore throat the next day, he went out briefly in the afternoon to mark some trees that he wanted to have cut down. By that Friday evening, his voice was quite hoarse, but he was still in good spirits. By the early hours of Saturday morning, December 14, Washington awoke feverish, very uncomfortable, and with labored breathing. He would die before the day ended.

As Washington lapsed into unconsciousness, he closed his eyes, his hand fell to his side, his countenance changed, and he died "without a struggle or a sigh." The great body that had endured so much, the great mind so steady in its operations and so sure in its conclusions, was stilled.

A nation and a world mourned. Even Great Britain claimed him as a native son.

Washington was a remarkable example of the many facets of character explored in this chapter. He demonstrates a truth that has endured throughout the millennia and that still applies today: When you are true to character, you possess a power of influence much greater than any title or position.

INSPIRATIONAL QUOTES

Be True to Character

"Be the change in the world you want to see."

— Mahatma Gandhi

"Labor to keep alive in your breast that little spark of celestial fire, conscience."

— George Washington

"Character cannot be developed in ease and quiet. Only through experience of trial and suffering can the soul be strengthened, ambition inspired, and success achieved."

— Helen Keller

"Strength of character may be learned at work, but beauty of character is learned at home."

— Henry Drummond

"Good character is not formed in a week or a month. It is created little by little, day by day. Protracted and patient effort is needed to develop good character.

A man's character is his guardian divinity."

— Heraclitus

"Be more concerned with your character than your reputation, because your character is what you really are, while your reputation is merely what others think you are."

— John Wooden, Legendary UCLA Basketball Coach

"Character may almost be called the most effective means of persuasion."

— Aristotle

"Life is a series of experiences, each one of which makes us bigger, even though sometimes it is hard to realize this. For the world was built to develop character, and we must learn that the setbacks and grieves which we endure help us in our marching onward."

— *Henry Ford*

"Character is the core of true success and being the Best that we can be. Being true to character is comprised of integrity, honesty, respect for self and others, and pride of workmanship."

— *Steven R. Shallenberger*

"Men acquire a particular quality by constantly acting a particular way. . . . You become just by performing just actions, temperate by performing temperate actions, brave by performing brave actions."

— *Aristotle*

"Associate with men of good quality if you esteem your own reputation; for it is better to be alone than in bad company."

— *George Washington*

Application

Begin a Thought Book

Acquire a spiral notebook in which you can capture your thoughts, insights, inspiration, and ideas. Number the pages and record the date as you go along. Create an index to record the pages of your most meaningful or significant entries.

Don't worry about structure or format; instead, focus on capturing the inspirations and insights of your heart and mind.

Your book will become a treasure for you— a friend and companion—so inside the front cover, in big letters, write your name and phone number and offer a reward for its return if you somehow misplace it.

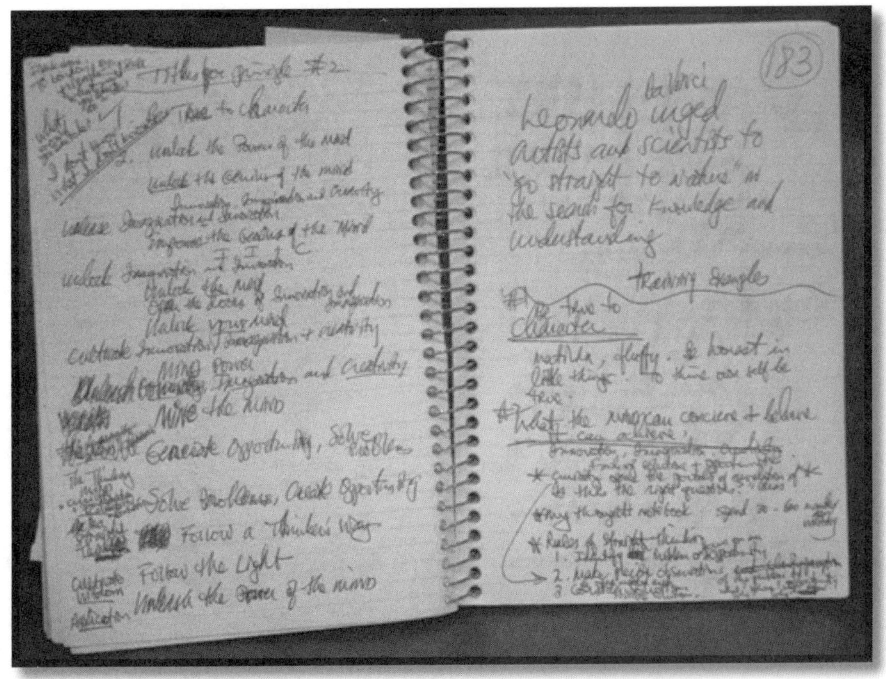

Individual Exercises and Application in Your Thought Book

Think about Ben Franklin's example of working on one virtue or principle a week for thirteen weeks and then starting over again. List areas of improvement that you would like to work on in terms of being true to character. What can you do this week to refine, improve, or learn more about yourself in this area?

Write down some elements of character that are your strengths. Then think about and record some areas you would like to improve.

When your actions are in harmony with principles of character, how does it make you feel? How does it make those around you feel?

What impact does your character have on you and others?

Consider writing a brief story about you and being true to character.

Write a story about someone you know or someone you observed who showed character.

List some of the individuals who have influenced your life for good and describe the level of character each one showed. Could you trust them?

Exercises and Applications with Others

Share one or two of the stories from this chapter and ask:

- When we do these things, how does it feel to us? To others?
- What is the impact on us? On others?

Share or give out to others your favorite quotes from this chapter.

In a Nutshell

1. Base your actions on principles of character: integrity, honesty, and respect for others.

2. Be honest in small things as well as big things, private things as well as public things.

3. If you aren't telling the whole truth, you aren't telling the truth.

4. Keep your word. Do what you say you will do. Be dependable.

5. Protect your reputation and your family's name.

6. Do what is right!

7. If you make a mistake, apologize, correct the mistake, and move on.

8. Be accurate in your descriptions. Underpromise and overdeliver.

9. Do not talk about others negatively in their absence. On the contrary, find something good to say about others.

10. "To thine own self be true and thou cannot then be false to any man."

11. Remember: Winners never cheat and cheaters never win!

12. Be principle-centered. Have the courage to stand up for what is right.

Guiding Constant 2

Use Your Imagination

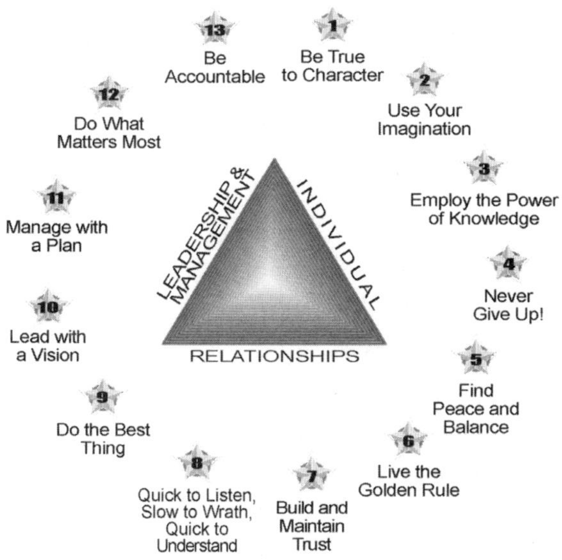

The Portal to the Best Is Imagination

CAN YOU GUESS THE NAME of the man who has likely brought more fun or laughs to more people—more joy to families—than any other man who ever lived?

He is the man who dreamed up Mickey Mouse, Donald Duck, and Pluto. He created a whole family of animated characters and went on to create incomparable family films that changed the world of cinema, and many of the principles of animation that he mastered are still being used today. Some of the greatest entertainment parks in the world carry his name.

He's Walt Disney—and with all he's done, we might say his achievement is among the best in today's world.

What made Walt Disney stand out? He loved to use his imagination. Walt regularly wrote things down in a rough form that in many cases later became reality—or the genesis for some other idea. He did research to supplement his ideas, and he found new ideas through regular meditation. He cultivated his imagination by always asking questions and by brainstorming with the people around him.

Coming up with new ideas and using his imagination became a habit. He regularly fired up his mind in such a way that it produced a constant stream of ideas, thoughts, and possibilities for entertaining others.

Think about the culture created by these films. The following list represents just some of the treasures he and his team have given us:

Snow White and the Seven Dwarfs
Dumbo
Sleeping Beauty
Mary Poppins
The Living Desert
Swiss Family Robinson
The Absent-Minded Professor
Pinocchio
Return from Witch Mountain
Lady and the Tramp
The Parent Trap
Old Yeller
The Mask of Zorro
Peter Pan
Fantasia
Bambi
Cinderella
Son of Flubber
The Shaggy Dog
20,000 Leagues Under the Sea
101 Dalmatians
Winnie the Pooh
Cars
Pirates of the Caribbean
Alice in Wonderland
The Chronicles of Narnia
Ratatouille
National Treasure
The Man from Snowy River
Toy Story
Finding Nemo
Aladdin
North Avenue Irregulars
Flight of the Navigator
The Apple Dumpling Gang
Pete's Dragon
Herbie Rides Again

What was the defining factor for Walt Disney? Simple: From a young age, he was always asking questions. He cultivated a strong sense of curiosity, followed his natural instincts, and worked hard. Work is an essential part of imagination, something that's easy to see through Walt Disney's experiences. Still another is the refusal to be defeated by what others might see as failure—something else Walt Disney demonstrated.

When he was just four years old, Walt's family moved to a farm. It was on the farm that Walt learned to love animals and first became interested in drawing. But just five years later Walt's father was forced to sell the farm because of poor health and low market prices for apples.

Walt wasn't one to sit by or give in to defeat: He got a paper route and woke up at three-thirty each morning to deliver newspapers to help his family. At sixteen, Walt worked with his father in a jelly factory—but he also decided to pursue his dreams by taking cartoon correspondence courses from the Academy of Fine Arts while attending his first year of high school, even though the hours were long and his workload was grueling. After returning from a year in France with the Red Cross Ambulance Corps, he took a job working for an advertising agency at the tender age of seventeen. It was there he learned the tricks of the commercial art trade.

Then he began making animated fairy stories. But when the distribution ran into financial difficulty and took all the money that had started coming in, Walt lost everything.

Picking himself up by his bootstraps, he moved to Hollywood, hoping to become a director. When that didn't pan out, he refused to give up. Instead, he returned to the drawing board to give cartooning another try. At twenty-four, he fell in love with and married one of his employees, Lillian, who would be his lifelong partner. Working hard, they sold enough cartoons and graphic designs to pay the bills.

Early in Walt's career, when things were a little rough in his scanty studio, he often noticed small mice crawling in his garbage can and around the room. One of them, a little mouse Walt named Mortimer, was the cutest of all and very mischievous. In fact, he was a little like Walt.

As Walt tried to imagine a possible cartoon series, he thought of that little mouse—and he decided to do a series about a mouse named Mickey. As part of the process, Walt developed the sound-and-action synchronization system that would be used in the production of all animated cartoons. Released in the theaters, the cartoon series became an overnight sensation. Mickey's movies and comic books appeared in twenty-seven languages and became an enormous international success.

Walt worked so hard that at thirty-one he suffered a nervous breakdown. Not one to be defeated, he fully recovered, wiser and smarter.

About that time, Walt decided that Mickey needed some friends, so he created a whole host of animated characters that became loved the world over. The rest is history, as Walt blessed the world with his imagination and talents. And he didn't stop with cartoons: Almost everyone has either heard of or been to Disneyland—a place that lives up to the sign at its entrance, proclaiming it "The happiest place on earth!"

Virtually everything around us today became a reality because people or organizations used their imagination. When the kernel of an idea was combined with opportunity, innovation brought us the electric lightbulb, automobiles, airplanes, radio, television, space travel, computers, the Internet, movies, athletic achievements, medical advances, cultural arts, commerce, cell phones, scientific exploration, renewable energy, and much more. Most exciting of all? The best is yet to come—and some of it will be developed in areas we can't yet fathom.

What Are the Key Components of Using Your Imagination?

There is plenty of room for new ideas and solutions. The best ideas, products, and services have yet to be invented. "The greatest picture is not yet painted," said Lincoln Steffens. "The greatest play isn't written, the greatest poem is unsung." All of it depends on imagination—and when you use your imagination, you open the portal to the *best* new ideas.

Does it seem impossible that new ideas are still out there? You don't have to look very far to see exactly what's possible! Just when it seemed all the great ideas had been used up, along came the *Star Wars* movie series, straight from the imagination of George Lucas and Steven Spielberg. Then, when it seemed impossible to beat that, along came J. K. Rowling with *Harry Potter*—a book that has been read by millions and that became one of the greatest blockbusters of all time.

Look at Mark Zuckerberg. His vision—a little thing called Facebook—resulted in a social network of hundreds of millions in the first few years. Zuckerberg's imagination led to a thriving collaboration of people that changed an organization as well as the global community.

The best books have not been written, the best movies have yet to be made, the best races have yet to be run, and the best ideas are still to come. How, then, do you come up with the ideas that will improve your life and the lives of others?

Five Ways to Fire Up Your Imagination

Imagination is a gift given to every person—you simply need to find ways to stimulate it, to use it, and to let it serve you. Five of these ways are outlined within this chapter. In the section that follows, we'll provide some examples of people who have used their imaginations, how they used them, and how their imaginations opened up new opportunities, solved problems, and inspired new directions.

Five Ways to Fire Up Your Imagination

1. Stoke your curiosity—What does your best look like? Questions help produce answers. So ask! *Who? What? Why? Where? When? How?* Is it ethical and in line with your character? Dream, dream, dream!

2. Collaborate and brainstorm—Consider all options. Everything is game. Invite others to join in the creativity.

3. Use mind-mapping to stir your imagination and clarity.

4. Walk away for a while—Let the subconscious mind do its work.

5. Write! Record your ideas, bursts of imagination, discoveries, thoughts, and dreams throughout the entire process of creating the best.

1. Stoke Your Curiosity

Curiosity is the heart of the matter. Invention is a creative process and your imagination *can* be unleashed. Some would say that your brain already has the solutions. Whether that's true or whether you can draw on your brain to develop, discover, and design the solutions, the fact remains the same—there is an unlimited source of creative power within you.

Imagination is not luck, but luck often contributes to it. Imagination is not dreaming, yet your dreams may play a role. Imagination is not guessing, yet guesses may open up new pathways of discovery.

Imagination can be fired up by curiosity. Take a look at one of the most significant inventions of our age: It can be argued that the core competency of the Wright Brothers was curiosity. As Bernard Baruch put it, "Millions saw the apple fall, but Newton asked why." Could it be possible that the invention of manned flight went to the team that was more curious, that asked more questions, that was more persistent?

Curiosity is a pathway to imagination because it creates questions in the mind—and the mind wants answers to those questions. The process of seeking answers results in more questions. As you continue to ask questions, they become more focused, and the quality of your questions improves. A better quality of questions results in a better quality of information. Einstein said, "The important thing is not to stop questioning. Curiosity has its own reason for existing. I have no special talents. I am only passionately curious."

The ability to ask questions helps to cultivate curiosity. Continually asking *How? What? Where? When? Why? Who?* helps you see things with greater clarity.

Born in 1847, American inventor, scientist, and businessman Thomas Edison patented thirteen hundred inventions. These inventions—including, but certainly not limited to, the phonograph, the motion picture camera, and the long-lasting, practical electric lightbulb—have greatly influenced life around the world. It staggers the mind to realize the number of Edison inventions that have impacted life as we know it. To name just a few, he invented and created a system to transfer electricity from a central station to homes and businesses; he improved the storage battery and developed a battery for an electric car; he designed a cement mixer; he invented a machine that could record sound; and he created a process for recording telegraph messages automatically (the ticker tape). None of these things existed until Edison came along with his powerful imagination.

How could one man accomplish all of that? He had a fired-up imagination and an insatiable desire to understand how things worked. His curiosity was boundless. His is a history that testifies to the power of curiosity and imagination.

When Edison was seven years old, his first teacher considered him incapable of learning—so his mother, who had been a teacher, took him out of school and taught him herself. Thus Edison, who has been called "one of the best informed men in the world on scientific subjects," had only three months of formal education.

Edison's mother taught him how to think, and he became an avid reader. It was from the encyclopedia that Edison first learned about chemistry and how to do experiments.

Edison worked in a lucrative position for a telegraphy firm until he was twenty-three, by which time he had saved enough money to open his own workshop. Between 1870 and 1876 he patented 122 inventions.

Giving up his efforts to simultaneously invent and manufacture, Edison established a laboratory at Menlo Park, New Jersey, in 1876. About this time he started work on the first phonograph and created his carbon telephone transmitter, which paved the way for the commercial telephone. In 1879, his practical incandescent lamp—what we know as the lightbulb—became a reality.

In 1885 he hit upon the idea of moving pictures and began work on the forerunners of today's motion picture camera and projector.

During World War I, Edison became president of the United States Naval Consulting Board, which was formed to develop inventions that would improve the defensive power of the Navy. He was credited with thirty-nine inventions of military importance—including, but not limited to, a listening-device for detecting submarines, an underwater searchlight, a water-penetrating projectile, a device for detecting enemy airplanes, and a telephone system for ships.

Edison made imagination a key part of his life, and he fed his curiosity with thousands of questions. He leveraged this curiosity and imagination by inviting others to join him in his quest for inventions and processes that would benefit humankind; one great example was his development of research and industrial parks solely for the purpose of encouraging invention. Edison would actually give a trusted associate an idea and then ask what the associate could do with it. What followed was his associates brainstorming, matching each other's ideas, playing off of each other's imaginations, and pursuing knowledge and application.

Edison not only developed a wide range of advances that improved life on a global basis, but he provided an amazing example of imagination, curiosity, and collaboration.

2. Collaborate and Brainstorm—Consider All Options

One of Edison's major accomplishments was collaboration—and we're now going to talk about stoking the fire of imagination through collaboration with others and brainstorming as you create a list of best ideas.

You may not realize it, but it's possible to brainstorm with yourself—that happens when you ask and answer the right questions of yourself. You may plant the seed. You may get the process going. You may create the structure. The more you think about a subject and seek to understand it, the clearer ideas become.

Even though it's possible to do that on your own, inviting others to provide their input or allow you to bounce ideas off of them can often help you break through a mental logjam.

Involving others in the imagination process significantly expands the quantity and quality of ideas, options, and solutions. In the right circumstances and environment, the results can be almost magic. Draw people around you who can positively add to this magic. Remember: achieving your sustainable best is seldom a solo journey.

Edison had his assistant, William Joseph Hammer, and ultimately a full research team. Orville had Wilbur. The Founding Fathers of the United States of America had each other and respected one another for the talents they possessed. You have your own circle of people to draw on for both questions and answers in your quest to achieve your personal best.

Marie Curie is a striking example of employing the power of brainstorming and working with others. Marie's stunning accomplishments were a result of her personal determination coupled with collaborating with key people; together they unraveled the mysteries of radiation, identified radioactive isotopes, and sought for the good these discoveries held for all humanity.

A Polish-born French physicist and chemist famous for her work on radioactivity, Marie Curie was a pioneer in the field of radioactivity and the first person honored with two Nobel Prizes—one in physics and the other in chemistry—an honor that resulted from her ability to collaborate with others. Curie was the first woman to win a Nobel Prize, and she is the only woman ever to win the award in two different fields. The first female professor at the University of Paris, she founded the Curie Institutes in Paris and Warsaw.

Her remarkable example of collaboration with others and use of brainstorming in her work is manifest by the well-deserved recognition that came not only to her, but to others involved in her work.

In 1896, Henri Becquerel discovered that uranium salts emitted rays similar to x-rays. Marie and her husband joined forces with Becquerel to study this new phenomenon, which Marie named *radioactivity*, and together they discovered what other substances also emitted these types of rays. In 1903, Marie completed her doctorate in physics and received—along with her husband and Becquerel—the Nobel Prize in physics for their discoveries in the studies of uranium and radioactive materials.

Marie's achievements include the creation of a theory of radioactivity, as well as the discovery of two new elements, polonium and radium. Under her direction, the world's first studies were conducted in the treatment of cancers using radioactive isotopes—the forerunner of today's radiation treatments for cancer patients.

Marie Curie left a wonderful legacy and spent much of her life working with others to create practical applications of her research that would benefit mankind.

Ways to Brainstorm and Expand Your Thinking

Some additional ways to think about brainstorming are illustrated in Edward de Bono's book, *The Use of Lateral Thinking.*

Vertical thinking, as introduced by de Bono, is the process of looking for *right answers.* It is logical and predictable. The goal of vertical thinking is to remove unworkable choices from the list early and often. Vertical thinking is "if, then" with the goal of finding a promising option or solution as soon as possible.

Lateral thinking is everything vertical thinking is not. As highlighted by de Bono, "Vertical thinking moves only if there is a direction in which to move, lateral thinking moves in order to generate a direction."Lateral thinking is used to generate ideas with the goal of developing many possibilities—and then going for even more. In lateral thinking, you consciously refrain from imposing on others your assumptions about what works best. When this kind of thinking is used, leaps in creativity come from open, fast, energetic creation of ideas. Lateral thinking values new patterns of thought, new directions, new ideas, and, especially, lots of options.

Lateral-thinking brainstorms can be used to reassess a process or pattern of decision-making or solution development and can lead to new levels of your best.

Brainstorming as a Team

Brainstorming is creating ideas in a brief get-together or collaboration with a small group where every idea, from the ridiculous to the sublime, is encouraged and recorded. The goal is to create an environment where ideas can flourish. Each new idea stimulates other ideas; the goal is quantity. Ideas are recorded, and judgment of any idea is suspended so that new ideas can keep flowing.

Some organizations have succeeded in institutionalizing imagination, collaboration, and brainstorming into their organizations as a way of doing business. It is part of what they do. This type of "institutional creativity" puts them at the forefront of leadership within their industry.

As mentioned, brainstorming may take place individually or collectively. For now, we'd like you to do a simple exercise with a brainstorming group.

To begin, identify the vision, issue, problem, or opportunity that you would like to develop. Use the following guidelines:

- Keep the group size at a manageable level; work in groups of four to ten.
- Present a vision, problem, issue, or opportunity and start throwing out ideas.
- Give yourself a time limit. Generally limit the brainstorm session to anywhere from ten to thirty minutes.
- Try to eliminate all interruptions or distractions. Turn off cell phones.
- Practice idea generation without judgment; the words "that will never work" are off limits.
- Repeat the process as often as needed.

A scribe should list all ideas and provide a copy to the key stakeholders after the meeting.

Once ideas are generated and recorded, some find it helpful to further divide the ideas into categories, such as those below:

Brainstorming Notes		
Ideas of immediate usefulness	*Areas for further exploration*	*New approaches to the vision, problem, or opportunity*

3. Use Mind-Mapping to Stir Your Imagination and Clarity

Mind-mapping has been used for centuries. Virtually every person who has had a significant impact on society from ancient to contemporary times has used some form of mind-mapping, even if it's as simple as sketching out ideas in a book.

Mind-mapping is a free-flowing and effective creative tool, process, and learning-retention technique for *visually* stimulating, organizing, and arranging ideas; and for determining interconnections, or relationships. This creative tool is fun to use to visually or graphically organize how primary concepts or issues connect with other concepts, ideas, or issues. Those connections are drawn in natural treelike diagrams.

The mind-mapping process allows you to create, organize, clarify thinking, and communicate your ideas into an effective representation of ideas, information, and data. It can be used on an individual basis or as a team exercise.

Start a mind map by *positioning at the center* some vision, idea, opportunity, challenge, or issue. You can start by using words, short phrases, and pictures that are connected to the central issue by connecting lines. The simplest form of mind-mapping is done in longhand, but mind-mapping also may be done with software that is specifically designed for this purpose.

Especially helpful to visual learners, mind-mapping invites you to use images, color, and words to breathe life into concepts and ideas. Mind-mapping then invites you to link the central concept or idea with related concepts and ideas. This process and structure allows you to think of things in a different way and enhances the creative process.

Mind-mapping actively engages both right- and left-brain thinking. It also utilizes both your creative and analytical skills in the process of idea refinement.

Mind-mapping may be used, among other things:

- To visualize and outline discussions, brainstorming sessions, or lectures.
- To organize thoughts or ideas that come to you through these discussions.
- To prepare information for presentations in a way that improves clarity.

One of the most valuable benefits of mind-mapping is that it can increase and support the creative process as you expand upon ideas, issues, and opportunities and as you try to solve perplexing challenges.

Following are practical examples of mind-mapping.

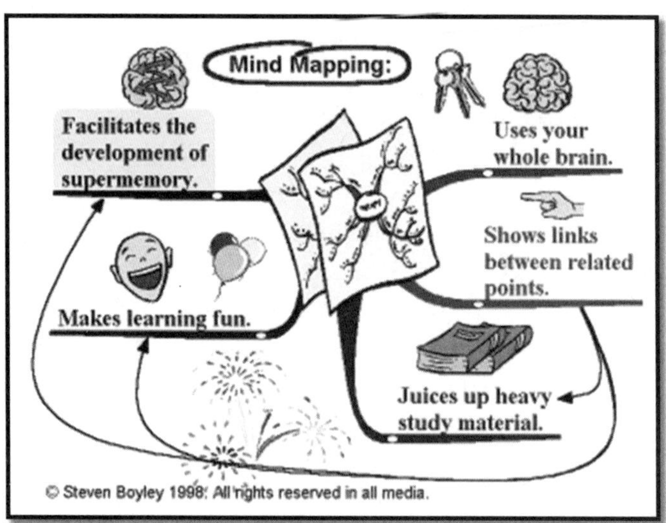

A summary and overview of mind-mapping

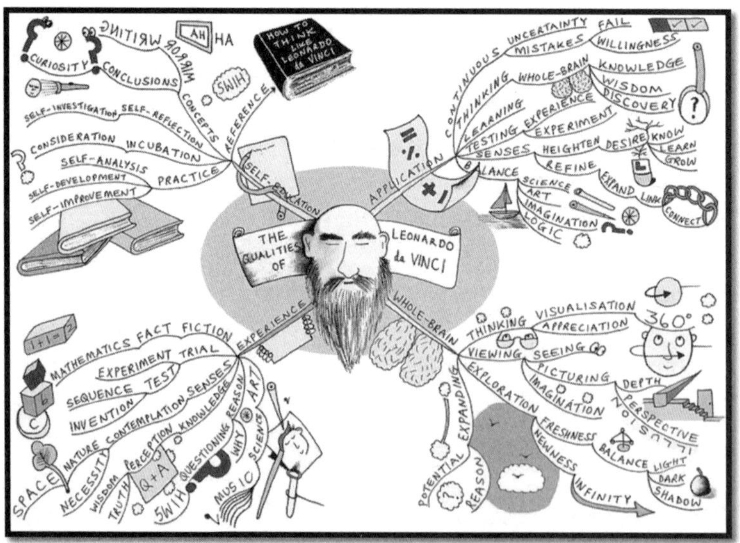

Capturing and presenting a large volume of information in a small space

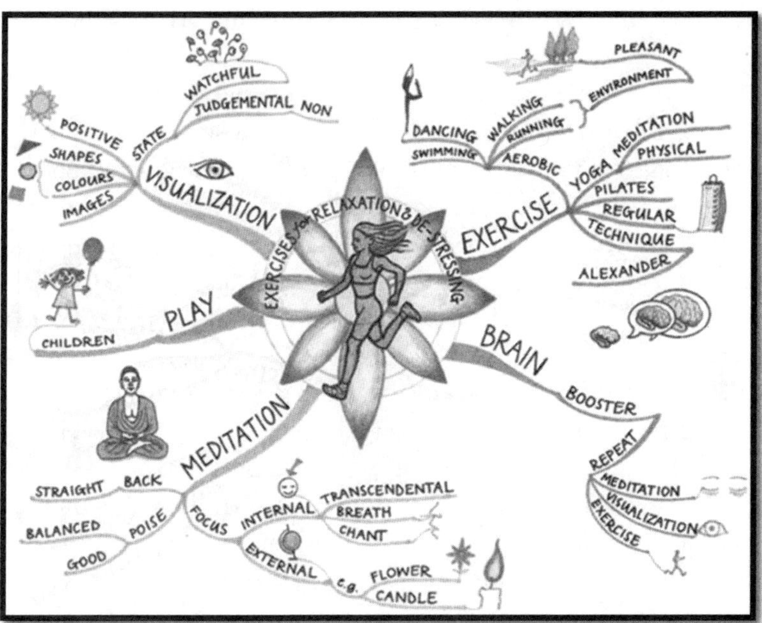

Reinforcing behavior and clarifying thinking

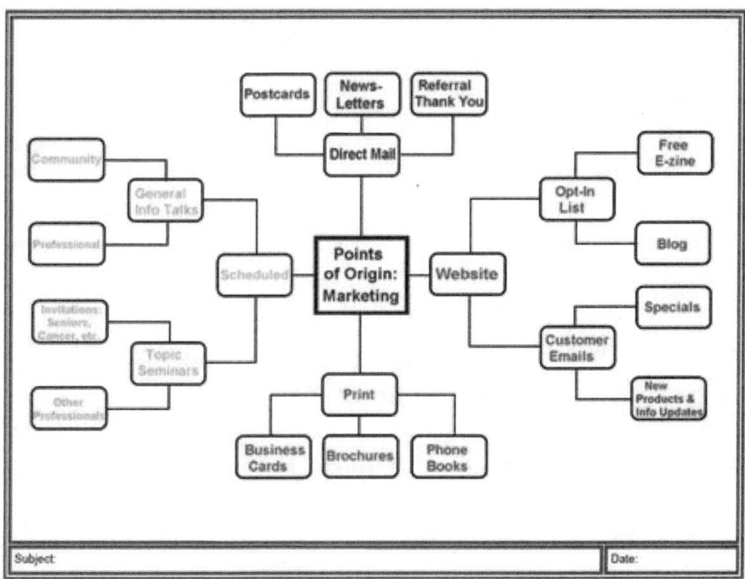

In this case, thinking about ways to market

4. Walk Away for a While—Let the Subconscious Mind Do Its Work

Walk away from your problem? Yes. Evidence published over more than a century reveals that many—maybe even most—significant leaps in science and other disciplines have occurred when people stopped thinking about the problem. Putting it on the shelf, walking away, and giving it a rest works. When you are working hard on a problem, your mind can get wrapped so tightly around it that you repeat the same arguments and review the same "facts" over and over. This prevents you from thinking creatively.

In "Images and Reality: Kekulé, Kopp and the Scientific Imagination," Alan J. Rocke tells the story of August Kekulé, a chemist who "changed the field of chemistry, and all of science" while sleeping.

Kekulé was riding on a London bus when, while in a "twilight state," he awoke with an image of atoms playing and forming bonds together. The pictures he drew of this image are credited as the beginning of the theory of chemical structure. Today we can see the molecule with powerful instruments, but Kekulé "saw" the molecule in a dream at a time of complete mental rest.

Years after his experience with illumination and the molecule, Kekulé was dozing once again by his fireplace when he "saw" an image of linked atoms in what looked to him like snakes intertwined in a circle biting their own tails. Kekulé deduced from this image that carbon atoms could form a hexagonal ring. He was describing what would become known as the benzene ring, a key molecule in industrial chemistry.

There are other notable examples as well. Einstein had a dream that he was sledding at night. As he went progressively faster, he felt he was traveling at the speed of light and noticed various colors in the stars. He later claimed that his entire scientific career was an ongoing meditation of the images in that dream.

It was on a fishing trip that Thomas Edison finally had a breakthrough in discovering the long-lasting carbonized bamboo filament that would allow the lightbulb to burn twelve hundred hours versus the previous best of forty hours. The idea of using bamboo came during a lull in fishing when Edison started examining a few threads from a bamboo fishing pole he was using while relaxing on the shore of Battle Lake in the present-day state of Wyoming. The trip had nothing to do with the lightbulb; he and other members of a scientific team had traveled to the area so they could clearly observe a total eclipse of the sun on July 29, 1878, from the Continental Divide. Edison had left the problem of the filament back at his lab in New Jersey, but his subconscious mind was ever active in quietly coming up with possible solutions.

Avoid the temptation to impose a schedule on your slow-down-and-relax strategy. Resist the urge to rush through your slowing-down time! "Walk away" means *walk away*. If you're afraid of wasting time by shutting down and spending some time away, use the word *incubation* instead. Incubation is defined as a time when the problem is "parked" in the subconscious and nothing visible seems to be going on. Incubation—or walking away—is a thought process in the midst of other processes.

The practice is to stop thinking about the issue and move on to something else for a time. You may find that writing about something completely irrelevant to the problem can help move the problem aside for a time.

5. Write

Writing underscores and reinforces the other four methods of using your imagination, because writing can be such a rich and vital part of boosting imagination. As you start to use any of these methods for developing your imagination, it's important to record the ideas or thoughts that come to you in a notebook.

There is power in writing. Writing on a regular basis will turbocharge your imagination and creativity, and you'll often find that the resulting ideas are totally serendipitous.

One of the greatest examples of writing is Leonardo da Vinci. Leonardo's "thoughts books"—notebooks in which he recorded thoughts, sketches, concepts, and images—were a personal incubation site for ideas and inventions. The image of Leonardo da Vinci is practically inescapable in these books. Some see him as the "quintessential engineer," one able to effectively combine scientific intellect with artistic creativity.

Perhaps best known as an artist, his name inevitably brings forth images of the *Last Supper* and the *Mona Lisa*. He was also an architect and a scientist. Yet if asked, he would ultimately refer to himself as an engineer. Driven by an unrelenting curiosity and an insatiable hunger for knowledge, da Vinci was an incredibly innovative thinker who perceived the world not only as his personal playground but also as one with unlimited possibilities. From his fertile mind grew designs of flying machines and instruments of war as well as practical theories and concepts in engineering, mathematics, and science, many of which were centuries ahead of their times. If da Vinci lived in our time, his accomplishments would have been considered astounding.

Following are a few samples from da Vinci's journals or thoughts books.

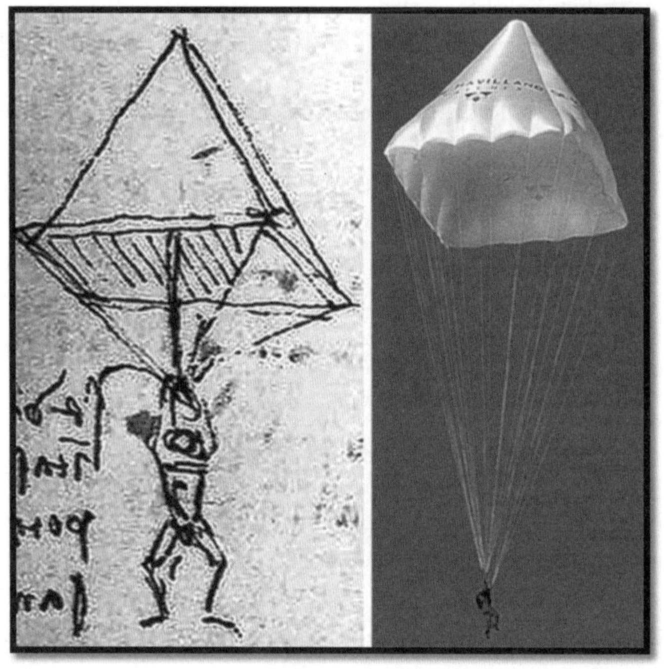

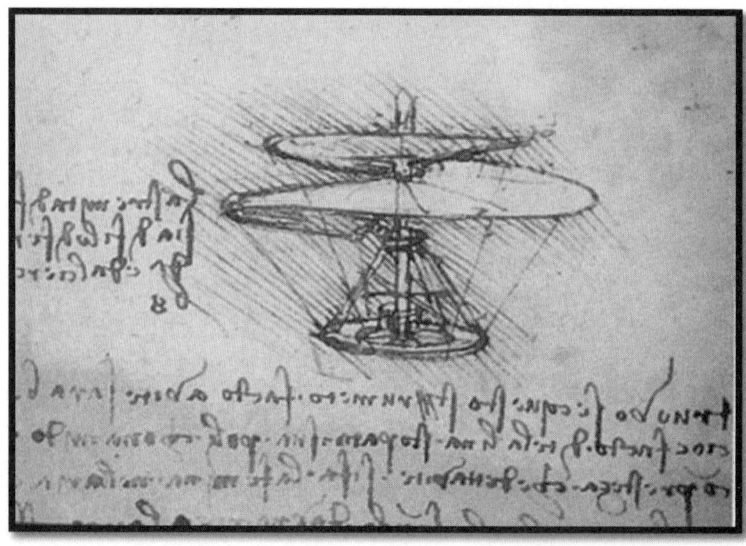

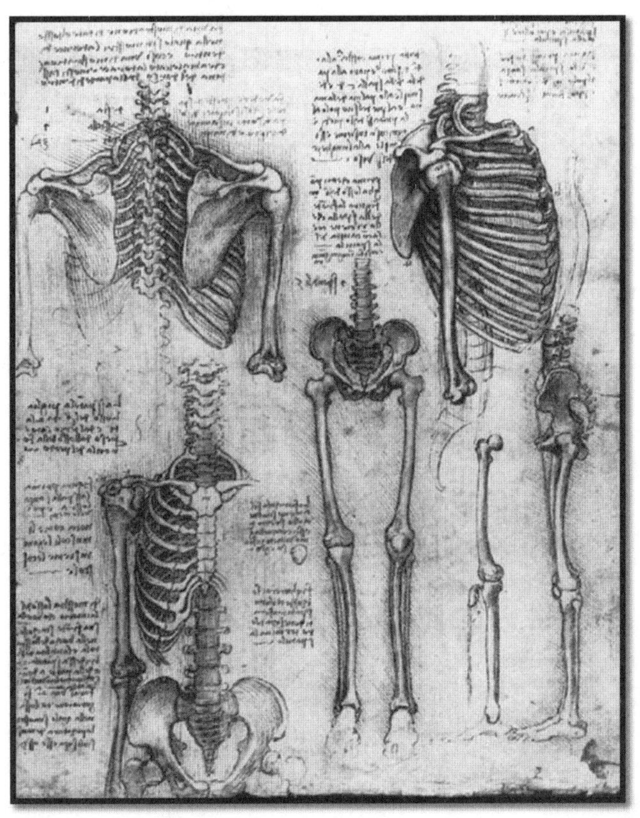

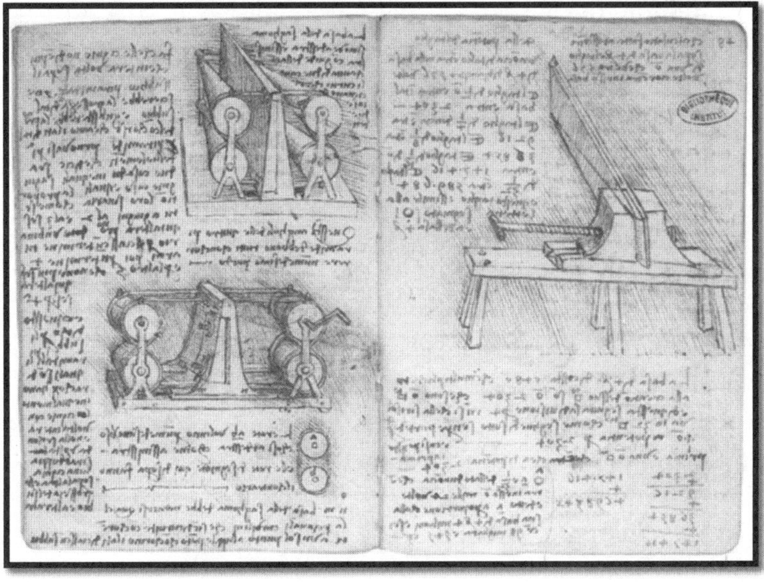

In 1976, John Reed was a senior vice president at Citibank. He had an experience with writing while on vacation in the Caribbean that led to a totally new way to serve customers. The ideas that came from his writing changed not only his bank but the entire industry.

While on vacation, John began to write random notes about business issues at home. He wrote thirty pages of ideas. As the ideas began to take shape, they formed into a blueprint for a new kind of bank—one that offered the national marketing of credit cards and street-level cash machines. Automatic tellers have now become a global way of life, providing twenty-four-hour-a-day service in even some of the most remote places of the world (see *OlinBusiness*, 2010, 2011.)

John Reed, Albert Einstein, Leonardo da Vinci, Anne Frank, Winston Churchill, Ernest Hemingway, Ralph Waldo Emerson, Henry David Thoreau, and Orville and Wilbur Wright all lived at different times and in different places but they had one thing in common: They understood how important writing in notebooks can be.

Sometimes your imagination can only be freed by writing. In fact, your memory and your inner self can be triggered simply by picking up a pencil or pen and poising it over your notebook.

Writing will show you a part of yourself that you've not seen before. Making entries in your notebook will have the effect of clarifying your direction, inspiring your creativity, and giving new importance to your thinking. Lewis and Clark fired a passion for exploration with their notebooks on finding the overland route to the Columbia.

Writing has significance and power because it combines the mind and the body, resulting in a focus not possible with other kinds of thinking. Writing in your notebook can create feelings of both peace and progress—peace as you write about the pressures of family or work life, progress as you record goals and make notes of your dreams for your life. Once you've written your vision down, it is continually before you and hard to erase.

Writing Can Be a Joy, Especially When You Don't Worry About Form

Writing can be a joy. "I don't like to write," writes Michael Kanin, "but I love to have written." You're not trying to be a "writer" but a recorder of your inner and outer world. Your thoughts and ideas are a revelation from your inner mind to your conscious self. Those thoughts are important. You're having them pretty much all the time, and it is time to give them air by recording them.

The act of writing opens up entire new vistas with majestic scenery. Harriet Beecher Stowe thought *Uncle Tom's Cabin* was written through her by "another hand." And according to the Talmud, "Every blade of grass has its angel that bends over it and whispers, 'Grow, grow.'"

The point is that writing connects you to your inner mind, which in turn is connected to a higher mind or higher source of inspiration. Even the legendary composer Johannes Brahms credited his inspiration to a higher power when he said, "Straightway the ideas flow in upon me, directly from God."

Writing fosters a creative process that enables you to, as Gyorgyi said, "look at the same thing as everyone else and think something different."

It is in these moments of creative illumination that answers to personal, relationship, and performance problems are revealed.

Your Will and Your Brain

Your creativity depends on understanding two realities. The first is that you can choose your response to what you see in the external environment. You may be a victim of constant change, especially regarding your external environment, but you are free to choose to achieve your best by responding proactively and with imagination. As Napoleon Hill said, "Every adversity, every failure, every heartache carries with it the seed of an equal or greater benefit."

The second reality is that you have an unlimited capacity for imaginative solutions. Thomas Edison said, "If we did all the things we are capable of doing, we would literally astonish ourselves."

Your brain stands ready. It is waiting to help you. It has all the power you need to creatively respond, even though you use only a tiny fraction of your brain on a daily basis. The brain is not troubled by the complexity of the problem or the depth of pain the problem has caused so far. It is an unlimited source of ideas, answers, strategies, and actions. Your job is to use your imagination.

INSPIRATIONAL QUOTES

Use Your Imagination

"Around here, however, we don't look backwards for very long. We keep moving forward, opening up new doors and doing new things, because we're curious . . . and curiosity keeps leading us down new paths."

— *Walt Disney*

"It is not the brains that matter most, but that which guides them—the character, the heart, generous qualities, progressive ideas."

— *Fyodor Dostoyevsky*

"Imagination is everything. It is the preview of life's coming attractions."

— *Albert Einstein*

"Imagination will often carry us to worlds that never were, but without it we go nowhere."

— *Carl Sagan*

"Without leaps of imagination or dreaming, we lose the excitement of possibilities. Dreaming, after all, is a form of planning."

— *Gloria Steinem*

"Disneyland will never be completed. It will continue to grow as long as there is imagination left in the world."

— *Walt Disney Company*

"Limitations live only in our minds. But if we use our imaginations, our possibilities become limitless."

— *Jamie Paolinetti*

Application

Individually

1. Identify a significant vision, issue, challenge, or opportunity in your life. What is your vision or goal in relation to the issue, challenge, or opportunity?
    a. Review the five ways to fire up your imagination.
    b. Like da Vinci, open your "Thoughts Book" and write the thoughts and ideas that come to you in regard to the idea you are focusing on.
    c. Let the stream of ideas flow and capture them on the pages.

With Others

1. Review one section from this chapter and teach it to others. Discuss some of the things that stand out. Ask, "How can we apply this in our daily lives?"
2. Use an actual example of something that would have significant impact in your life if you did it better. Identify the vision or goal. Write it down. Brainstorm on possible ideas or solutions that can help reach the vision or goal. Identify what you can do to implement the idea or solution.
3. Identify an issue in your organization that needs to be resolved and conduct a brainstorming session to come up with new ideas for solving the problem.

In a Nutshell

Ways to Fire Up Your Imagination

1. Identify an issue, a question that needs answered, an unmet need, or a potential opportunity. Use your imagination to develop best options, solutions, or alternatives.
2. Use questions that help to produce answers. Ask *Who? What? Why? Where? When? How?* Is the potential solution ethical and in line with your character?
3. Stoke your curiosity—what does your best look like?
4. Dream, dream, dream.
5. Collaborate and brainstorm—consider all options. Everything is game. Invite others to join in the creative process.
6. Use mind-mapping to stir your imagination and clarity.
7. Walk away—let your subconscious mind do its work.
8. Write—record your free flow of ideas, bursts of imagination, discoveries, thoughts, and dreams throughout the entire process of creating your best.

Guiding Constant 3

Employ the Power of Knowledge

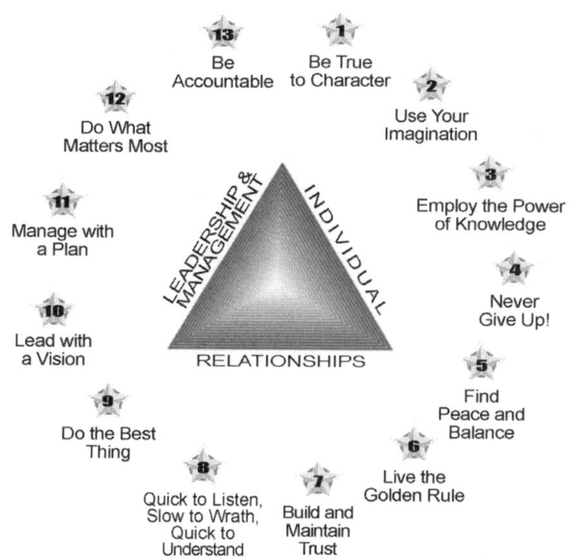

THE INSCRIPTION AT THE BASE of a statue located on the main quad at the US Air Force Academy depicting a falcon and her chick reads, "Man's flight through life is sustained by the power of his knowledge." The inscription uses words like *flight*, *sustained*, and *power* in relationship to knowledge. Indeed, one can be lifted and flight can be sustained by the power of knowledge.

The wings of knowledge and enlightenment can help you soar to great heights in your personal life, in your relationships, and at work. The lack of knowledge leaves you on the ground and at times renders you defenseless against the forces of the external environment.

Consider this: You will be the same in five years as you are today except for two things—the people you meet and the books you read. The message here is powerfully accurate—because inviting these factors into your life is not just random but involves choices you make. Even when you have a setback or tragedy strikes your life, employing the *power of knowledge* (gleaned from the people you meet and the books you read) helps you get to another level in life and helps you be your best. In order to apply it, you first have to acquire it.

What do you (or your organization) want to be like in five years?

If one of your desires is to be the best you can be, what can you do to get to that point? What principles, ideas, and thoughts should you cultivate (a ready mind and heart) and what seeds (knowledge) should you plant?

The fact is that your actions and behavior follow your thoughts. If you thoughtfully engineer what goes into your mind and your heart, these factors of change will have an enormous impact on your ability to achieve your dreams and realize the best you can be.

As you build upon what you have already accomplished and cultivate your unique qualities and characteristics, seek to associate with people (living and deceased) and read books (or CDs, DVDs, movies, music, hard copy, electronic, PDAs) that will move you closer to your goal of becoming your best. Doing these two things will stimulate your thinking and help to build your character. It's also essential that you avoid negative conversations and books that could keep you from your goals and even destroy your dreams.

You are the chooser and the maker, regardless of where you are today. If you are on top of your game today, what represents your best in the next five years? If you are broke, sick, stuck, or feel like a failure, start today to get on track and determine to be in a better place one day, one week, one month, and five years from now. That is the very heart of becoming your best. You can get to a better place; you have the power within you. So determine now to surround yourself with those who can help you get to a better place.

As you travel this journey toward becoming better, be a positive catalyst in that journey. Share the excitement of learning with those who are interested. Those who associate with you will feel the power of growth; even if you don't say anything, the impact of your journey will radiate from within.

The Power of Knowledge and Enlightenment in the Life of Helen Keller

The life of Helen Keller is a testament to the power of knowledge and enlightenment. In just a single year, her life became vibrant and full of possibility as a result of the people she met and the books she read.

Helen was born a healthy, normal child in 1880, but at nineteen months she contracted a disease later thought to be scarlet fever; as she recovered, it rendered her blind and deaf. Because she couldn't hear what others were saying, she couldn't imitate them; her only utterances were animal-like sounds.

When Helen was nearly seven years old, her parents, with the help of Dr. Alexander Graham Bell, employed twenty-year-old Anne Sullivan through the Perkins Institute for the Blind in Boston. When she came to live with the Kellers, she found Helen to be not only blind, deaf, and mute, but totally unmanageable as well. In her frustration at not being able to communicate, Helen screamed, wept, kicked, and bit. But through Anne's careful, patient, and dedicated tutorials, Helen learned not only discipline, but how to communicate.

Helen explains the transformation in her autobiography:

"The most important day I remember in all my life is the one on which my teacher, Anne Mansfield Sullivan, came to me. . . .

"I felt approaching footsteps. I stretched out my hand as I supposed it to be my mother. Someone took it, and I was caught up and held close in the arms of her who had come to reveal all things to me, and, more than all things else, to love me. . . .

"We walked down the path to the well house, attracted by the fragrance of the honeysuckle with which it was covered. Someone was drawing

> *water, and my teacher placed my hand under the spout. As the cool stream gushed over one hand she spelled into the other the word water, first slowly, then rapidly. I stood still, my whole attention fixed upon the motions of her fingers. Suddenly I felt a misty consciousness as of something forgotten—a thrill of returning thought; and somehow the mystery of language was revealed to me. I knew then that 'w-a-t-e-r' meant the wonderful cool something that was flowing over my hand. That living word awakened my soul, gave it light, hope, joy, set it free! There were barriers still, it is true, but barriers that could in time be swept away.*
>
> *"I left the well house eager to learn. Everything had a name, and each name gave birth to a new thought. As we returned to the house every object which I touched seemed to quiver with life. That was because I saw everything with the strange, new sight that had come to me. . . .*
>
> *"I learned a great many new words that day. I do not remember what they all were; but I do know that mother, father, sister, teacher were among them—words that were to make the world blossom for me, 'like Aaron's rod, with flowers.' It would have been difficult to find a happier child than I was as I lay in my crib at the close of the eventful day and lived over the joys it had brought me, and for the first time longed for a new day to come."*

Such is the enlightenment that comes from the power of knowledge. It literally liberates one from darkness.

In 1900, at the age of twenty, Helen entered Radcliff College; she graduated with honors in 1904. She authored a number of books, and she and Anne traveled extensively, giving lectures and raising funds for individuals with disabilities. After Anne's death, Helen continued to give encouragement to anyone who sought her help until a short time before her death in June 1968, shortly before her eighty-eighth birthday.

Dr. Carson Successfully Separates Conjoined Twins

Another inspiring example of employing the power of knowledge is found in the life of Ben Carson.

In 1961, eleven-year-old Bennie Carson was known for getting into trouble and being a slow student. When he got his report card, he had six Fs and two Ds. Ben went home and told his mother, "I'm dumb, Mom."

She replied, "You weren't meant to be a failure. You are a smart boy." New rules were implemented: no homework, no TV. He and his brother moaned. But there were good reasons for the rules. Raised as an orphan, Ben's mother married at the age of thirteen and within a few years found herself divorced with two boys. She didn't know how to read and wanted to be sure her boys didn't turn out the same way.

Ben's mother continued inspiring her boys to employ the knowledge available to them. When Ben once proclaimed, "My brain is dumb," his mother challenged him to use his imagination—and when he protested that he didn't have one, she asked him to finish a sentence: "Once upon a time there was a blue mouse," she began, then prompted, "Then what happened?" When Ben couldn't finish the sentence—still claiming his lack of imagination—she said, pointing to his head, "You have all the world in there. You just have to see beyond what you can see."

When Ben told his mother he wanted to be a doctor just like the one his pastor talked about in a sermon, his mother told him, "You can be anything you want to be in life, as long as you are willing to work at it. God will not abandon you."

Ben's mind was fired up, and he wanted to learn more and more. He was introduced to a library and started to study and learn in areas that interested him. The more knowledge he gained, the more exciting the process of learning became. Soon he went from last to first in his class, excelling in spelling, science, and math. He was totally turned on to learning. He kept hearing his mother's words: "You have all the world in there."

His teachers recognized that something profound had caused Ben to change. One day Mr. Jurek, the science teacher, invited Ben to look through a microscope at amoeba cells on a slide. When Ben asked what he was seeing, the teacher replied, "That is a whole new world, Ben. *You have just stepped into a whole 'nother world.*"

Ben was off and running! He never looked back. His desire to gain knowledge and the discipline with which he studied let him rapidly gain knowledge and insights that many others did not have. That year Ben was awarded the highest academic achievement in the eighth grade.

Ben Carson went on to attend Yale University, where he earned a degree in psychology. From Yale, he attended the University of Michigan Medical School, where his interest shifted from psychiatry to neurosurgery. After medical school, Ben completed his residency at the top-ranked Johns Hopkins Hospital in Baltimore. At age thirty-two, he became the hospital's youngest director of pediatric neurosurgery.

Ben Carson made history by being the first in the world to successfully separate a pair of twins joined at the head. A seventy-member surgical team led by Dr. Carson worked for twenty-two hours. An innovative procedure he created reduced the chance of the twins bleeding to death during surgery and made all the difference in the success of the outcome.

Dr. Carson's other surgical innovations were equally remarkable. He developed the first intrauterine procedure to relieve pressure on the brain of a hydrocephalic fetal twin. He also developed a procedure in which an infant suffering from uncontrollable seizures had half of its brain removed while the remaining half fully adjusted and carried on normal functions.

The surgeon who did it all was the same person who, as a young man in the eighth grade, believed he was stupid. His insatiable desire to gain knowledge, to learn, to read, to study, to ask questions, and to understand gave Dr. Carson the ability to become a doctor and to save lives in a way no one else had been able to do. By persistently and energetically seeking and employing knowledge, Ben opened new worlds of ideas to those within his profession. Literally, his thirst for knowledge gave him a whole new view of the world.

As you gain knowledge and enlightenment, you will acquire greater freedom and power to act and work toward the best in whatever you try.

How Is Knowledge Freedom and Power?

A simple yet stunning illustration can be found in Zambia's Mwense district. The natives of the district have been taught how to keep drinking water clean and how to remove the habitat of the mosquitoes that carry malaria. This knowledge gives the villagers the freedom to make wise choices. to establish a better quality of life from improved health practices, and to have power over the fatality of this disease.

Another example occurred in World War II; when they broke the Japanese communication codes, United States forces were able to intercept and understand critical attack information. As a result, the United States was able to anticipate the Battle of Midway, defeat one of the most powerful navies in the world, and make significant progress toward ending World War II.

These are just two examples of employing the power of knowledge. An amazing yet simple transformation occurs wherever knowledge is properly used.

Knowledge and Enlightenment Can Lead to You Being Your Best

Knowledge is defined as skills, facts, and information acquired through various means. It is what is known—it is things as they are. It is the result of experiencing, learning, and understanding.

To *think* you know is not to know. For example, you may presume that a particular trend in the economy will continue or that certain company strategies will produce anticipated results. To say that you *know* these two things is a mistake. They will be known only when the facts are in and the data has been collected—assuming, of course, that the facts and data are verifiable. The purity of knowledge is that it presumes nothing.

Knowledge is a foundation for achieving your best. "This is the nature of genius," said Deepak Chopra, "to be able to grasp the knowable even when no one else recognizes that it is present." Creating the best is a habit of doing things to ensure that you know all that is knowable and that you act on it with humility and confidence.

Knowledge, added to the foundations of character and imagination, extends your ability to achieve your best. To employ the *power of knowledge* is not just knowing; it is being enlightened enough to make the best decision leading to the best outcome. Knowledge is more than information. The power of knowledge entails properly employing information for good and effective results.

The goal of Guiding Constant 3 is to learn how to employ knowledge—knowledge that empowers you and lifts you to new heights of success in your personal life, in your relationships, and in your performance.

Six key factors can help you employ knowledge. Remember: You will be the same in five years as you are today *except* for two things—the people you meet and the books you read.

Six Key Factors That Help You Employ the Power of Knowledge

1. Hunger and thirst for knowledge. Read, meet, associate, and observe.
2. Regularly assess the external environment. "Change" can provide you with valuable opportunities or churn you up in its wake. Use the External Environment Assessment Tool.
3. Walk to the edge of the best—innovation and research. What's out there now? What does the best look like? Who has succeeded? Who has failed? What is the baseline or benchmark?
4. Ask for feedback. Feedback is the breakfast of champions!
5. Think straight—avoid being surprised.
6. Use the "light" of knowledge, wisdom, and judgment.

1. Hunger and Thirst for Knowledge

The story is told of a young man who approached Socrates as he sat by a lake. The young man told Socrates he would do anything to gain the wisdom Socrates possessed.

After a moment, Socrates stood up and motioned for the young man to follow him. He walked into the lake until he was waist deep in water. Then Socrates asked the young man what he really wanted. When the young man insisted that he wanted wisdom, Socrates pushed the young man's head under the water. The man struggled and finally surfaced, wondering what the philosopher was up to. Again, Socrates asked him what he wanted. The man responded, "Wisdom." Again Socrates shoved his head under water. The man struggled longer before finally coming up for air. For the third time, Socrates asked the man what he really wanted. When he pushed his head under water this time, Socrates held it there for almost an entire minute. The man finally fought his way up, gasping for air.

Socrates asked him in that moment: "What is it you want?" This time the man was honest. He said, "I want air!" Socrates smiled and responded, "When you want wisdom as much as you wanted that breath of air, you won't need me, and you shall get it."

So it is with knowledge. When you hunger and thirst for knowledge as much as you want air, you will get it.

Sometimes you need to focus on a desire or idea and hold it in your mind until you can choose the thing you desire—and that becomes your vision or goal. With a clear goal in mind, you can choose to act in ways that create the result you are after. Once you latch onto an inspiring and captivating vision or goal, it can provide you with the fire to pursue your dreams.

That's what happened to Ben Carson when he decided to become a doctor.

And that's what happened to a young boy in post-World War II Germany who decided to become a pilot.

Desire for Learning

Dieter Uchtdorf recounted, "I was eleven years old and living with my family in the attic of a farmhouse near Frankfurt, Germany. We were refugees for the second time in a period of only a few years, and we were struggling to establish ourselves in a new place far away from our previous home. I could say that we were poor, but that would be an understatement.

"During the difficult economic conditions of postwar Germany, opportunities for education were not as abundant as they are today. But in spite of limited options, *I always felt an eagerness to learn.* I remember one day, while I was out on my bike delivering laundry, I entered the home of a classmate of mine. In one of the rooms, two small desks were nestled against the wall. What a wonderful sight that was! How fortunate those children were to have desks of their own! I could imagine them sitting with open books studying their lessons and doing their homework. It seemed to me that having a desk of my own would be the most wonderful thing in the world.

"I had to wait a long time before that wish was fulfilled. Years later, I got a job at a research institution that had a large library. I remember spending much of my free time in that library. There I could finally sit at a desk—by myself—and drink in the information and knowledge that books provide. How I loved to read and learn! In those days I understood firsthand the words of an old saying: *Education is not so much the filling of a bucket as the lighting of a fire.*"

Because of the circumstances of his family's poverty, Mr. Uchtdorf appeared to have few options, but through an education he became an agent with the power to choose. He loved flying. He pursued a course to become qualified to fly for the German Air Force in a joint program with the United States. The course required that he first learn English. Mr. Uchtdorf did this successfully. The experiences and knowledge he gained enabled Mr. Uchtdorf to pursue a career that eventually led him to a position as a 747 jumbo jet captain—and ultimately as the chief pilot for Lufthansa Airlines.

From a young age, Mr. Uchdtdorf developed a great faith in God. Because of that faith and his capable leadership skills, he became an inspirational leader of a worldwide humanitarian religious organization influencing many millions of people for good.

There are two forces in the world: you can act or you can be acted upon. Throughout your life, you can either be *the agent* and act, or you can be *the object* that is acted upon. What's the difference? The agent has the agency—the freedom to act, the ability to choose. Knowledge and understanding are the keys to this freedom, the "wings" that give you flight into success. Once you've chosen to obtain knowledge, you are equipped with both the power and the disposition to work to achieve your best.

"Someone said there are always two choices open to us; two paths of choice," says *Harry Potter* author J. K. Rowling, "that show what we truly are, far more than our abilities." Or, we might add, our circumstances. You always have choices—even if only to choose your attitude at the moment. Complain, whine, and give up—or value your time and believe in your capacity to gain the knowledge that frees you to act and to succeed.

"Man's flight through life is sustained by the power of his knowledge." What does that statement mean? So far, we've learned that—like Helen Keller, Ben Carson, or Dieter Uchtdorf—you can learn to act and make the best of your circumstances. When you increase in learning and education, you increase your ability to act (your power) and you improve your circumstances. This is why "thirsting for knowledge" is a Guiding Constant and a source of power.

How Can You Light the Fire of the Power of Knowledge?

- Hunger and thirst to know all that you can about life and about every subject possible. Have an attitude of humility toward gaining knowledge. No matter how old you are, never think that you already know it all. Be *humble* about learning. Learning is an attitude.

- What types of people lift, inspire, and encourage you toward your best? Do you seek them out, listen, observe, ask for advice, and imitate the good that you see in them?
- What books, tapes, CDs, DVDs, and media help ignite your thinking?
- What university, college, or school—whether on-site or distance learning—can help you complete a single class or a degree?
- What seminars, conferences, organizational training, and webinars can help you?
- Gain knowledge through "Three-Person Teaching," also known as the Walter Gong approach. You capture information from the teacher. You apply information. You become the teacher. In other words, be a hungry learner, and then teach what you have learned to others. Then have them teach you.
- How can you develop a "brain trust" and associate with mentors and other positive associates in a way that helps both you and them in the process?
- Voraciously use the Internet to seek information, different sides of the story, and what is out there.
- Surround yourself with people who desire to achieve the best.

With the basis of a desire to learn, let's now move on to an enlightening tool that can make all the difference in your life: examining the external environment.

2. Regularly Assess the External Environment—Keep an Eye on Change

Change Is Constant

Knowledge is what you get when you ask what is happening in the external environment.

The *external environment* is everything that is happening outside your immediate surroundings.

It is important to realize that the external environment most often cares nothing about you. It can be cold, impersonal, brutal, and totally impartial.

It is Mother Nature, and it's unpredictable. If you know it's coming, you can often minimize its impact or seize the opportunity.

It's also important to realize that not everything in the external environment affects you. Your primary interest, then, are those things in the external environment that affect your internal environment—your personal life, your family, your business, your community.

The external environment is "change." These changing forces represent both a threat and an opportunity to you individually and to the organizations you are associated with.

Everyone is familiar with change. You've seen the change cycle take place numerous times as economies have gone up and down. Bull markets have become bear markets. In 2008, the economic bubble burst. Housing prices dropped rapidly; entire industries were crushed seemingly overnight. Millions lost their homes and their jobs. Organizations that were at the top of their game were either scaled back significantly or simply disappeared altogether. Virtually everyone was affected one way or another.

It is interesting to note that if we were carefully looking into the external environment—*using the power of knowledge*—we could have seen danger signs in the market, including increased debt levels, reckless spending, and more debt. We would have noticed investments in the lending industry that began to collapse as mortgage defaults started occurring. By seeing these trends, we could have made appropriate decisions to defend ourselves from the coming economic tsunami. We could have moved to higher ground by getting out of debt and making sure our job skills allowed us to support ourselves in tough economic times.

If we waited until the economic tsunami hit, it was much more difficult to respond.

It is important to remember that "what was good enough for yesterday often is not good enough for tomorrow." Change is ongoing. Just think about how different the world is today than it was five years ago.

It is absolutely vital to be aware of what is going on in the external environment (change) that may affect you for good or bad, both personally and professionally.

The External Environment

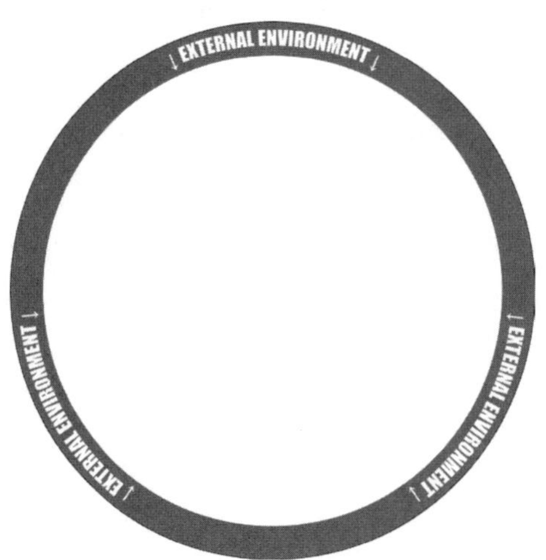

Ways You Can Explore the External Environment to Gain Much-Needed Knowledge

A. Use the External Environmental Analysis (EEA)

The External Environment Analysis is a tool you can use many times; with practice, you can get good at spotting issues coming at you *before* they hit. As a result, you have an opportunity to prepare in advance for things that could either harm you or that could benefit you.

This type of understanding and knowledge can literally make the difference between success and failure—and can shed a new light on everything.

To see how it works, draw a circle that fills half the page. You are on the inside of the circle (your internal world); the external environment is everything outside the circle that is coming in at you. At the top of the page, write your focus; it might include something like personal life, relationships, professional life, organizational issues, community issues, or issues in the country.

Now "look" outward to the external environment and note things that are "incoming."

Ask yourself, "What do I see?" Write down everything you see. Just let the ideas flow and record your observations as quickly as you can.

Spend part of your time looking for threats or dangers. Spend the rest of your time looking for opportunities.

Consider keeping your EEAs in a binder, notebook, or in your Thoughts Book. You will find that you gain new insights into the external environment each time you review your work.

B. Prioritize and Rank Your Observations by Biggest Threat or Largest Opportunity

Once you've finished the EEA—which could take ten minutes or ten weeks—prioritize your observations and issues by importance. In other words, prioritize them by what matters most.

What represents the biggest threat to you? What represents the largest opportunity?

Armed with this information, you are now in a better position to exercise leadership to get to a better place.

C. Anticipating Hidden Change in the External Environment

Ironically, what is real at any given time may be difficult to discern. Sorting out false information from reality can at times be challenging.

Realities hidden from your view are troubling. At times, there is little opportunity to know and respond. For example, ask the couple who closed on a new home a month before the economy crashed; if they had been looking for the right signs, they would have known that their home would soon be worth half of what they paid for it. Ask the airline captain piloting a passenger jet from LaGuardia Airport in New York to North Carolina how he could have anticipated a huge flock of geese flying into his path and shutting down both engines.

What can you do when it's not possible to know in advance? You can anticipate worst cases and prepare for them. In the case of the home purchase, you can plan an exit strategy for whatever might happen. You could ask yourself, "What home price can we afford assuming we lose our employment, cannot sell the home quickly, and have to live in it for several years?" Many who lost their homes to foreclosure in the recession of 2008–2011 made purchases based on the assumption that nothing would change. But conditions did change, leaving many with no option but foreclosure or short sales.

Let's look at the case of geese and the passenger jet. Crew members had anticipated and trained for all eventualities, enabling them to act instantly

to avert disaster. They employed the *power of knowledge and enlightenment* to save the passengers. In the case of US Airways 1549, instant decisions saved lives because the pilot anticipated potential changes.

That pilot—Chesley "Sully" Sullenberger III—and his crew are credited with saving all of the passengers. No stranger to safety and accident investigations, Sullenberger has assisted in several National Transportation Safety Board investigations, served as safety chairman of the Air Line Pilots Association, and founded an air safety company, Safety Reliability Methods. A graduate of the US Air Force Academy, he also received degrees from Purdue University and the University of Northern Colorado.

If there was ever a pilot prepared to take a "bird strike" and safely land his plane, it would be Sully. He was prepared because of the power that came from his knowledge of situational emergency preparation. He had prepared for this eventuality long before it happened.

D. Be Aware of Incorrect or False "Knowledge"

It is possible that "knowledge" may be accepted as real *when it is not*. People, organizations, or entire industries can become obsolete overnight by believing "knowledge" that proves to be incorrect or false. "There is no harm in providing subprime mortgages," said the bankers, real estate brokers, and many others associated with the recession of 2008–11. Because the external circumstances and internal fundamentals were operating on "knowledge" that proved false, the assumed strength of the financial and real estate industries disintegrated overnight. It is essential to have correct knowledge.

3. Walk to the Edge of the Best—Innovation and Research—What Else Is Out There?

What else is out there? What represents the best today? How can you improve on it? What does your best look like?

A good example of this type of thinking led Thomas Edison into taking a careful look at the lightbulb.

Building on the contributions of other inventors over the previous three-fourths of a century—*that's right, seventy-five years*—Edison made such dramatic improvements to the idea of the incandescent light that he became known as "the inventor" of the lightbulb.

The main problem Edison encountered with the lightbulb was its short life. It was certainly too short—and thus too expensive—for practical application. It was really nothing more than a struggling technology at the time. The materials were too expensive and were not easily accessible, and the processes for mass production were not practical.

After many experiments with platinum and other metal filaments, Edison, then forty years old, returned to a carbon filament. The first successful test was on October 22, 1879; the light lasted forty hours. Edison continued to improve this design and by November 4, 1879, filed for US patent 223,898 (granted on January 27, 1880) for an electric lamp using "a carbon filament or strip coiled and connected to patina contact wires." Although the patent described several ways of creating the carbon filament—including "cotton and linen thread, wood splints, papers coiled in various ways"—it was not until several months after the patent was granted that Edison and his team discovered a carbonized bamboo filament that could last more than twelve hundred hours.

Edison and his team started by reviewing what body of knowledge existed. Then they asked themselves, "Can we improve on what currently exists? What does the best look like?" Then they went to work to creatively solve the problem of the lightbulb's short burn time.

Ask yourself what additional information is available that has not yet been considered. What assumptions are you making—without even realizing it— that color your view of the external environment at this moment? What body of information or research already exists that defines the current best?

Another remarkable example of this process occurred in the spring of 1899, when Wilbur Wright wrote to the Smithsonian asking for information about experiments with flying.

Orville and Wilbur Wright, credited with inventing manned flight, started with learning everything they could about the external environment. "I wish to avail myself of all that is already known," said Wilbur Wright, "and then, if possible, add my mite to help on the future worker who will attain final success." They studied what had been done up to 1900 and began their own efforts after developing a full understanding. The reason? By learning all that was available to know, they could avoid the mistakes and build on the successes. Knowledge provided the Wright brothers with power that made them free to act.

While it seems obvious that a thorough study of the work already done would yield benefits, no one had done it before. No one had thoroughly analyzed what was going on in the external environment. Not only did the Wright brothers study others' efforts, their knowledge resulted in the ability to judge the merits of that work and make use of only the best knowledge—knowledge that was based on real science and not on assumptions or superstitions.

The simple questions they began asking in their bicycle shop resulted in more curiosity and more questions. After more than a thousand failed attempts, every time answering a new question, they achieved the dream of humanity—sustained flight.

Get the Facts or Leave it Alone, or the Conclusions You Come to May Be Your Own

I recently was visiting with an individual who is an "expert" in the energy field. We were discussing the solar generation industry and a key factor that may affect its future success. Our firm had recently completed about thirty solar installations, and we were reflecting on the future of the solar industry and how to best position our firm in the market.

I had heard that energy prices were expected to quadruple in the next ten years. My "expert" said, "I don't believe that's an accurate perspective." When I asked why, he said, "There are thirty-seven nuclear plants being built right now that will be coming online in the coming years. These plants will help to keep energy prices low."

This was a much different perspective than I had been operating on. Imagine if someone made a decision to build a solar infrastructure based solely on the apparent "information" that energy prices would go up four times in the next ten years, making solar energy more economically feasible—when that assumption may not be accurate. That perspective could have disastrous consequences, especially if the decision was based only on that information. Good questions to ask are, "What if the information I have is incomplete or false?" "How do I get the correct and complete information?" "Have I considered all of the possibilities in the external environment?"

Just three months after this discussion came the 9.1 earthquake and tsunamis in northern Japan, which heavily damaged the nuclear power plant; radiation leaked into the atmosphere. Because of massive shifts in the external environment, policymakers and people worldwide now question whether nuclear power is safe as part of a sustainable energy policy and portfolio.

4. Ask for Feedback: Feedback Is the Breakfast of Champions

General Mills has doggedly branded its Wheaties cereal as the "Breakfast of Champions." It's also safe to say, "Feedback is the Breakfast of Champions."

The ability to accept feedback and to correct your directions or decisions is a key indicator of the champions in personal development, relationships, and performance. Successful parents, spouses, employees, and executives boldly own their own ideas and will not let go of them without testing them.

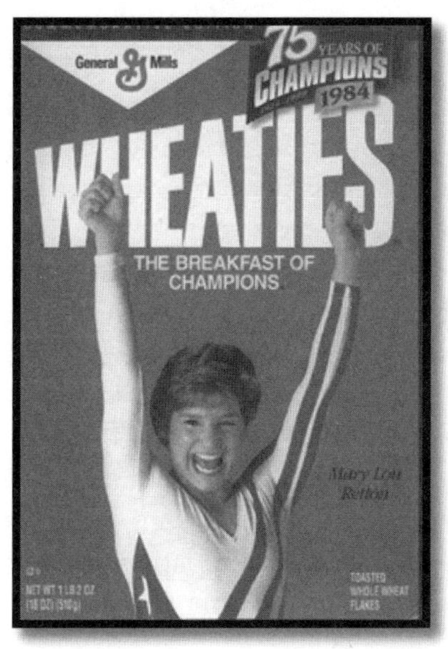

Champions know that success is inevitable; that there is no such thing as failure—only feedback. They know that the best way to forecast the future is to create it.

There are two keys to gaining knowledge through feedback. The first is to assemble a network of people who will provide honest, insightful opinions about what you are doing. Second is to know how to solicit and accept feedback with questions. You might ask, "Honey, does this tie work with this jacket?" or "The focus group data says the product will be a winner. What are we missing that could trip us up? What is out there that we don't see that could derail us and wipe out the success we are anticipating?"

A Feedback Network

People you respect—people who have experience and can be candid and honest about your performance, your relationship with your children, and the company's strategy or the product's potential—are worth their weight in gold.

This is a virtual feedback network. Think of feedback as a process of your subconscious. In your mind's eye, seat a number of the great minds at a round boardroom table. Shut your eyes and ask, "What would Edison do?" "What would Ghandi do?" Listen carefully to impressions from your subconscious mind.

How to Solicit Feedback

First, be prepared to accept feedback. Park your tendency to be offended or hurt when someone criticizes or fails to lavish praise on your latest idea. Be quick to listen, humble, open, and willing to learn from others. Refuse to blame others.

Create a culture of feedback and open communication. Foster feedback by complimenting those who give it and by taking it into account in visible ways. You can make it okay to provide feedback by how you respond to it. The most fruitful forms of feedback may occur in private conversations where there is no competition to be heard, no one-upsmanship, and no fear of speaking one's mind. Individual opportunities for feedback also give you the chance to follow up and praise the feedback provider.

Keep it simple. Think in your mind, *What should I continue? What should we start doing? What should I stop doing?* Keeping it simple also means being clear about what you want to know.

Ask the right people. Which members of your family, work team, or organization will provide honest opinions and keep your questions and their feedback confidential? You're not looking for real feedback if you're simply looking for validation of a decision already made or not looking for ways of doing something better.

Formal and Informal Feedback

Asking for suggestions and advice may best be done in informal moments. Questions can be asked while driving to a meeting, flying to a conference, or over lunch. "How can we improve our associates' training?" "What does the best look like for the company? For the group?" Informal feedback is useful for collecting information on processes, product development, strategy development, and even the skills needed by new hires. Opinions of all kinds inform our thinking and provide reality checks for the direction various activities are taking.

What should we continue?

What should we start?

What should we stop?

Feedback in your family or with others you work closely with may not necessarily be collected through a survey. That is why management by "walking around" can be so valuable. On the other hand, simple surveys such as a Continue-Start-Stop survey can be useful. This can be accomplished by writing three questions—What should we continue? What should we start? What should we stop?—on a piece of paper and asking for feedback.

Formal feedback can be collected through anonymous surveys. Even simple surveys, such as Continue-Start-Stop, can be formally collected. Survey tools are available for creating online surveys where data analysis is instant. You can construct simple polls in blog or discussion board applications. Contemporary tools with analytics such as Survey Monkey, Survey Gizmo, Zoomerang, and the likes are free or reasonably priced for professional versions. Tools such as Qualtrics and Checkbox provide industrial-strength survey capabilities. All are available today and are being continually improved.

5. Think Straight—Avoid Being Surprised

We are all thinking all of the time. But the capacity to "think straight" is a key to obtaining and clearly interpreting knowledge.

Unfortunately, all thinking isn't straight thinking. William J. Reilly wrote a classic piece about the invention of the air brake for trains. Apparently Westinghouse engineers believed such a task was impossible. They claimed they knew that by experience. Reilly *didn't* have experience, so he didn't let the Westinghouse assessment discourage him from finding the solution that ultimately resulted in a successful air brake for trains.

Straight thinking is thinking supported by evidence and stripped of assumptions, presumptions, and prejudices. Realize that you can assume that you understand when you actually do not.

How can you develop the ability to think straight? First, learn that mistakes in thinking are common and that you can anticipate them.

The Rules of Straight Thinking (adapted from the premise and rules of M. Russell Ballard, "Let Us Think Straight")

A. Straight Thinking Begins with Straight Listening

Carefully listening will help ensure that the advice, feedback, or data you are receiving is properly and wisely taken into account. The listener who is humble is also teachable. You may "hear" advice with your ears but not internalize it into your whole self, leaving advice to rattle around in competition with your status or your belief that you already know. Knowledge is all around you and available to you if you'll practice straight listening.

B. Straight Thinking Requires That You Move Methodically and Get the Facts

Getting the facts does not always happen quickly. A successful leader who wanted to stimulate thinking about the facts put a facetious sign on his desk that said, "Don't confuse me with the facts. My mind is already made up."

In his 1711 *Essay on Criticism*, Alexander Pope wrote "A little learning is a dang'rous thing." What makes a little knowledge dangerous is that you can presume to have enough—then make erroneous choices based on that presumption. "If a little knowledge is dangerous, where is the man who has so much as to be out of danger?" asked Huxley.

It is dangerous to think you know—according to Chester Barnard, that's the greatest barrier to knowledge. Thinking you have enough knowledge to act when you do not is dangerous at many levels.

C. Think Until It Hurts

Lord Thompson of Fleet, creator of an empire of more than four hundred businesses, said that we are averse to thinking. To be successful, you must "think until it hurts." Lord Thompson also said, "Sloppy, inconclusive thinking becomes a habit. The more one does it, the more one is unfitted to think a problem through to a proper conclusion"(Lord Thomson of Fleet, *After I Was Sixty* [London: Hamis Hamilton, 1975], 106).

> *"If I have any advice to pass on as a successful man, it is this: If one wants to be successful, one must think. One must think until it hurts. One must worry a problem in one's mind until it seems there cannot be another aspect of it that hasn't been considered. Believe me, that is hard work and, from my close observation, I can say that there are few people indeed who are prepared to perform this arduous and tiring work. But let me go further and assure you of this: While in the early stages, it is hard work, and one must accept it as such. Later one will find that it is not so difficult. The thinking apparatus has become trained; it is trained even to do some of the thinking subconsciously. . . . The pressure that one had to use on one's poor brain in the early stages is no longer necessary. . . . One's mental computer arrives at decisions instantly or during a period when the brain seems to be resting. It is only the rare and most complex problems that require the hard toil of protracted mental effort" (Thomson, After Sixty, 106).*

D. Build Up a Bank of Experience

Once again from Lord Thompson: "I was entirely convinced that, through the years, in my brain as in a computer, I had stored details of problems themselves, the decisions reached, and the result obtained; everything else was neatly filed away there for future use.

"Then, later, when a new problem arose, I would think it over and, if the answer was not immediately apparent, I would let it go for a while, and it was as if it went the rounds of the brain cells looking for guidance that could be retrieved. For by next morning, when I examined the problem again, more often than not the solution came up right away.

"That judgment seemed to come almost unconsciously, and my conviction is that during the time that I was not consciously considering the problem, my subconscious had been turning it over and relating it to my memory; it had been held up to the light of experiences I had had in the past years, and the way through the difficulties became obvious. I am pretty sure that other older men have had this same evidence of the brain's subconscious work."

"This makes it all very easy, you may say. But, of course, it doesn't happen easily. The bank of experience from which I was able to draw in the later years was not easily funded" (Thomson, *After Sixty*, 105).

6. Use the "Light" of Wisdom and Good Judgment

How do you develop good wisdom and good judgment? Where is common sense? Someone once said that good judgment comes from experience, and experience comes from bad judgment. Learning from mistakes is as valuable as any learning available. Horace Greely said, "Common sense is very uncommon." Why do you suppose this may be true?

Emerson says that "common sense is genius dressed in its working clothes." Common sense is the ability to see things as they are without filtering them through the lens of your own prejudice and then acting on that sense with good judgment.

Situations, Situations, Situations

While attending Vallejo High School in Northern California, I was fortunate to play on our championship baseball team. Our coach, Norm Tanner, had been a professional pitcher in the Boston Red Sox organization. I was a catcher, among other positions, and played throughout junior high, high school, and later, college. We saw a lot of very good teams and some that were not so good.

During the last part of each practice, Coach Tanner did what he called "situations." We would field the team, put runners on the bases, and create situations we might expect to find in a game. Using his Fungo bat, the coach would unpredictably hit the ball unpredictably somewhere to see how we would respond.

For example, he created one situation where runners were on first and third bases with one out. Then he bunted the ball down the first-base line. There was no time to think. What would we all do? If it's a somewhat short bunt, the catcher stays home—and the pitcher has to field the ball, check the runner at third base or home, and go for the sure out at first. If it is a short-short bunt, the catcher takes it, checks the runner on third base, and looks for the double play at second to first and goes for the sure out. If it is a medium bunt down first, the pitcher covers first and the first baseman makes the play on the ball, checks the runner on third, and goes for the double play or sure out.

And so it went. We ran hundreds and thousands of every situation imaginable. When game time came, we didn't worry about how we would respond. We were ready! This helped us to avoid "mental errors." It made us into a championship team in our league.

In raising children, in running organizations, and in making decisions as you go along in life, you may find this practice of reviewing situations in advance helpful. This practice frequently allows you to build on your experience to make good choices in the future, especially when the pressure is on.

How Do You Gain Wisdom?

- Ask for advice from others who have had experience.
- Gain your own experience firsthand. Feel the happiness and pain. Experience the trial and error, the hurt and the healing, the winning and the losing. You become seasoned through experience.
- Regularly go through situations and improve your ability to respond during pressure situations.

- Keep track of your *judgment quotient*—setting a goal and then seeing how close you come to achieving the goal or doing what you say. Keep track of your goals and how you perform on them. You can regularly track the judgment quotient in your organization. Did you achieve 105 percent or 75 percent? This helps you improve the competency of your judgment over time.

Common Sense and G*ood Judgment* Come from Experience

M. Russell Ballard shared the following experience: "I signed an Edsel franchise with Ford Motor Company. [The Edsel was] one of the most disastrous national marketing mistakes ever made in the United States. Ford Motor Company spent over two hundred million dollars producing an automobile that would carry the name of Edsel Ford, the father of Henry Ford II, who was then the president of Ford Motor Company. The sales promotion, anticipation, and the excitement were unbelievable. You can appreciate what it was like, being a relatively young businessman and having all the power of the Ford Motor Company brought to bear on me to encourage me to become the Edsel dealer for Salt Lake City. I wrestled with the decision. I said to my father, who was a great man in my life, 'Before I sign the franchise, I want to see the car.'

"They made special arrangements for us to fly to California to see the car. It was a big decision; it involved a lot of money, a lot of commitment on my part. *The minute my father and I saw the cars I had the distinct impression not to go ahead with the franchise.*" But, yielding to pressure, Mr. Ballard signed the franchise and later had to sell it as a great loss. He continues, "I can think straight now when it comes to those kinds of decisions because of what I suffered. Perhaps we need to understand that failure is part of life. We are not going to be successful in everything we do, but we never need to fail to learn the lesson, and to place in the bank of our memories those things that will then cause us to become increasingly powerful and successful in life."

Your cumulative experience pushes you to the edge of the best with a greater view than you have ever had.

I like to reflect on knowledge I've gained in my life and how it has contributed to the opportunities I have in life today. My interaction with leaders, associates, and mentors has had a permanent and profound impact on all that I do. I am grateful for the pathways of their lives and their positive influence on me. The interchanges I have had with people around the world as I have taught and discussed leadership and management has had a profound effect on me. The up-close and personal learning that has taken place with my wife, children, and family has taught me so much. Going to school, reading books, learning how to be a pilot, participating in athletics, having successes, and having failures have all contributed to sharpening my judgment and adding to whatever meager wisdom I may have. All of these things combine to provide a grand starting point to my new best.

Wisdom and judgment together constitute the light that allows you to employ the *power of knowledge* correctly.

Knowledge is a game-changer.

Take this exciting challenge about knowledge, and work to become *the best* at what you do. Have a discussion with those you associate with. What does the best look like for you?

You may work as a tradesman, student, professor, soldier, business-person, attorney, contractor, entrepreneur, teacher, salesman, mechanic, postman, artist, athlete, lawyer, banker, doctor, or in some other capacity. Whatever you do, there is one place where it is not crowded, even in your chosen field—at the top!

Whatever your occupation, you can become the "go-to person" through learning and hard work. By learning to be the best at what you do, you become trusted, you are given more responsibility, you improve financial opportunities, and you feel a greater satisfaction.

Ask the question among your associates: "What does the best look like in our lives? In our business? In our division? For our organization?" Now go to work, have some fun, and implement the best and most feasible ideas through employing the *power of knowledge*.

INSPIRATIONAL QUOTES
Employ the Power of Knowledge

"The more things you try, the more likely one of them will work. The more books you read, the more likely one of them will have an answer to a question that could solve the major problems of your life."

— *Jack Canfield*

"We have a hunger of the mind which asks for knowledge of all around us, and the more we gain, the more is our desire; the more we see, the more we are capable of seeing."

— *Maria Mitchell*

"Take the attitude of a student, never be too big to ask questions, never know too much to learn something new."

— *Og Mandino*

"As a single footstep will not make a path on the earth, so a single thought will not make a pathway in the mind. To make a deep physical path, we walk again and again. To make a deep mental path, we must think over and over the kind of thoughts we wish to dominate our lives."

— *Henry David Thoreau*

"The universe is full of magical things, patiently waiting for our wits to grow sharper."

— *Eden Phillpotts*

"Failure is instructive. The person who really thinks learns quite as much from his failures as from his successes."

— *John Dewey*

Application

"Choose to be in the top 5 percent of those working in your profession."
— Steve Shallenberger

Individual

Use the External Environment Analysis. In your notebook, your Thoughts Book, or on a piece of paper, complete an External Environment Analysis (EEA) on your personal or professional life. Prioritize the biggest threats or largest opportunities.

Write in your Thoughts Book about gaining knowledge; identify things you can do to gain greater knowledge and understanding in some key areas of your life.

List some of the most important and influential books that you have read. Then identify some books you can read that could have an important stimulating impact on your life.

List people that you have met, either directly or indirectly, who have had a significant impact on you. Then determine some people you can meet, directly or indirectly, that could have an important impact on your life.

Post the "In a Nutshell" somewhere you can regularly see and review it.

With Others
The External Environment Analysis

1. Pick either a relationship focus or organization focus, and complete the EEA.
2. List all of the items your group came up with.
3. Prioritize the biggest threats or largest opportunities.
4. Do you need to act on any one of them now?

Pick out one or two stories from this chapter. Teach the principle and stories to others.

Invite your associates to identify one area where gaining greater understanding would be helpful to them or others. Set a time to get back together, and report on what knowledge they gained and how they can apply it for good.

In a Nutshell

1. Hunger and thirst for knowledge. Read, meet, associate, and observe. Remember that in five years you will be the same as you are today except for the people you meet and the books you read.

2. Regularly examine the external environment. Change—the external environment—can provide you with valuable opportunities or churn you up in its wake. Use the External Environment Analysis tool to your advantage.

3. Walk to the edge of the best—innovation and research. What's out there now? What does the best look like? Who has succeeded? Who has failed? Who has used search tools? What is the baseline or benchmark?

4. Ask for feedback. Feedback is the breakfast of champions.

5. Use the "Continue, Start, Stop" tool to gain feedback.

6. Grow your knowledge by reading a book a month. Read a book that will stimulate your mind or teach you something related to your field.

7. Use the "light" of knowledge, wisdom, and judgment in making decisions.

8. Invest 3% of your income back into yourself. This can be an investment to a live event, DVD home study course, MP3's, books, personal coaching, etc.

Guiding Constant 4

Never Give Up!

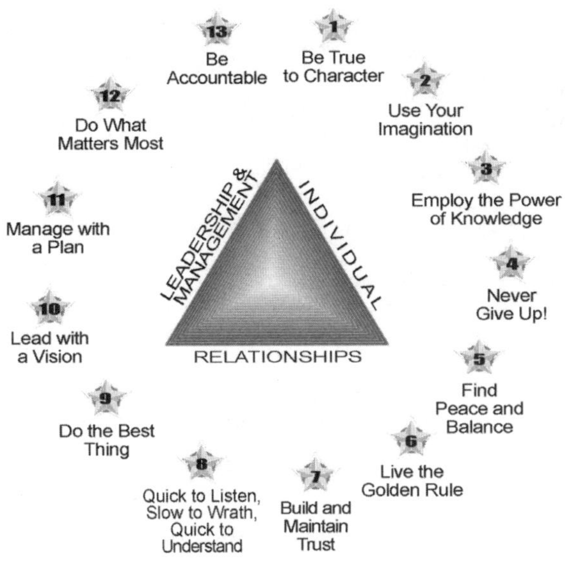

As World War II escalated, the British were demoralized by feelings of helplessness. Night after night, hundreds of German bombers dropped death and destruction on London, Manchester, and Reading. Night after night, people lost their homes or their workplaces or their lives. Children were sent to the country for safety; teenagers were trained to fly fighter planes. The headlights of cars were kept off, and black paper covered the windows of every home and business. Along with suppressing the lights of everyday life, the smoke and dust dimmed even the light of the sun. *Demoralized* doesn't seem adequate to describe what the British people felt.

In the midst of such despair, one man with a will to live and the vision for better days—Prime Minister Winston Churchill—turned British hearts

and minds toward hope with only thirty-nine words: "Never give in. Never, never, never, never—in nothing, great or small, large or petty—never give in, except to convictions of honor and good sense. Never yield to force. Never yield to the apparently overwhelming might of the enemy."

Churchill's comments, given as the commencement speech at his old preparatory school in 1941 aren't famous only because of the power and meaning of the words. His is also known as the shortest speech on record. When he sat down, sustained applause began as people stood as a witness that they would follow him with hope in the future. *Never Give Up!* was Churchill's rallying challenge at a time when the British needed to turn impending defeat into the will to win. Churchill's response inspired not only England but the whole free world.

This spirit of that message inspired Britain and her allies to fight back with great courage—not only for their survival as a nation, but for a world-wide victory over tyranny.

The British learned the hard lesson that the ultimate enemy can be within ourselves, where we each battle the urge to give up. Churchill's rally to a belief in victory is a rally we can each give ourselves. The truth? As Douchan Gersi put it, "Victory always starts in the head. It's a state of mind. It then spreads with such radiance and such affirmations that destiny can do nothing but obey."

Never Give Up! It is during moments of discouragement or despair—when you aren't sure if you can really make it—that success can be found as you reach deep down and fight back with courage, faith, and the spirit of keeping on.

J. K. Rowling and *Harry Potter*: Overcoming Failure

In 1990, while Joanne (J. K.) Rowling was on a four-hour-delayed train trip from Manchester to London, the idea for a story of a young boy attending a school of wizardry came "fully formed" into her mind. As soon as she reached her Clapham Junction flat, she began to write immediately.

After moving to Porto, Portugal, to teach English as a foreign language, Rowling married; the couple welcomed a daughter the next year but separated only a few months after her birth. The next month Rowling and her daughter moved to be near Rowling's sister in Edinburgh, Scotland. During this period Rowling was diagnosed with clinical depression and contemplated suicide.

Seven years after graduating from university, Rowling saw herself as "the biggest failure I knew." Her marriage had failed and she was jobless with a dependent child—but she described her failure as liberating in her 2008 Harvard University commencement address:

> *Failure meant a stripping away of the inessential. I stopped pretending to myself that I was anything other than what I was, and began to direct all my energy to finishing the only work that mattered to me. Had I really succeeded at anything else, I might never have found the determination to succeed in the one area where I truly belonged.*

In order to teach in Scotland, she needed a postgraduate certificate of education—something that required a full-time, year-long course of study. She began the course in August 1995 after completing her first novel and having survived on state welfare support. She wrote in many cafés, especially Nicolson's Café, whenever she could get Jessica to fall asleep.

"The Elephant House"—one of the cafés in Edinburgh in which Rowling wrote the first Harry Potter novel.

In 1995, Rowling finished *Harry Potter and the Philosopher's Stone* on an old manual typewriter; her agent submitted the book to twelve publishing houses, all of which rejected the manuscript. A year later she was finally given the green light (and a £1500 advance) by editor Barry Cunningham from Bloomsbury, a small publishing house in London. Although Bloomsbury agreed to publish the book, Cunningham advised Rowling to get a day job—he believed she had little chance of making money in children's books.

In 1997, Rowling received an £8000 grant from the Scottish Arts Council to enable her to continue writing. The following spring, an auction held in the United States for the rights to publish the novel was won by Scholastic for $105,000. Rowling said she "nearly died" when she heard the news.

In June 1997, Bloomsbury published *Philosopher's Stone* with an initial print run of one thousand copies, five hundred of which were distributed to libraries. The book subsequently won the Nestlé Smarties Book Prize, the prestigious British Book Award for Children's Book of the Year, and the Children's Book Award.

The rest, as they say, is history. Harry Potter is now a global brand worth an estimated £7 billion ($15 billion), and the last four Harry Potter books have consecutively set records as the fastest-selling books in history. The series, totaling 4,195 pages, has been translated, in whole or in part, into sixty-five languages.

The Harry Potter books have also gained recognition for sparking an interest in reading among the young at a time when children were thought to be abandoning books for computers and television (adapted from Wikipedia).

J. K. Rowling came to a point in her life where she felt like a failure. Instead of giving up, she stripped everything away and started building from there. Leveraging her unique talent, she worked on the story of Harry Potter. The result was a changed woman and a changed world.

J. K. Rowling isn't alone. Others have also suffered setbacks that were just as dramatic and discouraging. As just one example, Roger Bannister—the first person to break the four-minute mile—was horribly burned in a fire and was painfully disfigured. He came back, through much adversity, to become the fastest distance runner alive at the time.

What do we remember about J. K. Rowling, Helen Keller, Roger Bannister, and many others like them? We remember the good! We remember the satisfaction of coming back. We see examples of endurance, persistence, and never giving up. We remember the victories.

How can you overcome the obstacles in your way and achieve your goals, dreams, aspirations, and visions? The only way to do it is by never, never giving up.

What of Your Own "Bad"?

Regular people experience "bad" in many ways. Your "bad" can stop you in your tracks.

We had a memorable "bad" in our own family. About 6 P.M. one evening, our son David was in a serious accident that resulted in a critically broken neck. He was immediately put in a halo to keep his neck secure. At the time, he was scheduled to start law school in six weeks. How could he pick up the pieces? The brace prevented him from turning his head, he couldn't drive, and it was difficult to do any work at all. He was in pain and wasn't even sure he'd ever regain normal function. But he resolved to start law school on time. His "I'll show you" attitude did just that. He refused to give in or give up, and thanks to the help and support of his family, professors, and classmates, he recovered fully and not only started law school on time but graduated with his class on time.

Your "bad" may include such difficulties as "How will I pay my mortgage without a job?" "How can I ever trust again when he or she has betrayed me?" "How do I feel love and forgiveness ever again after her divorce from me is final?" "When will peace come into my heart over the loss of my two sons to a drunk driver?"

"Bad" in a company can upend momentum and effectiveness at work. The vice president of marketing gets the report that sales are continuing their downturn for the fourth consecutive month. The human resources manager learns she will be deposed regarding two lawsuits from employees—and the CEO lets her know there will be repercussions. The production team learns that two major suppliers will miss delivery dates, causing customer fulfillment issues that will further impact sales numbers—the sale isn't realized revenue until the product ships.

Bad things happen in all aspects of life—at school, at work, in marriage. Some of the bad things are part of the daily mix of living with and around

"I'm sorry, sir, but we can't break up the pair."

other humans. But some of the bad things are big things—life-changing events that can turn your life on end. In these moments, you might feel like it's impossible to recover or return to things as they were. But you *can* recover!

The good in life is often offset by the difficult. As a matter of fact, much of what you learn comes from adversity. Guiding Constant 4—Never Give Up!—empowers you to become your best in spite of, and sometimes because of, the odds.

Never Give Up! is an attitude, a process, and a mantra all rolled into one. To unlock your potential in the face of difficulty, crisis, or disaster is wrapped up in the will to go on. These are the times you discover what is within you. You have a choice when it seems that difficulties have locked all the doors—that choice is to stay in the game. Keep fouling off strikes until your pitch comes. Then hit it out of the park.

The Enemy Within

To achieve your very best you must defeat the enemy within. One of the biggest enemies to personal happiness and joy in the journey can be feelings of discouragement, loneliness, disappointment, defeat, or being overwhelmed. Beset by these kinds of feelings, you fail to win because:

- You give up before you give yourself a chance.
- You're afraid that the cost in terms of effort and other resources is too high.
- You believe the critics within (your own voice) and without (others around you who say, "You can't succeed").

Continuing to think you can win when success seems out of reach is not a gift but a decision you need to make. "Nothing splendid has ever been achieved," according to Bruce Barton, "except by those who dared believe that something inside of them was superior to circumstance."

You're Not Alone

When things are cruising along well it's hard to imagine that disaster is near. Ask those who lived through the 1920s and the ensuing Depression or the early 1940s and the onset of World War II. And then there was the summer of 2008 with its double-digit unemployment, stock crashes, and real estate downturns.

The urge to escape that economic disaster led many to leave the stock market, taking 30 percent losses on their way out. Jobs were eliminated and unemployment benefits were limited and short-lived. Entire companies run by the best-educated people on the planet disappeared in weeks. Everyone involved took an emotional hit, and many were left wondering what they could have seen and done to reduce the hardship.

You're not alone if you feel helpless when times are very, very difficult for you. But remember this: There is hope and there are options when you exercise a determination to fight back, to use your imagination, to employ the power of knowledge, and to search for your best.

It's not the crisis that takes you down—what takes you down is giving up. Those who don't give up prosper in the worst of times. They look around and find something to believe in. They change careers, offer a new service, start a business. They commit to something and go the distance. You can do the same thing.

Consider Abraham Lincoln's story. Remember, he wasn't always President Lincoln.

As a politician, Lincoln was *defeated* in his first try for the legislature, *defeated* in his first attempt to be nominated for Congress, *defeated* in his application to be commissioner of the General Land Office, *defeated* in the senatorial election of 1854, *defeated* in his efforts for the vice presidency in 1856, and *defeated* in the senatorial election of 1858.

"I am now the most miserable man living," wrote Lincoln to a friend. "If what I feel were equally distributed to the whole human family, there would not be one cheerful face on the earth." The depth of Lincoln's failures led him to despair of ever feeling happiness and success. But you know the history. What changed?

The fact that others have succeeded in the face of high odds against them doesn't always help you feel better, but examining their stories can help you figure out what to do next. Lincoln's example is obvious; now look at some people you may not have realized were failures before or while they were succeeding.

Thomas Edison was fired from his first two jobs for being "nonproductive." As an inventor, Edison made one thousand *unsuccessful* attempts before he finally invented a lightbulb that worked.

Michael Jordan, Hall of Fame National Basketball Player and one of the greatest professional basketball players ever, said this: "I have missed more than 9,000 shots in my career. I have lost almost 300 games. On 26 occasions I have been entrusted to take the game winning shot . . . and I missed. I have failed over and over and over again in my life." But permanent failure was not an option for Michael Jordan, because he knew this one great truth, as taught by Og Mandino: "Sound character provides the power with which a person may ride the [failures] of life instead of being overwhelmed by them. Failure is the . . . highway to success."

Mandino may have learned that failure is the highway to success from John Keats, who wrote, "Failure is, in a sense, the highway to success, inasmuch as every discovery of what is false leads us to seek earnestly after what is true, and every fresh experience points out some form of error which we shall afterwards carefully avoid."

Learning to Never Give Up!

Nothing is ever accomplished without the determination and dedication to see an idea, goal, or ambition to its completion. Just as a car will take you nowhere without an engine, all the good intentions in the world will prove useless without action. It's important to recognize the things that might deter you from your goals, then employ strategies to keep moving forward.

The quality of seeing something through, of overcoming overwhelming odds and bouncing back from serious setbacks, can be learned. Never giving up combines the three previous principles for becoming your best: Be True to Character, Use Your Imagination, and Employ the Power of Knowledge.

Four essential habits of never giving up can be learned and applied to help you through when things are tough:

1. Hold on to an inspiring purpose. Never give up!

2. Practice the power of positive thinking. Maintain only positive language. Eliminate negative language from your vocabulary.

3. Control what you can control.

4. Repeat the mantra: "I will persist! I will succeed! I will never give up!"

1. Hold on to an Inspiring Purpose. Never Give Up!

Victor Frankl, a prisoner in Jewish prison camps during World War II who later wrote *Man's Search for Meaning*, realized that the last true freedom he had was his mind. Frankl found that as he kept love in his heart and mind, even though he didn't know what had happened to his wife, he could lovingly envision her standing over him. This vision gave him a purpose to live and the ability to withstand the cold, pain, and oppression.

He looked forward to seeing her again. They might punish him, treat him harshly, and subject him to poor conditions, but they could not control what or how he thought. As he thought of his wife and the love he had for her, he found a quiet inner peace and motivation, even in the middle of the unspeakable tragedies that surrounded him.

What is the purpose that drives you forward?

Your purpose may be to be loyal to God, family, country, love, liberty, or freedom; to realize a powerful goal or an inspirational dream; a desire to live or some combination of these. Hold on to that purpose with a passion. Never let go of the things that matter most and that give you a reason to live and to push forward.

The more vivid and alive your purpose is, the more powerful your purpose becomes.

When you are discouraged, threatened, and beaten down, remember your purpose and push on until the night turns into day and the storm vanishes into brightness. It will!

Here's one of my favorite poems—one I've cherished for more than thirty-five years:

Just Keep On

Just a keep on a livin' and a keep on a givin'
And a keep on a trying to smile.
Just a keep on singin' and a trustin' and a clingin'
To the promise of an after while.
For the sun comes up and the sun goes down
And the morning follows night.
There's a place to rest like a mother's breast
And a time when things come right.
Just a keep on believin' and hidin' all your grievin'
And a keep on trying to cheer.
Just keep on a prayin' and a-lovin' and a-sayin'
All the things we love to hear.
For the tide comes in and the tides goes out
And the dark will all turn bright;
There's a rest from the load and an end to the road
And a place where things come right.

During my third year in college, I will never forget the profound effect of a summer job I had working for the Southwestern Company out of Nashville, Tennessee. I went door to door seventy-five hours a week selling educational books and Bible dictionaries in Aberdeen, Maryland.

My goal was to make enough money that summer to pay for the entire next year of school. Another goal was to keep my word and finish my work commitment for that summer.

After attending a one-week sales school in Nashville, I headed off to Maryland. My first day to work was a Saturday. I hit the doors at 8 A.M., just as they taught me at sales school. I was scared to death. I found a country road to start on and knocked on my first door. As I knocked, someone yelled from inside, "What in the hell do you want?" I shouted back, "Nothing!" and quickly moved to the next house.

As I approached the next house, I could hear large dogs barking inside the house. I hardly dared enter the fenced yard. So I stood on the sidewalk and clapped—like they do in South America—rather than ringing the doorbell. I felt like an idiot but waited patiently. Eventually a woman came out and I explained what I was doing; she invited me in. I worried a little that I might never be seen again but we had a great visit and she ended up buying the set of books. I had been working only one hour.

I got out my calculator; at this rate, I figured, I would make $16,000 by the end of summer. It was a good thing I had decided I would not stop until I had finished my work commitment, because I knocked and knocked and knocked but didn't get into another house that day. The next day was the same. I recalculated my earnings and figured that at this rate I would make $364 during the entire summer.

Eventually things settled down. I got into a regular work flow and accomplished my goal of making enough money to pay for the whole next academic year. But it was the hardest job I ever had because I had to keep going, muster up enough courage to knock on the first door each day, and stay positive in the face of constant rejection and discouragement. When I successfully completed that job at the end of that summer, I believed I could do just about anything.

The next summer I became a manager and made four times as much money. The following summer I expanded my management experience, and I made five times more than I did the previous summer.

These experiences gave me enough confidence to eventually buy my first company.

I would have *never* had that opportunity if I had given up when things got tough. What kept me going? I made a solid commitment to work the full period I had agreed to—and I wanted to be self-sufficient. I no longer wanted to take money from my parents.

The next year I was in love and engaged to be married at the end of the summer. So once again I had a passionate purpose: I wanted to make enough money to pay for our expenses for the academic year so we would not incur debt as we started a new family.

These purposes were so significant that they inspired me to be a finisher and to not give in.

Holding on to a powerful, vibrant purpose helps you never give up. It's absolutely important to hang in there—even when you feel most discouraged.

While the storm is beating down hard on you, keep repeating, "This too will pass." And as the day follows night, it will! The storm always subsides—and yours too will pass. The clear day will come and the radiant heat of the sun will shine again. Some things just take time to work through.

The bamboo plant is a great example. For the first three years you water it, care for it, and nurture it. Very little seems to happen to reward all your effort, as only a small sprout emerges from the soil. It appears that the plant is simply not growing. And then at some point between the third and fifth year, the tiny bamboo sprout can suddenly grow as much as three feet in a single day until it gets as high as ninety feet in a short period of time.

How can that happen? During the first three to four years while the plant is not growing above ground, it is actually growing below the surface of the ground, developing miles of an intricate root system capable of supporting its eventually massive height.

Life can be the same way. You may not see results at first, but as you labor, gain experience, and develop internal strength and capacity, your public success and capacity become more apparent.

2. Practice the Power of Positive Thinking

William James wrote, "The greatest discovery of our generation is that human beings can alter their lives by altering their attitudes of mind. As you think, so shall you be."

Don't allow yourself to think any negative thoughts. Fill your mind with positive literature, prose, music, and media—things like *Amazing Grace,*

Apollo 13, Rudy, Remember the Titans, The Sound of Music, The Legend of Bagger Vance, and *Rocky*. Stay focused on your vision and goals. Have faith and believe in a positive outcome. Remember that time spent thinking negatively is time not applied to creative thinking and solutions.

One night Edison's lab was destroyed by fire. The next morning he looked at the ruins and said, "There is great value in disaster. All our mistakes are burned up. Thank God we can start anew."

Former president of the United States Teddy Roosevelt shared the following inspirational quote: "It is not the critic who counts, not the man who points out how the strong man stumbled and fell, or where the doer of deeds could have done better. The credit belongs to the man who is actually in the arena; whose face is marred by dust and sweat and blood; who strives valiantly; who errs and comes short again and again . . . who knows the great enthusiasms, the great devotions and spends himself in a worthy cause; and at the best knows in the end the triumph of high achievement; and who at the worst, if he fails, at least fails while daring greatly, so that his place shall never be with those cold and timid souls who know neither victory nor defeat."

3. Control What You Can Control

Make a list of things you *can* control and go to work on that list. Don't dwell on things you *cannot* control.

Mary Kay Ash was the type of person who made an excellent contribution to the companies she worked for and who rose to the top in what was then a male-dominated corporate world. Working for several direct sales companies over a thirty-year period, she achieved considerable success. But even though Mary Kay had the title and the track record, she was not taken seriously by her male peers. In board meetings her opinions and suggestions were ignored, dismissed, or even ridiculed. The men she worked with minced no words in their judgment, pronouncing her guilty of "thinking like a woman."

Frustrated, she retired in 1963, intending to write a book to assist women in the male-dominated business world.

Sitting at her kitchen table, she made two lists. One list was all the good things she had seen in the companies where she'd worked; the other list was all the things she thought could be improved. As she reread her lists, she realized that what she had in front of her was a marketing plan for her ideal company. In just four weeks, her "book" had become a business plan and her retirement was over.

She rolled out her new business in September of 1963. Beginning with a storefront in Dallas and an investment of $5,000, Mary Kay Cosmetics earned close to $200,000 in its first year, quadrupling that amount in its second year. When Mary Kay took her company public in 1968, annual sales had climbed to more than $10 million.

Mary Kay authored three bestselling books, and her business model is taught at the Harvard Business School. She received many honors, including the Horatio Alger Award. *Fortune* magazine has named Mary Kay Cosmetics one of the Ten Best Companies for Women and one of the one hundred best companies to work for in America.

At the time of Mary Kay's death in 2001, Mary Kay Cosmetics had 800,000 independent beauty consultants in thirty-seven countries, with total annual sales of more than $2 billion. Never underestimate the power of a person with a mission! And never, never underestimate the power of never giving up and never giving in.

Here are several ways you can take control of your life through positive action:

- Make a list of all of the things you can do to help solve the problem.

- Consult with a mastermind group that can be of help. From the recommendations of this mastermind group, add to your list of things that can help you solve the problem.

- Pick out some of the items on your list of things you can control, and develop a plan of action to implement them.

- Ask yourself, "How do I bounce back? How do I recover from where I was? What is the worst that can happen?" Then go forward with the plan you have implemented.

By controlling the things you can control, and *not worrying* about the things that you can't control, you will feel more confidence and peace and you will experience progress.

4. I Will Persist! I Will Succeed! I Will Never Give Up!

The greatest antidote to discouragement is determination. The extraordinary quality of persisting, enduring, and persevering through the hard times, and continuing to move forward in faith provides encouragement and hope. This kind of focused persistence invites opportunity and gives you the power to work through challenges.

There are many examples where a second—or third, or fourth, or fifth—effort ultimately won the day. For some, winning was actually a glorious, successful failure.

One of the greatest examples of this type of perseverance and persistence was provided by Sir Ernest Shackleton, captain of the *Endurance* (an appropriately named vessel), who became trapped in the massive ice floes of Antarctica in 1915. Crew members battled their way for six weeks through a thousand miles of packed ice. Only a day's sail short of its destination, the *Endurance* became locked inside an island of ice.

Imagine your ship, manned by twenty-seven crew members, slowly being crushed by an early winter as enormous sheets of ice closed in on the ship. Your crew can hear the wood planks starting to splinter. You now have to move to the ice sheets with your three lifeboats and supplies. The nearest land is an island five hundred miles away. You will likely have to wait out the winter until the ice starts breaking up.

That was the scenario faced by Shackleton and his crew. The chance of survival seemed slim—and it was a real risk that once they were free of the ice, ten months later, they could completely miss the island because of a navigation error.

What happened? They successfully survived the ten months on the ice. Once it started breaking up, they successfully—and incredibly—navigated to Elephant Island.

After reaching the barren island, Shackleton left most of his crew there for a later rescue. His plan was to travel with a small party an additional 780 miles over the Antarctic Weddell Sea in one of the remaining boats, again risking navigation errors, to find help at a whaler's outpost.

Shackleton left twenty-two crew members behind. He and the remaining five crew members sailed until the sails ripped, then rowed 779 miles to the South Georgia whaler's outpost. The mariners there were amazed to see Shackleton and his small crew; they had assumed that all were lost at sea.

But Shackleton didn't stop there. He acquired a ship to return to Elephant Island and rescue his crew. "I don't know how he did it," said British explorer Duncan Carse forty years later after traveling the same route over the Weddell Sea, "except they had to." Shackleton had pledged to save all twenty-seven members of his crew. Not one was lost. Shackleton had a clear purpose that allowed him the strength to endure, persist, and persevere.

The inspiring results of this type of effort and endurance can also be seen in business, sales, sports, and relationships—in dealing with setbacks, overcoming adversity, conquering health issues, mourning the loss of a close family member or friend, or feeling seriously down.

"I Will Persist Until I Succeed"

Among the most inspirational lines ever written are found in Og Mandino's *The Greatest Salesman in the World*:

> *I will persist until I succeed. . . .*
>
> *The prizes of life are at the end of each journey, not near the beginning; and it is not given to me to know how many steps are necessary in order to reach my goal. Failure I may still encounter at the thousandth step, yet success hides behind the next bend in the road. Never will I know how close it lies unless I turn the corner. . . .*
>
> *I will never consider defeat, and I will remove from my vocabulary such words and phrases as quit, cannot, unable, impossible, out of the*

> *question, improbable, failure, unworkable, hopeless, and retreat; for they are the words of fools. . . . I will remember the ancient law of averages, and I will bend it to my good. . . .*
>
> *Never will I allow any day to end with a failure. . . . Nor will I allow yesterday's success to lull me into today's complacency, for this is the greatest foundation of failure. . . . So long as there is breath in me, that long will I persist. For I know one of the principles of success—if I persist long enough I will win.*
>
> *I will persist! I will win!*

One of my favorite childhood stories—one that illustrates the power of persistence—is the mythical "Little Engine that Could":

> *A little railroad engine was employed about a station yard for such work as it was built for, pulling a few cars on and off the switches. One morning it was waiting for the next call when a long train of freight cars asked a large engine in the roundhouse to take it over the hill "I can't; that is too much a pull for me," said the great engine built for hard work. Then the train asked another engine, and another, only to hear excuses and be refused. In desperation, the train asked the little switch engine to draw it up the grade and down on the other side. "I think I can," puffed the little locomotive, and put itself in front of the great heavy train. As it went on the little engine kept bravely puffing faster and faster, "I think I can, I think I can, I think I can."*
>
> *As it neared the top of the grade, which had so discouraged the larger engines, it went more slowly. However, it still kept saying, "I—think—I—can, I—think—I—can." It reached the top by drawing on bravery and then went on down the grade, congratulating itself by saying, "I thought I could, I thought I could."*

Sometimes you're dealt a hand you simply can't control—one you certainly don't deserve. The only way through a situation like that is to not give up—to instead say, "I think I can, I think I can" as you look for ways to succeed and to get over the top.

In Spite of Overwhelming Odds

As illustrated previously, I have always been grateful for the inspiring example of Helen Keller's life as she and her family lived the principle of Never Give Up!

As mentioned earlier, Anne Sullivan arrived to find a child who did nothing more than scream, weep, kick, and bite—but she refused to give up. Despite Helen's profound handicaps, she proved to be an eager and brilliant pupil. With Anne's constant companionship and help, Helen later went to school, learned how to use a special typewriter, and learned to read Braille—not only in English but also in Latin, Greek, French, and German.

She also learned to understand spoken words by placing her fingers on the speakers' lips and throat—something she started doing at the age of ten with Anne. After much practice she could imitate the sounds by feeling the movements and vibrations of her own lip and throat.

This girl who could once only utter animal-like sounds gained admission to the prestigious Radcliff College and graduated with honors four years later. She spent the rest of her life working on behalf of those with handicaps. Imagine if Helen's parents or Anne Sullivan had given up on Helen. How different Helen's life would have been. How different our world would have been.

What would have happened if Bannister, Shackleton, Keller, Lincoln, J. K. Rowling, or thousands of others had given up? How different would our world be today!

It's the same for you as you journey along life's pathway. Remember that you have unique skills and abilities and that your best often is realized through a spirit of determination, endurance, and faith in yourself—and faith that things will ultimately work out. May you never give up!

INSPIRATIONAL QUOTES

Never Give Up!

"Magic is believing in yourself, if you can do that, you can make anything happen."

— *Johann Wolfgang von Goethe*

"Happiness lies for those who cry, those who hurt, those who have searched, and those who have tried for only they can appreciate the importance of people who have touched their lives."

— *Anonymous*

"Accept challenges, so that you may feel the exhilaration of victory."

— *George S. Patton*

"Don't live down to expectations. Go out there and do something remarkable."

— *Wendy Wasserstein*

"I can choose to rise from the pain and treasure the most precious gift I have—life itself."

— *Walter Anderson*

"All endeavor calls for the ability to tramp the last mile, shape the last plan, endure the last hours toil. The fight to the finish spirit is the one characteristic we must possess if we are to face the future as finishers."

— *Henry David Thoreau*

"Nobody wants me down more than I want up!"

— *Molly Brown, a famous survivor of the* Titanic

"You have brains in your head. You have feet in your shoes. You can steer yourself in any direction you choose. You're on your own. And you know what you know. You are the guy who'll decide where to go."

— *Dr. Seuss*

Application

Individual

1. Think of a time when things got tough in your life. What did you do to overcome the challenges you faced?
2. How did it feel to overcome your challenges?
3. List in your Thoughts Book traits and components you see as necessary if you are to persist, persevere, and never give up!
4. Identify an inspiring purpose that can drive you forward when challenging times come.

With Others

1. Pick one of the stories in the Never Give Up! section and teach it to others. Use a personal example from your own life.
2. Ask, "How does this principle apply today, and how can it be a powerful force in my own life and the life of our organization?"

In a Nutshell

How do you develop the spirit, attitude, and habit of never giving up?

Here are a few suggestions that help to build this extraordinary force, as a habit, in your life:

1. Lock on to an inspiring purpose. Never give up!
2. Reflect on the Thirteen Guiding Constants and make adjustments in your plan as needed to get to a better place.
3. Practice the power of positive thinking. Use only positive language. Eliminate negative language from your vocabulary.
4. Control what you can control. Make a list of what you can control and focus on those items. Refuse to dwell on things you cannot control.
5. When the going gets tough, the tough get going—endure, persist, and persevere. I will persist. I will succeed.
6. Be like the little engine that could. I think I can, I think I can. I knew I could, I knew I could.
7. You are never too young, too old, or too discouraged to give it a shot. Let your motto be: I will never give up.

Guiding Constant 5

Find Peace and Balance

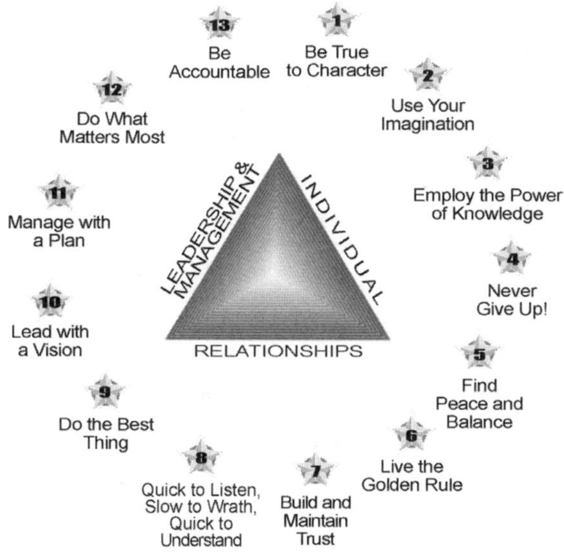

The old monk sat meditating by the side of the road with his eyes closed, his legs crossed, and his hands in his lap. Suddenly his prayers were harshly interrupted by the shouted, insistent demand of a Samurai warrior. "Old Man! Teach me about heaven and hell!"

The monk slowly opened his eyes and replied to the mighty Samurai with utter disdain in his voice, "Teach you about heaven and hell? I can teach you nothing. You're dirty. You smell. Your blade is rusty. You're a disgrace, an embarrassment to the Samurai. Get out of my sight."

Furious with rage, the warrior's face turned crimson as he raised his sword to slay the monk and screamed, "I will kill you for your impertinence!"

"That is hell," said the old monk gently, just as the sword began to fall upon his neck.

The Samurai was overcome with awe at the compassion and surrender of the monk who had dared to risk his very life to show him hell. Filled with gratitude, he lowered his sword, his eyes filled with tears.

"And that," said the monk, "is heaven."

Inner peace—a quality that resided deep within the monk's soul—is what you are feeling when you are happy. Peace is illusive. It requires a mind that is mature in the things that matter most: being true to character, doing your best, being trustworthy, and so much more.

One of the Greatest Threats to Peace is Stress!

"The time to relax," muses Sydney J. Harris, "is when you don't have time for it." As fruitless as this sounds, it sums up the relationship between what you know or sense would be best and what you actually choose to feel and do.

One of the greatest threats to peace is excessive, unproductive stress.

The Effects of Stress

Stress is difficult for scientists to define because it is a highly subjective phenomenon that differs for each person. Things that are stressful for some individuals can be pleasurable for others. People also respond to stress differently—some blush or eat more while others grow pale or eat less.

There are numerous physical as well as emotional responses to stress; it can have wide-ranging effects on emotions, mood, and behavior. Equally important but often less appreciated are possible effects on various systems, organs, and tissues throughout the body, as illustrated by the following diagram.

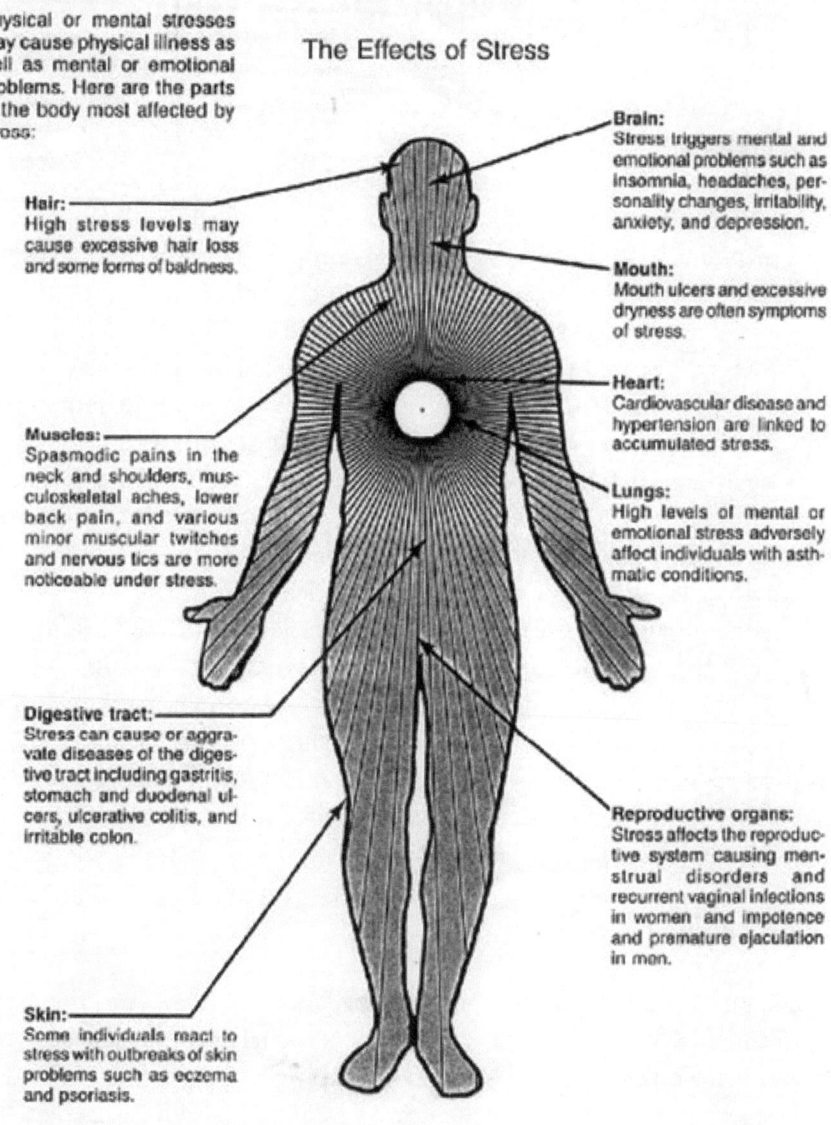

According to the American Institute on Stress, numerous emotional and physical disorders have been linked to stress, including depression, anxiety, insomnia, heart attack, and stroke. In fact, it's hard to think of any disease in which stress cannot play an aggravating role or where any part of the body is not affected.

There are different types of stress. At the right time, stress can be positive and can help you stay on the edge when needed. But a different type of stress can be destructive. It's the relentless, pounding, pressure-cooker type of stress. Some suggest that this type of stress is one of the top threats to health.

Some stress is self-inflicted; you likely feel stress when you fail to meet expectations for what you think you *should* accomplish or when you violate commitments to principles. Some stress is imposed by others, such as when a spouse pulls away from the marriage or a commitment is ignored.

As real as stress feels, it is susceptible to your will and desire for peace. Will Rogers captured the absurdity of some of the pressures we impose on ourselves when he said, "Half our life is spent trying to find something to do with the time we have rushed through life trying to save."

Regardless of where stress originates, understanding the nature and source of stress will enable you to either subdue it or use it for good in pursuit of peace and balance.

Living the Guiding Constants you are learning in this book can be a great source of peace. Reaching for a higher level of these Guiding Constants can help remove anxiety, fear, and stress. The stress of a broken trust can be avoided by being trustworthy and seeking to reset the relationship through apology and forgiveness. Relationships give life meaning and motivation. When your relationships are out of sync and when someone you care about begins to pull away there is a way to maintain or recover real peace and overcome the stress.

Understanding Peace

Stress, rage, and fear are products of how you see and react to the external environment. Your thoughts, attitudes, and beliefs produce consequences. If you believe people are out to get you by making you fail, look bad, or feel bad, then you will act, make decisions, and choose feelings that reflect that belief.

Conversely, if you believe people are out to help you by making every effort to enable your success and help you feel great, then you will act, make decisions, and choose feelings that reflect that belief.

Peace is rare because it requires you to change your attitudes and thoughts. Why? Because you are the only variable in the whole equation that you can control.

If you believe your happiness is due to forces in the external environment, then you are stuck. You're left with an assumption that is not true—that the world is causing your feelings. In that scenario there is no way out because you can do nothing to change the external environment. You can blame, kick, and scream all you want about the banking system, inflation, high unemployment, low housing values, heat, cold, rain, and whatever else is bothering you, and it won't change a thing. All it will do is disrupt your peace.

Believing that the world is causing your fear, anxiety, or stress is a habit of thinking that you've likely learned from others. In truth, your own thoughts are the cause and the reality of your life. "By changing your thoughts," said the Dalai Lama, "you immediately get inner peace."

You've certainly heard people say, "What you see is what you get." You probably haven't interpreted it quite this way, but here's what it really means: Whatever the mind can conceive and believe, it can achieve, according to Napoleon Hill. You can create negative feelings just as surely as you can create positive feelings. Gandhi taught, "Man always becomes what he believes himself to be. If I keep on saying to myself that I cannot do a certain thing, it is possible that I may really become incapable of doing it. On the contrary, if I shall have the belief that I can do it, I shall surely acquire the capacity to do it, even if I may not have it at the beginning."

This is as true for the development of peace as it is for acquiring something physical or learning a new skill.

Yes, external realties may create a heavy burden on you—you might lose a loved one, a business, your health, or your job. But your mind can anticipate these "possible" external realities—and you can control your response to them. You can employ your inner power and use the Guiding Constants to achieve the best—including the best feelings of peace.

Understanding Balance

Zig Ziglar says that "being successful means having a balance of success stories across the many areas of your life. You can't truly be considered successful in your business life if your home life is in shambles." The same thing applies to any aspect of your life that may be "in shambles."

Your car provides a good metaphor for balance. Your car performs best when the tires are in alignment, the oil is fresh, and the windshield is clean.

In the same way, your life works best when your goals are aligned with your values and all other things are in balance.

Einstein said, "The most important human endeavor is the striving for morality in our actions. Our inner balance and even our very existence depend on it." *Balance* means understanding that the meaningful life is manifest in a number of dimensions. Weighting one over another will eventually cause a train wreck. Whether it is in your relationships, your personal health, or some other area, an overemphasis on one thing will always cause suffering in another.

That's why balance is not just a "nice to have" quality that you can take or leave as time permits. It is critical—now. Balance is a matter of doing what matters most, planning for maintaining your priorities, and holding to your plan.

Many pressures distract you from peace and there are too many opportunities for being off balance. To find true happiness, you must find both peace and balance. Peace and balance are the yin and yang of life that supply the energy and perspective to create a sustainable best in your life and your organization.

Six Ways to Find Peace and Balance

1. Take time to find peace and balance. Realize that peace and balance are critical factors in life's success.

2. Regularly evaluate your balance. Evaluate where you are today and work to maintain balanced growth in your life. Strive to be a well-rounded and whole person.

3. Access your inner self through meditation.

4. Laugh often!

5. Cultivate patience.

6. Tap into the power of faith.

1. Take Time to Find Peace and Balance

Why take time to find peace and balance? As your world becomes increasingly busier with many competing demands for your attention, it is more important than ever to pause and center yourself. Effectively taking time to reflect, to evaluate, to build your reserves, and to live in balance leads to greater peace and is among the things that matter *most.*

Forces for Peace and Balance

The forces for peace are not new. You've undoubtedly practiced some of them before: ending unnecessary hostility, shedding emotional baggage, forgiving completely, and leaving judgment to a higher source. All are good beginnings.

Take time to meditate and quiet your mind. Cultivate trust, develop character, and live the Golden Rule. Apply your knowledge in creative ways to achieve your best, to do the right thing, and to do what matters most. When you are fully alert to each of the Thirteen Guiding Constants and how they function in your life, you will find that peace and balance have surfaced in your inner self.

2. Regularly Evaluate Your Balance

Specifically taking time to reflect on peace and balance and taking *action* that builds peace and balance will allow them to take deep root within you. If you get so busy that you simply don't take time to "catch your breath," the punishing cost can show up in many areas of your life—including reduced quality of your relationships and your overall happiness in life.

Guiding Constant 5, Finding Peace and Balance, is founded on building your inner strength. The more self-reliant you are, the greater your capacity to work effectively with and help other people. Through self-reliance come confidence, inner strength, and peace.

Develop the abilities and capacities of the Circle of Self-Reliance in your life. These include:

Physical and Emotional Fitness—Exercise and develop a sense of well-being. Build emotional reserves. Get plenty of sleep. Eat a healthy diet.

Mental Fitness—Gain knowledge and stay sharp mentally. Exercise your brain. Think healthy thoughts.

Financial Fitness—Establish a wise financial philosophy for getting out of debt and for building a retirement fund.

Security and Safety Fitness—Don't take unnecessary risk. Be sure you are safe and secure.

Social and Relationship Fitness—Build strong and healthy relationships. Be able to laugh and enjoy life.

Spiritual Fitness—Cultivate a tenderness and sensitivity of spirit. Do good; leave the world a better place. Help others.

The Circle of Peace and Balance is first an inner circle where the body, soul, heart, and mind are found. The outer circle—which measures your fitness—focuses us on those things that matter most to your peace and balance. In an irony not lost on anyone, it is possible to give too much time to one or more of these elements and find yourself out of balance. To be physically and financially fit is good, but to use your strength and means across all components is best.

Evaluate Where You Are on a Scale of 1 to 10
Begin with a Self-Evaluation of Peace and Balance

To determine where you should begin in restoring peace and balance, take the "number and dot" test. The purpose of this exercise is to think of balance and peace like a wheel. If the wheel is round on all sides, it will roll perfectly well. If the wheel is lopsided, it will be a rough or more painful ride.

How is your balance? To find out, you'll use a number between 1 and 10, with 1 being closest to the center of the circle and 10 being on the outside rim of the wheel—in other words, 1 indicates that you're totally out of balance and 10 means you're fully in balance.

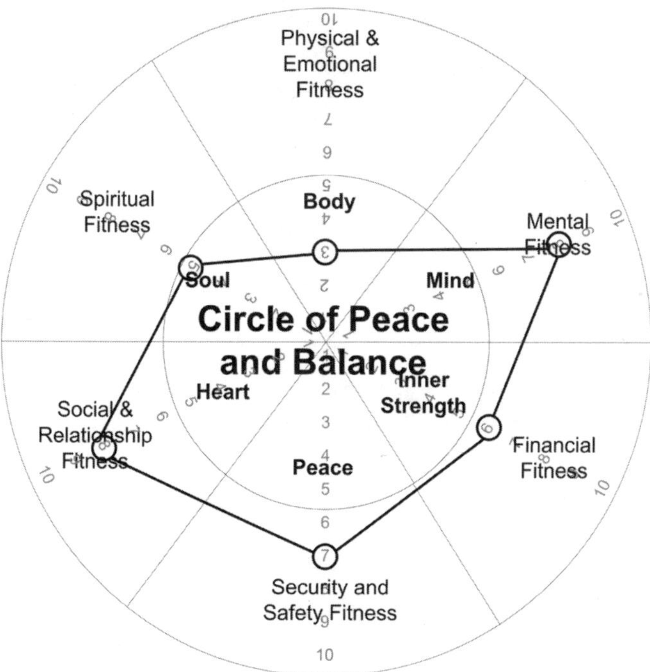

Rate yourself in each portion of the circle. Place a dot to indicate the number in that piece of the pie. If your financial fitness is above average but not perfect, circle the 6 or 7. If your mental fitness is very good but still improving, circle the 8 or 9. If your physical fitness is very low, circle a 2 or 3. Do the same for each of the categories in the circle. Now connect the dots and see where your balance may be off.

This exercise can immediately reveal areas for closer examination in your overall pursuit of balance and peace.

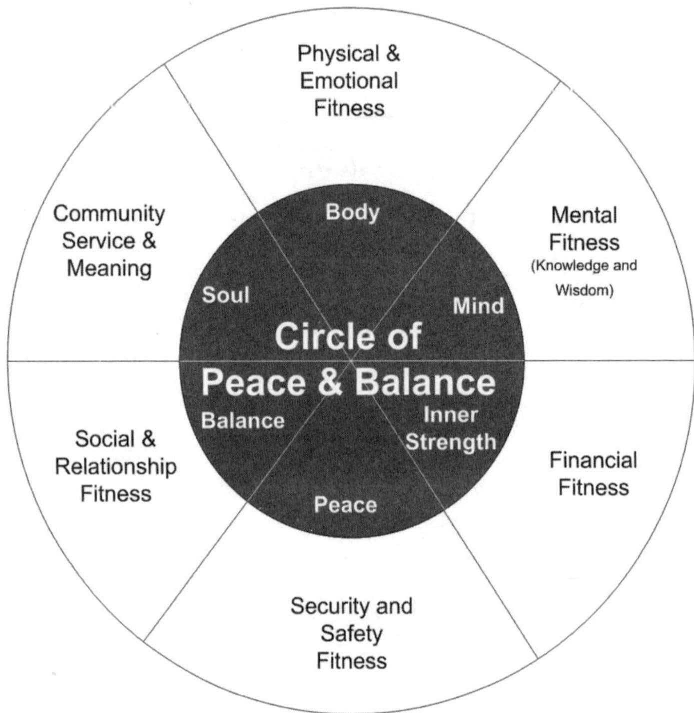

In the diagram above, physical and emotional fitness and spiritual fitness are rated low, indicating an area you should focus on in pursuit of peace and balance.

Examples of things that bring renewal and balance:

- Exercise—walk, jog, bike, or play basketball, tennis, or racquetball.
- Read a book.
- Listen to mentally stimulating materials while you walk, jog, or bike.
- Do something nice or thoughtful for someone else. Be kind.
- Reflect on your vision and goals. Let these goals inspire you and reinforce your actions.

- Determine to direct your life from within instead of reacting to things without. Take the high road; leave the low road to others.

- Be patient and simply listen to others. You can always respond later.

- Listen to soothing, quiet music. Take time to listen to nature.

- Carry a positive attitude. Take all negative comments and thoughts out of your vocabulary. Walk a little faster and with a sense of direction. Acknowledge and recognize others.

3. Access Your Inner Self Through Meditation

Reflection and meditation are processes for accessing inner strength and the power of your mind. There are three sources of inner strength that you may tap into through the inner recesses of your mind: your inner healer, which helps you maintain your health; your inner self-awareness, which keeps you aware of important issues in your life; and your inner counselor, which helps you answer perplexing questions or problems. You may also invite special counselors or friends (deceased or living) to assist you.

Create an environment around you that is positive and quiet—a place where you can be productive and can feel peace. Slow down. Listen to peaceful music and media. Read Thoreau's masterpiece, and then create your own Walden Pond.

Accessing Your Inner Self

In this peaceful environment, learn to meditate in order to communicate with your inner mind. Keep the process simple by doing the following:

- Close your eyes and relax. You may prefer to relax by lying down on the floor or a bed or by sitting in a chair.

- Take several deep breaths. Fill your lungs completely and fully exhale. Feel the heaviness of your hands, arms, and legs as you let them totally relax.

- Imagine a serene, safe, and peaceful location. (Mine has a view of the ocean in front of me and mountains behind me, with a view of beautiful meadows.) Use your mind's eye to find a place that is inviting, warm, and comfortable.

- When you arrive at this place, you may "go to" or focus on one of three minds:

    a. The inner healer
    b. The inner self-awareness
    c. The inner counselor

You'll find yourself in a semi- or subconscious state, focusing on your inner mind.

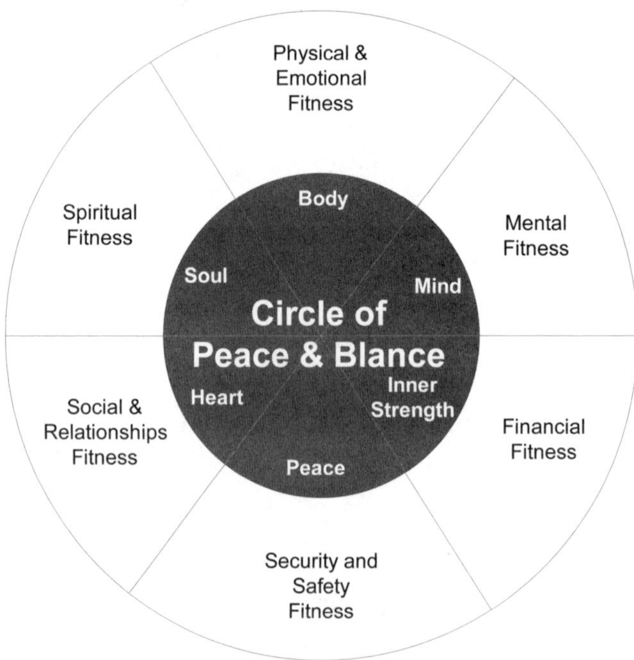

- In each of these mindsets or locations, reflect on any of the facets of the Circle of Peace and Balance to find answers to questions or concerns. Or you may choose to simply focus on an issue that concerns you. If it is health related, your body frequently has the answers and in some cases may be able to heal itself (as in the case of a bad headache). The body can teach you much—you need only ask it. Occasionally you will merely fall asleep because what you need is sleep. As you focus on your inner counselor, you may pose a question or describe an issue that is important to you. Answers will come. Work to avoid mental multitasking while focusing on only one area per "visit" to your inner counselor.
- After three to ten minutes, return to your fully conscious state and slowly open your eyes.

After a time of reflection and meditation, you will find that you typically feel completely at peace and refreshed.

You may repeat this process anytime. Even a two- to three-minute break in the middle of the day can allow you to travel in your mind to your place of peace and shut out all competing thoughts. Communicate with your inner mind in this peaceful place, and listen to its messages. When you open your eyes again, you will have new insights and ideas and can focus your energy on achieving the best result for the issues you are tackling.

4. Laugh Often!

Laughter and a sense of humor are infectious. The sound of laughter is far more contagious than a flu bug—and when laughter is shared, it bonds people and tends to increase happiness.

Laughter triggers healthy physical responses in your body. Laughter and a sense of humor strengthen your immune system, increase your energy, reduce your pain, and are an effective antidote for stress. Humor can lighten burdens, brighten spirits, inspire hopes, connect you to others, and help you to stay alert and focused. Well-placed and tasteful humor helps build a more constructive environment.

Applied at the right time, laughter and a good sense of humor can change the atmosphere of a tense situation to one that is more inviting and relaxed. Humor can completely change the tone of a meeting or situation so the participants can more easily put things into perspective and get on to a positive solution. One of the extraordinary things about laughter is that it can change things quickly and it can affect everyone.

With so many positive benefits, the ability to laugh easily and frequently is an extraordinary force for good in overcoming challenges, strengthening relationships, and building both physical and emotional health. And humor gets you to a better place, where you can see the world from a more relaxed, healthy, positive, enjoyable, and balanced perspective.

Want to Dance?

A good example of turning tension into humor came from our kitchen. One of the challenges of our kitchen of twenty-three years was the narrow passageway, or "choke point," at one end, between our refrigerator and pantry. It could be a bit irritating if two people were trying to get by at the same time.

One of those times happened between me and my wife Roxanne at a time when we were both under pressure and in a hurry. We each took two steps one way and then two steps the other way. Then she asked, "Would you like to dance?" Rather than being annoyed, we both started laughing and hugged as we danced. The humor of the situation changed the whole feeling. As a matter of fact, we still laugh about it, and it has led to our being able to enjoy more moments together rather than getting irritated at one another.

Gardner's Stories

Gardner—one of our board members and a brilliant consultant and businessman—has developed the rare gift for creating laughter in the middle of an overly intense situation. For example, at just the perfect time, Gardner would say something like, "Did you hear about the two older ladies driving down the street? They ran a red light. Doris was worried about Viola's driving but didn't say anything. They then ran another light, and Doris thought maybe she should say something but didn't. Finally after running a third red light, Doris said, 'Viola, what are you doing? You have run three red lights in a row!' Viola then replied, 'Well, Doris, I thought you were driving!'" Everyone would laugh. Then Gardner would say, "Now that we know who is driving, let's put our heads together and solve this issue. We can do it!" Amazingly, it always seemed to work. It didn't really make any difference what the story was, but it worked magic, and we had more fun getting the job done. Gardner is now ninety-two years old and still on our board.

Movies and Soundtracks

One of the enjoyable things in life is to watch funny movies or listen to comedians, especially with others, so you can share the funny lines and moments later.

Watch Out for That Post in Prague, Czech Republic

Seven members of our family were visiting the Czech Republic in downtown Prague. As we walked along the sidewalks enjoying the views, I ran smack into a post that was about three and one-half feet tall. I didn't see it coming at all and it wiped me out. I hit it straight on, and I went down. I was hurting, but my family was laughing so hard that there was no way I could really get upset.

We laughed about me hitting that post for at least an hour—in fact, we laughed until we cried. Ten years later, my family still warns me about any potential "posts" or "poles" as we walk along the street.

One Person Can Influence Many

One of our sons married a beautiful young lady who knows how to laugh. She is intelligent and has good judgment. If something becomes intense, she just laughs it off and turns the whole situation on its ear—and things are no longer intense. Her attitude has influenced our entire family, and we are grateful for her happy spirit. What a wonderful ongoing difference it has made in our family.

Anatomy of an Illness

Norman Cousins, the former managing editor of the *New York Post*, became gravely ill. In his memoir, *The Anatomy of Illness*, Cousins said that comedies, like those of the Marx Brothers, helped him feel better and get some pain-free sleep. Cousins attributes his recovery to vitamin C, a healthy diet, and being able to laugh.

Research at a number of prominent medical universities is discovering that, indeed, laughter seems to have lifesaving effects on the body. Laughter appears to lower blood pressure, increase blood flow, and promote oxygenation of the blood. Humor reduces stress hormones, such as cortisol and adrenaline, while increasing memory and learning. In a study at Johns Hopkins University Medical School, humor during instruction led to increased alertness and higher test scores.

Cultivate laughter and a tasteful sense of humor. Have some fun. Laugh with friends. Tell some jokes. See if you can change stressful counter-productive situations into happier, more positive situations through appropriate humor. Be more spontaneous. Let go of defensiveness. Express your true, best, good-natured feelings. All of these behaviors can lead to greater peace.

5. Cultivate Patience

Things don't always go as planned. You experience setbacks. People cut in front of you. You get stuck in traffic and arrive late. Somebody or something else is too slow. There are times when you suffer adversity, sickness, injury, or injustice. Each of these circumstances can add a great deal of stress and anxiety to your life and can rob you of peace and productive relationships.

Not having patience is like driving with one foot on the gas pedal and one foot on the brake. It is a bad practice and drives everyone crazy in the process. With time, it damages you and the car.

I am grateful for the profound comment by Sri Chinmoy: "Patience is not inertia. . . . Patience has the steady movement of growth and is always accompanied by peace. This peace can never be mistaken for inertia which is always accompanied by restlessness."

In other words, patience is a force for good that brings calm to your soul as you live life and have the opportunity to grow and learn.

Patience is a state of mind, and it requires practice. As with anything else that you work on or practice, you become better at it the more you work on it.

I chuckled over the following quote because it is reflective of how we sometimes approach patience: "O Lord, please give me the patience I need, and do hurry up about it." The fact is that patience is developed as a state of mind over time.

Ben Franklin shared, "He that can have patience, can have what he will."

Take a deep breath. Go deep within the wellsprings of your soul and focus on things that matter most when you feel agitated. Focus on gratitude, health, happiness, peace, love, relationships, loyalty, sustained progress, and improvement, doing what is right and best with honesty and character. Go to a place of peace and perspective. All of these things help you practice patience and stay focused on the big picture.

There will be times when circumstances demand action now. Even then, be patient with your immediate and necessary response.

When you are patient, the world will come to you. Solutions will come. Understanding and peace will come. Trust the process. Be patient.

When I think of patience, I think of George Washington leading a ragtag army to victory over *eight* long, trying, seemingly impossible years. I think of Nelson Mandela in prison for twenty-seven years, inspired by the poem "Invictus," doing hard labor and ultimately becoming the president of South Africa. I think of Victor Frankel in the death camps of WWII, Beethoven writing music while deaf, and Ben Carson gaining knowledge. I think of Thomas Edison, Marie Curie, and Isaac Newton patiently working through experiments, Florence Nightingale changing health care, Helen Keller emerging from a silent and dark world to one of beauty, Ronald Reagan working through lost elections to become president of the United States, Walt Disney suffering through financial and health hardships to revolutionize the world of entertainment, Mahatma Gandhi and William Wilburforce patiently working to help the world be a better place. The list of those that cultivated patience goes on and on. Patience is at the very heart of healthy progress, growth, change, getting to the best, and finding peace.

6. Tap into the Power of Faith

You may seek guidance, strength, and direction from a source greater than yourself. *No burden, no discouragement, no challenge, no problem, no disappointment is too big* when you feel help and strength from a source greater than you.

Regardless of how you define it, when you draw on this power you tap into a source of strength, comfort, and direction that gives you a greater capacity to overcome every obstacle, challenge, misery, sadness, and setback you might encounter. This is one of the greatest sources of peace and comfort available to humanity.

The Prayer at Valley Forge

There are few examples more moving than that of George Washington seeking and receiving help, peace, and direction at one of the darkest and most lonely hours of his life—as he sought to lead his troops and a new country to independence, freedom, and liberty.

Twenty-six-year-old Isaac Potts was a resident of Valley Forge, and as a Quaker was opposed to the war. He supervised the grinding of the grain that George Washington ordered the neighboring farmers to bring to his army. Potts recalled that while riding in the woods, "I heard a plaintive sound, as of a man at prayer. I tied my horse to a sapling and went quietly into the woods and to my astonishment, I saw the great George Washington on his knees alone, with his sword on one side and his cocked hat on the other. He was at prayer to the God of the Armies, beseeching to interpose with his divine aid, as it was ye crisis and the cause of the country, of humanity, and of the world.

"Such a prayer I never heard from the lips of man. I left him alone praying. I went home and told my wife . . . what I had seen and heard and observed. We never thought a man could be a soldier and a Christian, but if there is one in the world, it is Washington. We thought it was the cause of God, and America could prevail.'"

Washington's faith in a power and a cause greater than him provided him with a deep peace and confidence in the middle of the raging storm. He knew that all would work out well in the end.

The Marquis de Lafayette and General Peter Muhlenberg, both generals serving with George Washington in the Revolutionary War, had a similar experience. As they entered a barn near Washington's headquarters, they saw their commander in chief kneeling, saying nothing but looking to heaven.

They recount that "they saw the Father of his Country kneeling, on some of the hay thrown down from above for later supply to the horses—the cloak cast back from his noble figure, his hat lying beside him, his hands clasped and raised to heaven, and his closed eyes looking upward as only the eyes of faith can do. . . . [Washington's] face, as Peter Muhlenberg sometimes spoke of it later, was grandly sad and sorrowful, seeming entirely wrapped in awful contemplation of human weakness and that eternal might which could alone supplement and make it able to do its duty in the world."

They quietly retreated from this scene virtually speechless and subdued by the example of their leader.

It was a short time later that ultimate victory was achieved at Valley Forge over the mightiest military force in the world at that time. A free nation was born.

Gettysburg, Pennsylvania

About eighty years later, the United States was in its greatest crisis since becoming a new nation, embroiled in a civil war over slavery. The Confederate army was moving in for battle against the Union forces at Gettysburg. The result of this battle would likely decide the fate of the United States of America. There was the threat that victory by the forces of the South would cause Washington, DC, to be seized. Everyone was gripped by fear.

In the midst of such fear, Abraham Lincoln was calm—and only later did he explain why. "I went to my room and got down on my knees in prayer," he wrote. "Never before had I prayed with so much earnestness. I wish I could repeat my prayer. I felt I must put all my trust in Almighty God. He gave our people the best country ever given to man. He alone could save it from destruction. I had tried my best to do my duty and found myself unequal to the task. The burden was more than I could bear. I asked Him to help us and give us victory now. I was sure my prayer was answered. I had no misgivings about the result at Gettysburg."

The type of strength, guidance, and peace that Washington and Lincoln experienced is not reserved for great leaders. It is available to every single human being, including you.

A Multimillion-Dollar Setback

Early in my career, one of the firms I owned and was president of was growing rapidly. We thought we were making a solid profit—after all, we had employed four full-time CPAs to account for operations. But when the dust settled, it quickly became apparent that we had actually lost millions of dollars on our operations.

We had a significant line of credit with our bank and obligations to other creditors. I had personally guaranteed all the loans, and it appeared everything that I had worked to build for an entire decade was at risk. The loans and obligations were called with a demand for payment. I simply didn't have the money, though I had pledged all of my assets.

I imagined that our terrible financial situation would make the news, resulting in public humiliation. I made the decision to work to satisfy every obligation rather than file bankruptcy, even if it took the next ten years.

There were many late and lonely nights as I searched for answers and solutions to accomplish this goal. After two years of fighting the battle, I was once again up late at night, not knowing how I could go on any longer. I saw no answer to the heavy challenges that I faced and no way out of the situation I was in.

At the end of my rope, I remember kneeling down and indicating to my Maker that I was at the end of my rope, and I just didn't know what to do next. The experience is so vivid in my mind that I can remember the exact spot where I knelt. I said, "I will work as hard as I can, but I turn my life over to Thee. Wherever I end up is where I will go." As I concluded my prayer, a feeling of peace and calm came over me that has remained. In the ensuing years, things turned out better than I could have ever imagined. I was able to ultimately satisfy—in one way or another, through give and take—every obligation. I am still astounded by what transpired after that experience.

So when you feel like you are at the end of the rope, there is a place to turn that is bigger and larger than you. It will show the way, guide you through, and bring peace to your soul.

INSPIRATIONAL QUOTES

Find Peace and Balance

"Indeed, the major obstacle to you achieving the outcomes that you hope for in life are your thoughts."

— *Victor Frankel*

"The unexamined life is not worth living."

— *Socrates*

"If I have ever made any valuable discoveries, it has been owing more to patient attention, than to any other talent."

— *Sir Isaac Newton*

"The time to relax is when you don't have time for it."

— *Sydney J. Harris*

"For every minute you remain angry, you give up sixty seconds of peace of mind."

— *Ralph Waldo Emerson*

"Forgiveness is freeing up and putting to better use the energy once consumed by holding grudges, harboring resentments, and nursing unhealed wounds."

— *Simons*

"The only way to bring peace to the earth is to learn to make our own life peaceful."

— *The Buddha*

"I do not want the peace which passeth understanding; I want the understanding which bringeth peace."

— *Helen Keller*

Application

Here are a few suggestions for bringing peace and balance into your life:

Individual

1. Complete the balance assessment in your Thoughts Book and mark the date.

2. Make a plan to improve your balance.

3. Go to the inner chambers of your heart and mind. Visit a secure and peaceful location that is special to you. Visit your inner counselor, inner healer, or inner self-awareness. This type of meditation is extremely powerful.

4. Do relaxation exercises.

5. Consider praying, and record your impressions in your Thoughts Book.

6. Assess how you feel you are doing with patience. Think about what you can do to consistently exercise patience.

7. Set up an exercise plan.

8. Listen to peaceful and calming music.

9. Tell some good and well-placed jokes.

With Others

1. Complete the Balance Assessment for your organization, team, or family.

2. Discuss with teammates what you can do to improve balance.

3. Discuss what the impact might be on you and others.

4. With your team set some goals regarding balance.

5. Watch a funny movie with work associates, friends, or loved ones.

In a Nutshell

Steps to Peace and Balance:

1. Manage stress by getting to a more peaceful place. Even though you may live in a stressful world, carry your own peace within you.

2. Take *time* to find peace and balance. Realize that peace and balance are critical factors in life's success.

3. Regularly evaluate your balance. Evaluate where you are today and work to maintain balanced growth in your life. Strive to be a well-rounded and whole person.

4. Peace and balance can come through meditating and accessing your inner self.

5. Laughter and a sense of humor are great medicine.

6. Cultivate patience.

7. Tap into the power of faith.

PART TWO
STRONG RELATIONSHIPS

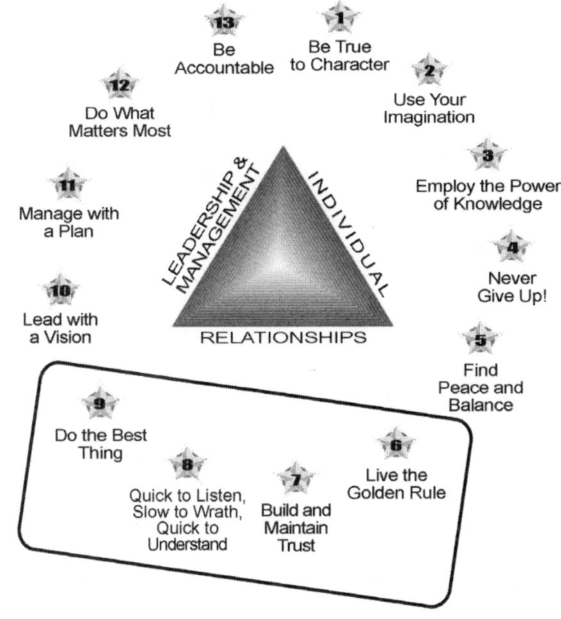

Trust, Collaboration, and Strong Interpersonal Associations

"Come my friends, 'tis not too late to seek a newer world."

— *Tennyson*

In part one we examined strong individuals and discussed how to develop and build character, competency, and capacity. It was a focus on the within. Once you are effectively working on the within, you have a map that enables you to improve the without.

Part two will focus on helping you develop or strengthen trust, improve collaboration, and build strong interpersonal associations—qualities that allow for the best results. Their value comes in limitless possibilities and the power to change your world.

Guiding Constant 6
Live the Golden Rule

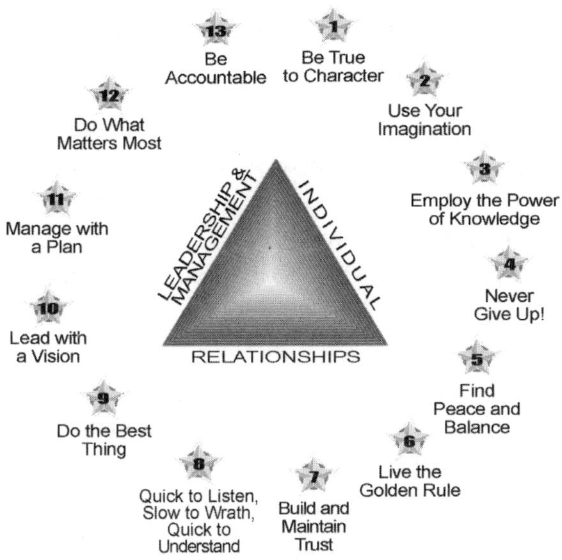

The Heart of the Matter
They've Stolen Everything!

My family and I were on the final leg of a one-hundred-and-twenty-mile journey that had involved multiple buses and ferries to travel from Bariloche, Argentina, to Puerto Montt, Chile. The bus had stopped once or twice to let people off when a German couple suddenly jumped up and yelled, "They've stolen everything! They've taken all of our money, our passports, everything!"

The bus driver pulled over so we could all help search for the couple's backpack that contained "everything." We quickly confirmed that, indeed, the backpack was gone.

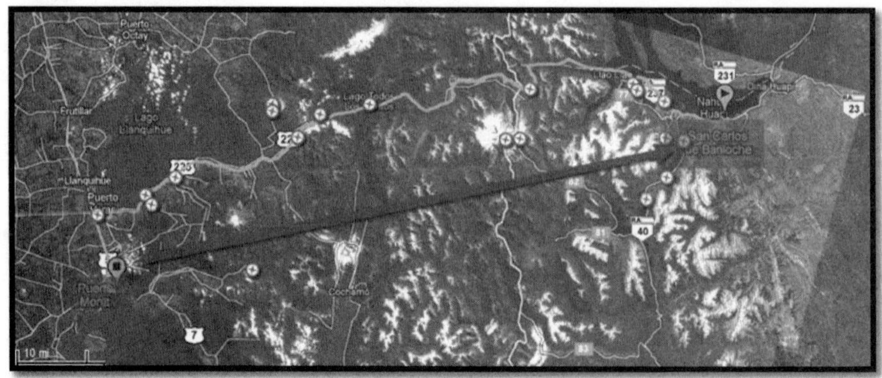

The German couple was distraught. What could they do? They didn't even have money to make a phone call. They spoke no Spanish. They were emotionally devastated over the loss of their passports, credit cards, and ID. The cruise they had scheduled to begin the next day would not happen without tickets. They couldn't even get back to the port where their cruise was to depart. All seemed hopeless. What could they do?

What If That Had Been Us?

I thought how easily the plight of our fellow travelers could have become ours. We were on the same bus. We were just as vulnerable to thieves or to somehow losing our valuables. As I watched the German couple talking to one another, I thought, *Well, I have about $200 in my wallet, and we're leaving for home this evening. Perhaps that amount could help.*

I indicated to the woman that we wanted to help and asked how much they needed. After checking with her husband, she said, "We need $500."

Since I had already measured my willingness and ability to help at about $200, I thought, *This will test my humanitarian resolve.* After a brief conversation with my family, we pooled all of our money and found we had a total of $540. We decided that we could get to the airport and make it home with our credit cards and $40 in cash for our taxi to the airport. *No problem,* I thought.

As the experience unfolded, many things went through my mind. I admit that *No problem* wasn't really my prevailing attitude for a few moments. But two things set the course for our eventual decision. First and foremost was the question, "What would we want someone to do for us in that same situation?" Second, we decided that if we really wanted to help, we couldn't worry about not seeing our $500 again—especially if there was a chance it could make a difference to this couple.

We gave the $500 and concluded our trip. After returning home, we received this e-mail from our new German friends:

Dear Steve,

I am writing this e-mail from Puerto Natales to say thank you so much for your confidence you showed us by giving us money without knowing us. I am expecting my husband back today from the embassy in Santiago de Chile with a new passport. We had a difficult time, many phone calls and re-arrangements to get a new passport for him. The police were not helpful at all, they let us sit in the police station several hours.

We will arrive back in Germany on January 19. I will transmit the $500 US to you then asap.

We would also like to invite you and/or your family in our house should you or your kids ever be visiting Germany. We live close to Heidelberg and some more nice places which are worth for a visit. Our son went to school for one year in the US, and my husband is travelling a lot in the US, so we would be really happy to welcome you.

They repaid the money long ago—but better than any amount of money are the friends we made from Germany.

A Rule in Every Age, in Every Culture

The Golden Rule—reaching out and helping each other—is established in both ancient and modern writings by philosophers, statesmen, religious leaders, and politicians as a means to a civil society and positive relationships.

Confucius is credited with the word *golden* in "The Golden Maxim," written in 479 B.C., but the essence of this rule is found in Christianity, Hinduism, Judaism, Islam, Taoism, Buddhism, and in the ancient Greek philosophies. The idea of the Golden Rule is found in every culture.

During our Chilean adventure, the values of the Golden Rule were easily understood by both an American and a German culture. While the precise wording may differ, it's a standard that is exercised and esteemed throughout the world in all types of wisdom literature.

The Golden Rule Around the World

Religion	***Golden Rule***	***Source***
Buddhism	*One who, while himself seeking happiness, oppresses with violence other beings who also desire happiness, will not attain happiness hereafter.*	Dhammapada 10. Violence
Christianity	*All things whatsoever ye would that men should do to you, do ye so to them; for this is the law and the prophets.*	Matthew 7:1
Confucianism	*Do not do to others what you would not like yourself. Then there will be no resentment against you, either in the family or in the state.*	Analects 12:2
Greek Philosophers	*Do not do to others what would anger you if done to you by others.*	Isocrates
Hindusim	*This is the sum of duty: do naught unto others which would cause you pain if done to you.*	Mahabharata 5,1517
Islam	*No one of you is a believer until he desires for his brother that which he desires for himself.*	Sunnah
Judaism	*That which is hateful to you, do not do to your fellow. That is the whole Torah; the rest is the explanation; go and learn.*	Talmud, Shabbat 31a
Nigerian Proverb	*A person who picks something and decides to make it his own ought to think how he would feel if he was the person who lost the property he picked.*	Yoruba

Regardless of language or source, we know two things about the Golden Rule. The first is that virtually everyone can quote it. The second is that if we actually lived it, the world would be much different. Napoleon Hill said the Golden Rule "both equals and transcends in importance" all other laws of personal power and achievement.

It's highly probable that the Golden Rule is quoted more often than it is lived. What could be simpler than to say, "Do unto others as you would have them do unto you"? And yet we give in to impatience or insensitivity, forgetting to notice when others are in need and forgoing the opportunity to serve.

Living Selflessly

If we want our first impulse to be one of service, we will be most effective as we teach our heart and mind principles of generosity and empathy. It is helpful to decide in advance to look for opportunities to be of service and to suspend judgment—both of the people you might help and their circumstances. As you do these things, you develop the selflessness that is at the heart of living the Golden Rule.

An old Jewish story tells of exactly this kind of unselfishness. Brothers Abram and Zimri owned a field of grain and worked together to harvest it each year. Abram had a wife and seven sons; Zimri had no family. Each year at harvest, they divided the sheaves of grain equally.

One night as Zimri sat alone by his fire, he thought, "It isn't fair that we share the harvest equally. Abram, my brother, has seven sons and a wife, and I have no one." And so Zimri went out to the field in the evening, carefully removed a generous third of the sheaves from his portion of the harvest, and placed them on Abram's pile. Then he returned to his home and sat by the fire.

That same night Abram sat by his fire thinking about Zimri; he said to himself, "I have a wife and seven sons, and Zimri has no one. It would be more fair to give Zimri the larger share of the harvest." So later that night he went to the field and removed from his pile of sheaves a generous third and put them on Zimri's pile. Then he went back to his home and sat by the fire with with his wife and seven sons.

When Abram and Zimri went out to work in the field the next morning, both noticed and were puzzled that the piles were exactly the size they had been the day before. That night both brothers again went quietly to the field to repeat their efforts of the previous night. This time, however, each saw the other removing the sheaves. Realizing what had happened, they embraced with their hearts full of gratitude for each other (Clarence Cook, *Poems* [University of California Libraries: January 1, 1902], 6–9).

This Guiding Constant, the Golden Rule, has the power to transform every relationship—whether family, friend, colleague, or boss. The power in the Golden Rule is the power of a noble character driven by the desire to reach out and lift others. But the benefit is not exclusively for others. There is a deep inward benefit to self from living the Golden Rule.

The Golden Rule Is Reciprocal

To live the Golden Rule means to seek the best thing, something that is related to the law of the harvest. The premise of the law is simple: you reap what you sow—in other words, you "get" what you give. Here's how it works: Do you want to receive justice and fairness? Then give justice and fairness. Do you wish others would notice that you need help and then help you? Then recognize and give help to others.

Assume that you live the Golden Rule in all of your roles. You apply it in your dealings as a helpful neighbor, in showing kindness to your family, in standing up for those you work with, and in supporting a total stranger. There is no doubt that your actions will benefit all these people. But there is another beneficiary: you.

Living the Golden Rule in a genuine way produces significant returns for you. You will have more peace. You will feel more confident and satisfied with your life. Your opinion of yourself and your belief in what you can accomplish will grow. You will find that you are a person you can trust to do the right thing—the best thing.

These "returns" on your investment of time and means are not the reason you decide to be a person who helps others. But these returns expand the benefit of every conscious effort to live the Golden Rule and extend this benefit over time.

Our family still talks about our experience with our German friends in Chile. We reflect on the privilege and positive influence these types of experiences have been for us. As a result, we see ourselves as people who may be able to make a difference, and we are encouraged to continue to live the Golden Rule. We believe it is doing the best thing.

No Time to Think

My wife, two of our children, and I learned in Chile that when it comes time to step up, we must have already decided that we would live the Golden Rule. We had emotionally said yes way before our German friends cried out, "They've stolen everything!" If we had needed to discuss what to do and worried whether we could afford to help, the opportunity would have passed.

Our commitment in advance to live the Golden Rule preempted any paralyzing thoughts about the risk of losing the money. We were already willing to suspend judgment. We didn't need to know the end from the beginning in order to "do unto others."

This disposition to give up resources in order to help someone in need wasn't automatic. It was a choice for us—a choice we made when we set the vision and goals for our family. We had to ask, "What is our vision for ourselves and our family members?" Once we discovered the vision of our best, we committed to live the Golden Rule. It has taken practice and we are not always as aware and ready as we could be, but we cherish those times when we do live the principle.

Relationships and the Golden Rule

The week I wrote the first draft of this story, I was reminded of the "They've stolen everything" tragedy of our German friends. It was one year later. We exchanged e-mails, reminding us both of the bond that was forged by the connection between someone in need and someone prepared to help. It really doesn't matter anymore who helped whom. We are connected.

The internal commitment to "do unto others" is personal. One of the main benefits of living the Golden Rule, however, is building more positive relationships. *Imagine you and your partner fully living the Golden Rule. What would that be like?* What would the best look like in your relationship? Would there be more listening *and* understanding? Would there be more forgiveness and giving the benefit of the doubt? But marriage isn't always that way, is it? And why not? Why is the Golden Rule—an adage so many subcribe to—so difficult to live?

The Golden Rule can be difficult to live because it asks you to change. It's natural to think first of your own needs and interests—but that kind of thinking can be an enemy of living the Golden Rule. Even though your survival depends on taking care of yourself, your relationships depend on taking care of each other. The Golden Rule is so powerful because it embodies so much of what you want to be and do.

The self-interest side of you may think, "Yeah, why can't everyone live the Golden Rule in his or her dealings with me?" The truth is, selflessness can be emotionally risky. *Learning to live the Golden Rule means working on your character.* It means trusting and being trustworthy. It is a call to something higher in you.

A Call to Something Higher

John F. Kennedy made a famous call to do the best thing when he asked Americans to imagine what it would be like to have to walk to the back of the bus, drink from a separate fountain, or eat at a different lunch counter because of skin color. He suggested that if we could hold the sadness and injustice of racism in our hearts, we would change how we treat others—and that could change the world. Kennedy believed that the power of the Golden Rule was real, that there was a harvest waiting for those who sowed it with their actions.

Gandhi invited you to be the change you want to see in the world. Would the world be better if you treated others with selflessness, empathy, compassion, and generosity? We do these things because they are right. And in the process, we change the world for good one person at a time.

The Golden Rule can be practiced in small ways to help prepare you for the larger Golden Rule moments you will encounter. Imagine you are stopped far from a stop light, and it's clear that it will take two or more cycles for you to get through the light. Now imagine that several drivers are trying to enter the road from the right. What will you do? Will you keep inching forward so they can't get in front of you? Or will you pause, create a space, and wave them into the line?

Your self-interest tells you that if you let the cars in line ahead of you, it will just take you longer to get through the light. But what does the Golden Rule ask of you? It asks you to do your best to feel what the other person feels. If *you* were the one sitting on the side of the road with no opportunity to merge, what would you want the drivers on the main road to do? Now the answer is clear. When you suspend self-interest, you can quote *and* live the Golden Rule.

We're Already There—Why Not Do Something?

A severe storm had caused delays and cancellations of flights at Chicago's O'Hare Airport. Thousands of stranded or delayed passengers were impatient, cross, and irritable. Among those in trouble was a woman, a young mother standing in a long line at the check-in counter. Her two-year-old child was on the dirty floor at her feet and she was pregnant with another child. She was sick and weary to the bone.

Her doctor had warned her against bending and picking up anything heavy, so as she moved slowly with the line she pushed her hungry and crying child with her foot. People who saw her made critical and cutting remarks but none offered help.

Then a man approached. With a smile of kindness on his face, he said, "You need help. Let me help you." He lifted the dirty, crying child from the floor and held her warmly in his arms. Taking a stick of gum from his pocket, he gave it to the child. Its sweet taste calmed her. He explained to those in the line the woman's need for help, then took her to the head of the line, spoke with the ticket agent, and soon had her checked in. He then found seats where she and her child could be comfortable, chatted for a moment, and disappeared into the crowd without giving his name. She went on her way to her home in Michigan (Gordon B. Hinckley, 2002).

This man lived the Golden Rule while others stood back as if to scold a young mother in distress.

The Higher Way

The Golden Rule is a higher way, a way many might find incomprehensible. Living the Golden Rule can seem counterintuitive. Would someone voluntarily give up a collegiate softball game victory to live the Golden Rule by reaching out to an opposing team member? In his book, *Finish Strong—Teen Athlete* (2009), Dan Green tells the story of an individual and a team that did just that.

Western Oregon University's Sara Tucholsky had no idea that the first and only homerun of her career—and her last swing of the bat—would become a national media sensation.

With two runners on base and her team down a run to Central Washington University, Sara hit a homerun to centerfield. As she rounded first base, she missed the bag. When she turned to tag the base, she injured her knee. Able only to crawl back to the base, Sara was told that she would be called out if her teammates came to her aid. If a pinch runner checked into the game, her homerun would count only as a single.

Players and fans alike were stunned when Central Washington first baseman Mallory Holtman, the conference's all-time homerun leader, asked the umpire if there was any rule against opponents helping an injured player around the bases.

She was told that there was not. Together, Holtman and shortstop Liz Wallace picked up Tucholsky and carried her around the bases, stopping at each bag to allow Sara to touch it with her good leg. "It was the right thing to do," Holtman said in an interview on national television after the respectful act of sportsmanship was witnessed by millions on ESPN and became a YouTube sensation.

The three runs sent Western Oregon to a 4–2 victory, ending Central Washington's chances of winning the conference and advancing to the playoffs.

"It's a great story," Western Oregon coach Pam Knox said, "something I'll never forget. The game's about character and integrity and sportsmanship, and it's not always about winning and losing."

As it turns out, the players who helped Sara had no idea of the circumstances surrounding the run or that the story would make national headlines. "We didn't know that she was a senior or that this was her first homerun," Wallace said. "That makes the story more touching than it was. We just wanted to help her." The gesture left Sara's Western Oregon teammates in tears. "I hope I would do the same for her in the same situation," Sara said.

Central Washington coach Gary Frederick called the act of sportsmanship "unbelievable."

"In the end, it is not about winning and losing so much," said Holtman, who initiated the act. "It was about this girl. She hit it over the fence and was in pain, and she deserved a homerun."

Who is Mallory Holtman? What do we know of her character? Who are her parents and when did she learn not just to quote, but to live the Golden Rule? Why wasn't she concerned about ridicule from her own teammates? Where was the "winning is the only thing" machismo? Why didn't Mallory and her team just quietly take the victory and say that the injury "was sad for that girl, but it's just part of the game"?

The question isn't about Mallory Holtman. The question is about you. The story of "the homerun that almost wasn't" is an invitation for you to develop and hold on to the type of generosity, fairness, and service demonstrated by those team members who lived the Golden Rule.

Don't Make It So Difficult

The academics and philosophers ask, cynically perhaps, "How do you know how another person wants to be treated?" They want you to doubt that you can understand how someone of a different culture, gender, or religion wants to be treated. They want you to believe you might actually offend such a person with your offer of help. Don't listen. Don't fail to live this principle because you assume it's too difficult.

If we had worried about possibly offending our German friends with our offer of help, the moment would have passed. If the Jewish brothers had stopped to think of fairness in terms of sheer numbers of mouths to feed instead of love and mutual respect, there would have been no moment of brotherly bonding. If the Good Samaratin had ignored the bleeding victim at the side of the road . . . and on it goes.

There is too much brazen confrontation in every society today. Is the emphasis on individual rights making you feel entitled to "push back" when you're cut off or deprived from getting what you want? Displacing rudeness and selfishness with the Golden Rule one person at a time may not change the world, but it *will* change *your* world and *your* relationships.

Qualities

It's simple to state the Golden Rule. Living it takes more. Civility, kindness, and charity are at the heart of living the Golden Rule.

Practical Civility

What if living the Golden Rule was a life-and-death proposition? If you don't think it could be, take a drive and see how many people you can cut off, how long you can drive the speed limit with traffic stacking up behind you, or how many hand gestures you can dish out before a potentially life-threatening altercation occurs.

Driving isn't the only situation in which you might be at risk. A friend told of standing in a line to check baggage when he received a viscious verbal attack for butting in line. My friend is not one who would butt into line, and he thought he was in the proper place before his assailant ever arrived. His first impulse was a natural one: to stand his ground and assert his right to be there. But he lives generously, looking for chances to help. He simply backed up and invited the man and his wife to step in front of him. Even though his first impulse was a negative one, he allowed generosity and civility to rule his response.

Living the Golden Rule means caring more about *what* is right than *who* is right.

Practical Kindness

"We were in a restaurant, and I noticed an elderly couple with a helium balloon tied to their table," related a pastor. "When I asked them what the occasion was, they told me it was their 50th wedding anniversary. I was glad and sad for them. Glad, because they still cherished each other. Sad, because they were all on their own. No family, no friends. As I went back to our table, I thought that I should pay their bill. I tried to do it anonymously, but the restaurant manager was curious: What is this, who are they to you, who are you, why are you doing this? I told them I was a church pastor and felt prompted to do it. The elderly couple was stunned speechless at the counter when told a total stranger had paid their bill. They were nearly in tears."

Two months later, the pastor was surprised to find that his anonymous act of kindness had been written up in *Woman's Weekly*. It was a random act of kindness that subsequently touched the hearts of thousands.

Practical Charity

To act with charity sometimes involves a contribution to a charitable organization—but it also involves exhibiting charity in your view of the world and the things you do for others. This concept is well illustrated by an old Jewish story of a Rabbi talking with God about heaven and hell.

"Come," said God. "Walk with me, and I will show you hell." Together they walked into a room of cold, rough stone. In the center of the room, atop a low fire, sat a huge pot of quietly simmering stew. The stew smelled delicious and made the Rabbi's mouth water. A group of people sat in a circle around the pot, each of them holding a curious, long-handled spoon. The spoons were long enough to reach the pot but the handles were so long that every time someone dipped his spoon into the pot and tried to maneuver it to his mouth, the stew spilled. The Rabbi could hear the grumblings of their bellies. They were cold, hungry, and miserable.

"And now," God said, "I will show you heaven." Together they walked into another room, almost identical to the first. A second pot of stew simmered in the center; another ring of people sat around it, each person outfitted with one of the frustratingly long spoons. But this time the people sat with the spoons across their laps or on the stone beside them. They talked quietly and cheerfully with one another. They were warm, well-fed, and happy.

"Lord, I don't understand," said the Rabbi. "How was the first room hell and this room heaven?"

God smiled. "It's simple," he said. "You see, they have learned to feed each other."

In the process of seeking the best for those around you, you also receive. This is the perfect practicality of charity. This is also the perfect practicality of living the Golden Rule.

Living the Golden Rule

At its core, living the Golden Rule is both unilateral and unconditional. It is not dependent on how others treat you, but it is a fundamental mindset and condition of the heart—of *how* you think of and treat others. *Ironically, because of the baggage that can build up in some of your closest relationships, you sometimes practice the Golden Rule least with those you most love and care about.*

How Is Living the Golden Rule Unilateral?

Living the Golden Rule in everyday life is unilateral because we each define it for ourselves, according to our background and experience. Your opportunity is to be consistent in feeling empathy and acting on the principles of kindness, generosity, forgiveness, gratitude, and civility.

Living this "rule" is also unilateral because you don't expect reciprocal treatment. You give freely and generously without concern for what may be returned to you. To presume a *quid pro quo* takes the "golden" part out of this principle of service to others.

How Is Living the Golden Rule Unconditional?

Living the Golden Rule is unconditional because you act without judging. Whenever you begin to judge, you risk talking yourself out of helping others. Your silent argument might be, "This person was foolish and doesn't deserve to be helped." Your living the Golden Rule does not free others from the consequences of their actions, nor do their bad choices release you to blame them and move on without serving.

Let your mind travel back in time to the robbed and beaten traveler on the side of the road to Jericho. What do you suppose was going through the minds of the priest and the Levite as they passed by the traveler? That he was probably a robber himself? That he had brought his beating on himself? That other matters were pressing and could not be delayed? If living the Golden Rule is conditional, you may not give it a chance.

Think about the college softball game. What a different outcome if the opposing team had said, "It's too bad that Sara couldn't finish running the bases. We would look foolish if we helped her. Besides, there is probably some rule against it anyway." You can explain your inaction away by claiming that it's complicated or not your problem. But truly living the Golden Rule is simple. You simply treat others with the same kindness, understanding, respect, and generosity that you hope others show you.

Every choice to live the Golden Rule builds character and has the potential to ennoble—raise, elevate, and magnify—both giver and receiver.

One Person Can Make a Difference

The story of a young woman and a group of soldiers provides a powerful illustration of the Golden Rule. On Christmas Day in 1941, a troop train pulled in to North Platte, Nebraska. The passengers—a group of surprised soldiers—were greeted by North Platte residents who not only distributed baskets of food and treats, but provided welcoming words and heartfelt smiles.

The original plan had actually backfired. Expecting to meet a train of Nebraska boys, the five hundred North Platte residents who met the train found themselves instead passing out encouragement and food to the soldiers from Kansas.

The reaction of the soldiers and the good feeling created in the town caused Rae Wilson, the twenty-six-year-old sister of a company commander in Nebraska's Company D, to write an editorial in the *Daily Bulletin.* She encouraged the town to "give back to our sons and other mothers' sons 100 percent. Let's do something. . . .'" What she was really saying was, "Let's do unto their boys what other mothers would do unto our own."

Each and every day during the entire war, three thousand to five thousand soldiers came through North Platte between 5 A.M. and midnight for a ten-minute stop. That brief stop became so memorable that the "boys" spoke emotionally of it fifty years later. At the end of the two wars as many as eight thousand troops had stopped on as many twenty-three separate troop trains every day. The food, treats, and time were all donated by residents and nearby farmers.

On April 1, 1946, the last day the canteen was open at North Platte, the final train stopped. Eleven soldiers got off just as three volunteers were cleaning up and closing the canteen for good. The volunteers had just made a large pot of coffee for themselves, but they gave it to the soldiers instead.

A total of six million soldiers knew who Rae Wilson was—if not by name, at least by the love and homemade food they received as a result of her vision.

Does Anyone Know Who I Am?

The world is full of examples like Rae Wilson. Rae Wilson's goal, of course, was not to be known but to give. What would that decision—to give of your time and means in the spirit of the Golden Rule—look like for you?

It's not very complicated at all. Simply ask yourself how you would hope to be treated and then treat others the same way.

Here are a Few Examples of How We May Hope to be Treated by Others

- *I would hope others would be patient with me.*
- *I would hope others would forgive my insensitivities, transgressions, frailties, and thoughtlessness.*
- *I would hope others would recognize and acknowledge my skills, strengths, and abilities.*
- *I would hope that others would never talk behind my back, and if they had an issue about me, that they would share it directly with me.*
- *I would hope that in my absence others would speak positively of me and stand up for me.*
- *I would hope that others would not offer "cold pricklies" but "warm fuzzies" in their judgment of and feedback to me.*
- *I would hope that others would be aware of my feelings and circumstances and that they would provide encouragement when needed.*
- *I would hope that others would be "quick to listen" and "slow to wrath," with a desire to really understand my feelings and thoughts.*
- *I would hope that others would be a good, positive influence and would have a good attitude around me.*
- *I would hope that others would provide clear guidance, correction, or direction when needed, without holding back, but would also be considerate.*
- *I would hope that others would bring out the best in me.*
- *In awkward situations, or dealing with harder issues or differing opinions, I would hope that others would try to understand my point of view.*
- *I would hope that others would know what my aspirations and goals are and would help me reach them.*
- *I would hope that others would help me feel comfortable in their presence.*
- *I would hope that others would treat me with kindness regardless of my color, cultural background, gender, religion, or political persuasion.*

If that's how we hope others would treat us, then we must treat others that same way! May that be the commitment of our heart, mind, and actions.

Victor Frankl recalls, "We who lived in concentration camps can remember the men who walked through the huts comforting others, giving away their last piece of bread. They may have been few in number, but they offer sufficient proof that everything can be taken from a person but one thing: the last of the human freedoms—to choose one's attitude in any given set of circumstances."

May we find fulfillment and joy as we unilaterally and unconditionally *live the Golden Rule.*

INSPIRATIONAL QUOTES

Live the Golden Rule

"May I do to others as I would that they should do unto me."

— Plato

"We have committed the Golden Rule to memory; let us now commit it to life."

— Edward Markham

"None of you [truly] believes [in this rule] until he wishes for his brother what he wishes for himself.

— Al-Nawawi's Forty Hadiths

"All things are our relatives; what we do to everything, we do to, ourselves. All is really one. "

— Black Elk, a Native American

"Come my friends, tis not too late to seek a newer world."

— Tennyson

"The sage has no interest of his own, but takes the interests of the people as his own. He is kind to the kind; he is also kind to the unkind: for Virtue is kind. He is faithful to the faithful; he is also faithful to the unfaithful: for Virtue is faithful."

— Tao Teh Ching, Chapter 49, Taoism

"Speak not injurious words neither in jest nor earnest. Scoff at none although they give occasion."

— 65th of George Washington's Rules of Civility

"Treat your inferiors as you would be treated by your superiors."

— Seneca 1st Century

Application

Individual

1. It can be motivating to think of an example of someone living the Golden Rule for you. What sacrifice of time, effort, and/or means was made for you? Write the experience in your Thoughts Book to preserve it for future use with family or others.

2. Consider memorizing one or two quotes or a story from this chapter. Write the quotes in your Thoughts Book.

3. Think of specific examples in your life of how you might live the Golden Rule.

With Others

1. Share with others one of the stories or quotes from this chapter or from your own experience. Discuss why the quote or story has meaning for you.

2. Determine together how applying this principle can be helpful in your organization.

3. Make living the Golden Rule a goal this week. Write down three things you would like to do this week toward that goal.

In a Nutshell

Living the Golden Rule can be practiced with everyone—from loved ones to those you don't even know. Any way you live it, the world will be a better place.

1. Living the Golden Rule is a principle of conduct taught in virtually every country, culture, and religion.

2. How can you leave the world a better place?

3. The Golden Rule is practiced naturally by those who have developed an awareness of the needs of others, empathy for their condition, and a desire to help them.

4. Living the Golden Rule is a call to set aside your self-interest and reach for something higher.

5. Civility, kindness, generosity, and charity are the heart and soul of living the Golden Rule.

6. When you live the Golden Rule you have the courage to convert the feelings of your heart into action and service.

Guiding Constant 7

Build and Maintain Trust

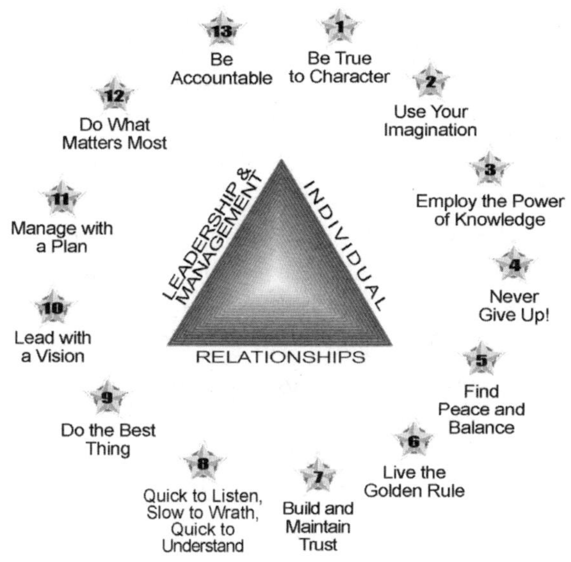

Trust

About thirty seconds after *Apollo 12—not Apollo 13*—lifted off the pad and headed toward the moon, the telemetry readings in Mission Control became garbled and nonsensical. The engineers at their consoles stared at their screens blankly, uncertain what to do and unsure what had happened. The astronaunt serving as Capcom capsule communicator could still talk to the capsule, so they knew the capsule was still on its journey and the astronauts were still alive. What they did *not* know was that the astronauts were surrounded by a cacophony of flashing warning lights and alarms.

No one knew what had happened or what to do. After staring at the garbled screen in front of him, the young electrical, environmental, and communication systems controller John Aaron turned from his console to flight director Gerry Griffin and said, "Flight, try sce to aux." Griffin had no idea what Aaron wanted. Neither did the Capcom astronaut—but he nontheless did as directed and passed the message on to the three astronauts in the capsule. Both Griffin and the Capcom asked Aaron to repeat the message.

Once he repeated it, there was no further discussion. The message made as little sense to Pete Conrad—the commander inside the capsule—as it had to Griffin and the Capcom. Again the command, "Try sce to aux," came through the radio, and Conrad exclaimed, "What . . . is *that*?"

But the astronaut to his right, Alan Bean, knew exactly what it was.

Bean had seen the signal conditioning equipment (SCE) switch during a training session a year before and remembered where it was located. He quickly reached up and flipped the switch from its normal power source to auxiliary (aux) power. Within seconds, the consoles in Mission Control began to come back on line and fewer of the warning alarms and lights were flashing in the capsule.

After checking his now-functioning screen, John Aaron asked that the astronauts be instructed to reinstall the fuel cells. The rest of the consoles came back on line, and the capsule returned to normal. Later examination revealed that the capsule had been struck repeatedly by lightning shortly after launch, damaging the electrical system. Because of the expertise, curiosity, and memories of Alan Bean and John Aaron—who had both seen something similar only once before—the mission proceeded to the moon successfully.

Milt Heflin pointed out that the switch used to control the power source for the SCE was designed only for testing on the pad. It was never intended to be used during a mission, which is why the flight director and the Capcom, an experienced astronaut, had never heard of it before. *It took a supreme act of trust* on the part of the flight director, the Capcom, and the mission commander to accept and relay the message that enabled Alan Bean to find the switch and save the mission.

That was Milt Heflin's point. *An amazing level of trust must exist in Mission Control for any mission to work.* Everyone in Mission Control is an expert in his or her field, and sometimes the flight director must trust a young, less-experienced individual in order for a mission to succeed. The same junior engineer, John Aaron, later played a vital role in the successful and now-famous return of the crippled *Apollo 13.*

The Power and Complexity of Trust

The story of *Apollo 12* illustrates both the power and complexity of trust. The success of the mission required humility, willingness to let go, and complete trust in the team by those in charge. It required the knowledge and memory of systems controller John Aaron and astronaut Alan Bean. Without all those combined factors, the system malfunction on *Apollo 12* would have aborted the mission and may have resulted in disaster. With those combined factors, trust flowed up and down the chain of command in a system of interdependence.

If NASA had been characterized by low trust and an unwillingness to take the risks that a trusting environment fosters, the story of *Apollo 12* may have ended far differently. Those in command didn't question the solution provided by the younger engineer. Instead, they passed the message on to the flight crew, the flight commander permitted a fellow astronaut to flip the switch, and trust was rewarded as a flight crew and mission were saved from tragedy.

Trust among team members—whether that team is family, a partnership, a production crew, an operating room staff, or top management—will enable achievement of the best.

Not only is trust a key to becoming your best, it is the glue that holds relationships together in life. Almost every action begins with trust.

There Is No Escaping Trust

Trust can be misunderstood because it is not easily defined. You routinely jump in your car and drive yourself to work or the kids to school, trusting that other drivers will not intentionally collide with you. There is no escaping trust. You trust that the milk has been pastuerized, that winter will end, that the doctor is right when he says your chest pain is just bronchitis. You have to trust that the bank will keep your savings safe. You exercise trust every moment of every day; *trust is the central principle of every action you take.*

Sometimes you also withhold trust. Consider again the examples in the previous paragraph. You wait a few seconds to accelerate after the light turns green because you *don't* trust the other drivers. You smell the milk in a newly opened carton to make sure it's fresh. You seek a second opinion on the bronchitis diagnosis. You move your money from the bank to the broker. But even those behaviors are based on trust: you act the way you do in those scenarios because you've lost trust.

There are a myriad of ways in which you demonstrate trust. You trust you will wake up when you go to sleep. You trust that our foreign aid reaches the starving poor. You trust that the power company will deliver and that the last employee to leave the building actually locked the door. You trust that eyewitnesses are accurate, that your car repair was actually necessary, and that the baby formula is not tainted with something harmful.

When you send your daughter off to school for the first time, you trust that her teachers will be kind to her, that her classmates will accept her, that her questions will be answered patiently, and that she will remember that you love her. Consider the trust she places in you when she walks out the door to go to school.

You trust that your employees give their full effort, that the supplier meets specifications, and that the purchase order will be paid. You trust that the car will start, the sun will come up, and the roof won't leak. The requirement to trust never ends.

Trust Is Like a Reservoir

In many senses, Guiding Constant 7—Build and Maintain Trust—is like a reservoir.

Look at how a reservoir is built. To begin with, it's man-made. A location is chosen, the impact is anticipated, and a dam is designed and built. Once the dam is finished, the river fills the reservoir—a process that can take years. The water that builds up behind the dam creates resources used by people in the vicinity of the reservoir. If the dam is not built and cared for properly, it can fail with catastrophic results.

With time, the reservoir becomes vibrant, giving life and stability to all around it. When well maintained, it can usually withstand any outside pressure. And when the reservoir is full it provides confidence. The power, strength, and potential for good in a reservoir is a metaphor for all that trust can be—both for you as an individual and for society worldwide.

When built with care and properly maintained, a reservoir provides quality of life for millions of people who draw on its resources for electricity, water, transportation, and recreation.

The reservoir is a wonderful metaphor of trust: It must be thoughtfully built and cared for over time. In a real sense, trust results from consistent actions. As you continue to build and maintain trust, filling your "reservoir," it's easy to solve difficult problems; you experience power, confidence, and strength. But if your reservoir of trust is low, it can be difficult to solve even the easiest of problems.

Living Guiding Constant 7

We purposely use the words *build* and *maintain* in the title of Guiding Constant 7 because those words describe the nature of trust. Building and maintaining reservoirs of trust means that you regularly do the things that strengthen your relationships. When you do something that weakens, threatens, or damages the trust someone has in you, it weakens your capacity to be successful together. When you do things that add to the level of trust, your capacity to work together and be effective increases.

The Fuel of Trust

Another way to think about trust is as a quality that can be measured.

Consider the fuel tank of your vehicle: it may be empty or full. When your gas tank is full, you feel confident. But when your gas tank is almost empty, you feel stressed and worried—and you have to take immediate action or the engine will quit. That scenario is especially stressful if you are on an isolated road in a remote area or in the middle of a busy freeway.

The quality of gas that you put in a fuel tank makes a big difference as well. If the gas put into an aircraft engine is tainted, the engine may sputter or even quit. That's particularly disconcerting when the plane is in midair.

Trust can be looked at the same way. High levels of quality trust build healthy, robust, and energetic relationships.

The Best Meter

Gauges and meters have long been used to indicate quantity.

Using it as a metaphor, a "gauge" or "meter" is also a simple way to analyze the levels of trust in each relationship. The higher the levels of trust on the meter, the stronger the relationship and the better you feel. The lower the levels of trust on the meter, the more strained and ineffective a relationship can be. The meter effectively measures both quality and quantity as registered by the "needle."

We call it the Best Meter, and it can be used to measure trust and the impact of your actions. Good actions cause the meter to go up; bad actions cause the meter to go down.

In other words, the needle moves to the right with positive actions and to the left with negative actions. Visualizing your actions this way helps you see the importance of both the quality and quantity of our actions.

The Best Meter allows you to look at and measure each and every relationship in terms of Bad, Good, Better, Best. The meter immediately connects to your inner self and produces a "read" on how the relationship is going.

If you detemine that the level of trust in the relationship is bad or fair, you need to do something to move the needle to the right. Genuine action pushes the needle in the right direction and strengthens the relationship. Insincere, fake, or going-through-the-motions action pushes the needle to the left, and you end up worse than where you started.

When the needle on The Best Meter is on the right, your relationship is solid and you feel good. When the needle is at the best, things are great! You are highly effective in the relationship.

Metaphors of Trust

In *The Seven Habits of Highly Effective People*, Stephen R. Covey uses the powerful metaphor of comparing levels of trust with an emotional bank account. You can either make deposits to or withdrawals from the emotional bank account by your actions. This powerful analogy clearly demonstrates that the actions you choose in your daily life will either strengthen or weaken your relationships.

Each of these metaphors—a reservoir in building trust, a bank account affected by deposits or withdrawals, or trust portrayed as a meter—is helpful as you consider ways to strengthen relationships by building and maintaining high levels of trust.

What *actions,* then, can you take to build and maintain trust? How do you keep the meter at good, better, or best?

- **Take a Best Meter Test for Valued Relationships**

In your mind's eye, The Best Meter may be used to analyze each of your relationships that matters. The test can quickly be done with your spouse or companion, family members, friends, colleagues at work, clients or customers you are meeting for the first time, and all others you interact with in the course of your daily life.

Give it a try: In your mind's eye, use The Best Meter to measure your relationship with your spouse or companion. What do you see? What is the meter doing? How does it feel? Where does the needle register? Try to be honest with yourself. If you want a real revelation, ask your spouse how he or she would rate the relationship on The Best Meter.

Do the same thing with a family member, a customer who has a complaint, or a work associate. Where does the needle register?

Your feelings are almost always right. But if you want a reality check, there are other ways to get an accurate reading and verifiable feedback, such as dialogue and surveys.

Once you have an accurate reading of the trust level in the relationship, you can take specific steps to do something about it.

- **Take Action That Drives the Needle to the Right**

What can you do to build and maintain trust—and consequently drive the needle to the right on The Best Meter and keep the reservoir filled?

The following *actions* are things you can do to create strong and sustainable relationships that flow naturally:

1. Fuel trust with the three Cs—character, competence, and capacity.
2. Be worthy of trust.
3. Act now to build and maintain trust at high levels.
4. Respect social contracts.
5. Build and rebuild trust.

1. Fuel Trust with the Three Cs—Character, Competence, and Capacity

Trust results from interdependence. You trust others to have character as you rely on their integrity, courage, and honesty—and they on yours. You trust others to be competent when you rely on their knowledge and ability. And you trust others to manifest their character and competence consistently through their capacity to maintain their effort—the endurance to see something through to the end.

Over the years, you've developed a great deal of trust in your auto mechanic. His decades of experience are evident in his tremendous workmanship; you never have cause to question his decisions or his work. He often finds less expensive ways to accomplish necessary repairs and you're confident that he will never try to take advantage of you. You've recommended him and his shop to numerous friends, all of whom have expressed the same sort of trust in him. But despite his skill and the quality of his work, would you go to him if you learned you needed surgery to remove a brain tumor? Of course not. You would seek out a trusted surgeon to perform that sort of operation. Part of trust depends on the appropriate training and background of the person in whom you invest your trust. Trust is impossible without competence.

The more opportunities you have to see a person act with integrity, the more you trust—and the farther the needle on the meter moves. You look for evidence that the people you relate to value what you value—that a person consistently lives those values (character) and consistently performs (competency). "Trust only movement," says Alfred Adler. "Life happens at the level of events, not of words. Trust movement." This is the same as saying, "Trust the actions that demonstrate character, competence, and capacity."

The balance between character and competence is crucial. Unless you are careful, you can mistake competence for character. When someone sounds and looks like he knows what he is doing, you may mistakenly presume he also has character. You might also ignore signs of a weak character because the evidence of competence is so compelling.

The balance between character and competence may be difficult to determine. As an example of imbalance, consider a highly competent employee who is unproductive and untrustworthy because of an addiction. To understand how important the balance is, visualize character and competence as conjoined twins that can never be surgically separated because they are joined at the head and heart. Separating such twins would kill both of them. That's how important the balance is between character and competence.

Trust is not just a way to protect yourself from harm or disappointment. It is the means of building character, competence, and capacity. As trust is consistently exercised, trust levels become extremely high. At that point, you and those you trust discover new and awesome abilities never before imagined.

You depend on the character, competence, and capacity of others to help you live safely and successfully and to help you achieve your goals, however lofty or mundane. In fact, you rely on the character, competence, and capacity of unseen thousands as you go about your life. You also depend on others to not hinder you. Becoming your best is virtually impossible without character (integrity and honesty), competence (knowledge and ability), and capacity (strength to deliver, dependability, and being a finisher).

2. Be Worthy of Trust

Focus on what you can do to be worthy of trust and to build and maintain trust—things that consistently drive the needle on The Best Meter.

A July 1999 *New York Times*/CBS News poll revealed that 63 percent of people interviewed believe that in dealing with "most people" you "can't be too careful"; 37 percent believed that "most people would try to take advantage of you if they got the chance." In other words, if you want to influence people, your first job is to let people see that you can be trusted. How can you do that?

The same poll revealed that 85 percent expect the people they "know personally" to "try to be fair." Could it be that simple? Let people see who you are, help them feel like they *know* you personally, and your trust ratio automatically triples. Think about things you've undoubtedly heard: "He's okay—I *know* him" or "It's not that I don't trust her, I just don't *know* her."

This second action builds on the first: Being worthy of trust requires that you demonstrate your character, competency, and capacity over time. There are a number of ways to be worthy of trust; consider the following:

- Do high-quality, high-quantity work and finish it when you say you will.
- Be consistent so others will see you as reliable.
- Be predictable: Always follow through on what you say you will do. Return phone calls and respond to e-mails. Be timely and responsive.

- Be open in communicating commitments, and be willing to have your performance measured. Communicate intentions and motives so your actions are transparent.

- *Give* trust. As with most other things in life, you get what you give. In other words, giving trust often results in returned trustworthiness.

- Be sensitive to the needs of others around you by putting their interests before your own.

- Show that you care about others through being kind, helping them achieve their vision and goals, respecting them, and keeping their confidences.

- Share your values by being very clear on how you feel about trust, character, competency, and capacity. Your clarity establishes a baseline for others to measure your actions against.

When people find you trustworthy, they prefer to deal with you. Opportunities for growth and progress come to those who are trusted.

As you achieve your own vision of trustworthiness and meet the expectations of others, you experience peace and balance in your life. Your relationships are more rewarding, you are better able to resist negative influences, and you build self-respect because you know you can be trusted.

Conversely, when you are not trustworthy, you are more likely to view others as untrustworthy—and you may behave selfishly and cynically by "getting them before they get me." Because trust is reciprocal, you develop it by developing your own trustworthiness first.

When you are trustworthy, you develop another capacity at the same time: you develop the ability to trust yourself. Living a life of trust creates greater self-confidence.

When you trust yourself:

- You trust your inner voice.

- You trust in your competence and are secure enough to listen and measure all input.

- You trust in your character because you have the power that comes from consistency.

- You are a full reservoir with resources that are deep and powerful because you work on your competence, character, and capacity.

- You have the confidence to trust your own judgment and are not swayed by the opinions of others.

Remember: Trusting yourself is a prerequisite to trusting others.

3. Act Now to Build and Maintain Trust at High Levels

To build trust, you need to define it. A common understanding and language for trust will enable you to understand how it is built and maintained. The dictionary says that the party giving trust is "to have a firm reliance on the integrity, ability, and character of a person or thing."

At first, you measure trust as you make decisions about a person. How do you think the person is likely to act in any given situation? How has the person acted in the past? What conclusions can you draw? Trust builds if you can predict that the person is reliable.

Next, trust is shared. You align your goals and values, working individually and mutually to achieve a common goal and vision. Because you both care about the same thing, you have a social contract—even if unspoken or informal—agreeing that trust is of mutual benefit and includes caring and concern for each other and for a shared vision.

You don't go around giving and receiving trust without behaviors on which to base that trust. Sadly, trust can either be developed or destroyed when problems arise—and either can occur rapidly. A sudden loss of trust can be devastating.

A great example can be seen in customer service. When the customer service team finds out that customers are upset, team members usually respond right away by saying, "We need to build trust." In fact, trust with customers is built like trust in any other relationship—by actions that establish trust. There's that moment of truth when a company shows it can be trusted—the moment when the customer confronts the company and the company's core values show.

What follows is an adaptation of some apologies I found in a blog post by Seth Godin in which he describes the variety of ways companies respond to customer complaints. I'll give you a few of the ten Godin listed. The first few invite mistrust. The later ones start to demonstrate how trust is built. As you read each one, notice its impact on trust (after you stop chuckling or rolling your eyes, that is!).

Customer Service Call Responses

Response 1	"You can always take your business elsewhere." *"Thank you, I will, and so will all of my friends." (Trust plummets.)*
Response 2	"It's not our fault." *This is not an apology; the company wants you to believe it is the victim.*
Response 3	"I'm sorry you feel that way." *This is not an apology. Roughly translated, the company is saying, "Your feelings are your problem. It gripes me that you feel that way. If you didn't feel that way, I would be happy." How does this affect trust?* *This response may sound empathetic at first glance, but it refuses any responsibility for the problem and places all of it on the customer. (Trust drops.)*
Response 6	"I'm sorry if I did something wrong." *This is getting to an apology and starting to rebuild trust. But it does not accept responsibilty, using* if *as a subtle disclaimer. You are not acknowledging that you did anything wrong; you're still hoping that you haven't. (Trust really isn't moving yet.)*
Response 9	"We're sorry that we caused this problem" or "We're sorry that we let this happen."

This is a full apology and is what we all want to hear when reporting a problem. Trust is starting to build, but more is needed. The customer might say, "Well, all right, these things happen. What are you going to do to fix it?" This is better but there is still a best way to rebuild trust with your customer.

Response 10 "We're so sorry that we caused this problem. Please know that we take this very seriously. This is a huge oversight on our part. I will immediately notify my supervisor, and we will review our procedures to ensure that this cannot happen again. In the meantime, that is no consolation to you for our lack of service! What can we do to regain your trust? We will be sending you a little surprise as a token of our appreciation of having you as a customer."

This apology might continue until the customer interrupts—and even then it goes on a little longer. (Trust is being built.)

A company I have been associated with for many years performs energy-savings audits and services for homeowners and small business owners. One of our customers said his air conditioner wasn't working properly. He was unhappy with us: Even after we performed a tune-up service, the unit wasn't blowing out cool air. So here's what we did: One of our associates visited with the customer so we could understand the problem in detail. Next, our technicians arrived within hours to correct the problem. Finally, one of our associates delivered a gift and reviewed the customer's feelings about the service to make sure his expectations were met. We didn't talk about what was right—we simply followed our company's mission statement, "We treat people right." By the time we left, the Best Meter registered at a ten—the highest possible level. Our challenge as a company is to have our service register as a ten on the first visit.

There are many great stories of customer service that cement trust between the customer and the company. For example, Nordstrom gives a refund on tires—something it doesn't even sell—and accepts the return of items purchased at competing stores. Another example is the FedEx driver who is stuck in traffic and who walks the packages to the FedEx terminal a mile away to make sure they will be delivered the next day as promised.

Warren Benis calls trust the major leadership challenge of today and tomorrow. Why is trust so important? Interpersonal trust results in greater creativity, teamwork, and productivity. Trustworthy managers are reliable, fair, open, competent, and loyal. This kind of trust inspires the people who experience it to become their best.

Trust is crucial to every happy and successful relationship; everything you do in life is built on trust. It's a concept worth repeating: High trust enables you to solve the most difficult of problems with ease. Low trust makes it difficult to solve even the easiest of problems.

You help build trust through being kind, exercising patience, listening, completing a task, consistently delivering results, doing what you say, and so on. When the trust account balance is positive, you feel strong and confident in your relationships. But when the balance in the account is running low or close to empty, your relationships can become seriously strained. And when deposits to the trust account stop altogether, relationships can die.

Stephen M. R. Covey, son of Stephen R. Covey, wrote an excellent book in which he suggests how to establish a powerful trust account balance. In *The Speed of Trust*, he teaches that "Trust is the hidden variable in the formula for organizational success. The old paradigm was that Strategy x Execution = Results. The new paradigm is that Strategy x Execution x Trust = Results."

Covey outlines a number of behaviors that can help fill your reservoirs with trust:

- Say what you mean, and mean what you say.
- Demonstrate respect (people crave respect and acknowledgement; give it!).
- Be transparent (hiding things creates mistrust, openness creates trust).
- Right wrongs (don't say you are sorry—behave as though you *are* sorry).
- Show loyalty, particularly to those not present.
- Get better (show your commitment via continuous improvement; results create credibility).

- Confront reality.
- Clarify expectations.
- Practice accountability.
- Listen first (and be quick to listen).
- Keep commitments (model the desired behavior; walk your talk).
- Extend trust (trust creates reciprocity; extend it conditionally to those who are earning trust, abundantly to those who have established trust).

Reflect on people who have either gained or lost your trust. What did they do? Not do? Do any of those behaviors apply to you? Who trusts you? Why? Who distrusts you? Why? Covey said, "Trust changes everything." Are there areas of your life—professional or personal—where you could create more trust? Building reservoirs of trust will result in power and growth. The power of trust will fuel your pursuit to become your best in all you do.

4. Respect Social Contracts

Without character, trust is almost impossible to develop. Sure, contracts are written to define and structure trust. Employment contracts attempt to optimize the benefits of working together. Real estate contracts containing hundreds of pages of documents are created to protect buyers, sellers, and lenders. Attorneys write agreements between parties exchanging resources such as time, money, and goods.

But despite all of the money and time spent on formalizing trust relationships, trust is largely unenforceable. Few contracts will prevent a breach of trust or even ensure a satisfactory remedy in the event of such a breach. The best contract you can rely on is the social contract where trusting interdependence is assured and binding because of the character, competence, and capacity of the parties to the unspoken trust agreement.

Imagine the shift in resources that would occur if everyone were to manfiest character in fully reciprocal trusting transactions and relationships. Such a condition is hard to imagine in an environment saturated with examples of fraud and focused on the importance of obtaining power and money. You see it every day in the news media, entertainment, business school courses, and even boardrooms.

In some circles, taking advantage of someone by being clever seems to be valued more highly than trust. Those who subscribe to this philosophy will learn that trusting relationships bring more peace, balance, success, and happiness than all of the power and possessions they can accumulate.

The resources or advantages acquired through dishonesty become a house of cards. Look at the historical result of choosing cleverness over trustworthiness. Madoff Securities, Enron, and WorldCom are just the tip of an iceberg. The fraud and lies involved in these and other cases like them were huge breaches of trust resulting in heartbreak, embarrassment, and even suicide.

Major companies like these—and even the economies of whole nations—risk complete financial failure because of the loss of trust and its foundational personal quality, character. At even greater risk is individual peace and balance—the ability to live "good" in the midst of a race to live "well." When trust is absent, chaos reigns. There is little hope for a foundation on which even the simplest pursuits and decisions about relationships, business, and education—about anything really—can be made.

Trust cannot be legislated, policed, contracted, forced, or bought. The greatest source of trust is a combination of character, competence, and capacity. Trust sits solidly as a foundation under your efforts to become your best—within and without.

5. Build and Rebuild Trust

Trust can and often should be rebuilt. Trust is based on your willingness to be vulnerable. A breach of trust can cause you to retreat from that vulnerability to protect yourself from further damage. Not all relationships are able to survive a broken trust. However, true success going forward depends on interdependence, and interdependence depends on trust. It is difficult to achieve your best without trust, and you should allow others to rebuild trust just as you would want to be forgiven by those whose trust you violated.

How is trust rebuilt? It takes considerable time, because consistent high-quality and high-quantity actions are necessary.

If you trusted and were wronged, be willing to reconcile and forgive the breach of trust. Be patient as you allow time for the rebuilding process to work. Be willing to talk about the withdrawals and about rebuilding the balance.

If you're the one who broke the trust, tell what happened and apologize. Describe how you will better manage similar events in the future. Be absolutely genuine; a trusting relationship cannot be rebuilt for appearance only. Your sincerity will be clear as you make restitution—as you do something concrete to show that you want to repair the violation of trust. Recommit to the trusting relationship, and be trustworthy from this point on.

The Powerful Influence of Trust

An experience with one of our sons taught me that you can have little or no lasting influence without trust. Although we had always been friends, I realized the balance in our trust account was low and needed deposits—sincerely made deposits.

"How are you doing?" I asked.

"Fine."

"How is school?"

"Fine."

"What is happening at school that gets you excited?" I tried again.

"Nothing."

I asked myself what was I doing to build trust in my relationship with my son. The answer, unfortunately, was not a whole lot. I began to think of things he liked to do that would allow us to enjoy time together in hope of strengthening our relationship. We both liked basketball, so I started inviting him out to shoot hoops in the evening. That simple thing changed everything. Trust slowly started to build.

At this time in his life, he was also not being very sensitive to his mother, and she had about had it with him. Hard feelings were developing. A few days later, I happened to walk in the house when they were arguing; he was being rude and offensive. I wanted to take him out! I took a deep breath, walked over to him, and whispered in his ear, "I love you. You are better than this." This respectful and measured action, based on a relationship of high trust, had an impact on our son.

He dropped his hands and walked into his room. Thirty minutes later he came back to the kitchen, approached his mother, and said, "Sorry!" Then he walked out. That may not sound like much to you, but it was the first time in three years that I had heard him apologize for anything. What is more significant is that he never again raised his voice and has been consistently respectful to his mother in the many years since. Trust was rebuilt to its highest level.

What made the difference? I trusted him to be "better than this." My actions gave him a desire to act on his own in a way that strengthened relationships. There were no lectures—just positive actions. Because of conscientious and deliberate acts to build trust, we replaced hostility with greater affection, effective feedback, and clear expectations. I showed him respect and built our relationship over time through shooting hoops and spending other time together. The result was a continuous upward momentum toward becoming the best in our family relationships. Rebuilding trust is well worth every effort.

Built and rebuilt, trust infuses relationships—both personal and professional—with the strength to endure whatever challenges may occur. When you are offered trust, it inspires and motivates you to be your best. And when you offer trust to others in confidence and good will, you forge the kinds of associations that encourage them to become their best as well.

INSPIRATIONAL QUOTES
Build and Maintain Trust

"Put more trust in nobility of character than in an oath."

— *Solon*

"I hope I shall always have firmness and virtue enough to maintain, what I consider the most enviable of all titles, the character of an honest man."

— *George Washington*

"Trust is the bandwidth of communication."

— *Karl-Erik Sveiby*

"Trust thyself: every heart vibrates to that iron string."

— *Ralph Waldo Emerson*

"I think we may safely trust a good deal more than we do."

— *Henry David Thoreau*

"I had to trust a team and they had to trust me to get me to the moon. And the size of that team was 256,000 people. And I trusted them. And they got me to the moon."

— Apollo 12 *Astronaut,*
Alan Bean

"Our distrust is very expensive."

— *Ralph Waldo Emerson*

"The best way to find out if you can trust someone is to trust them."

— *Ernest Hemingway*

"Trust men and they will be true to you; treat them greatly and they will show themselves great."

— *Ralph Waldo Emerson*

Application

Individual

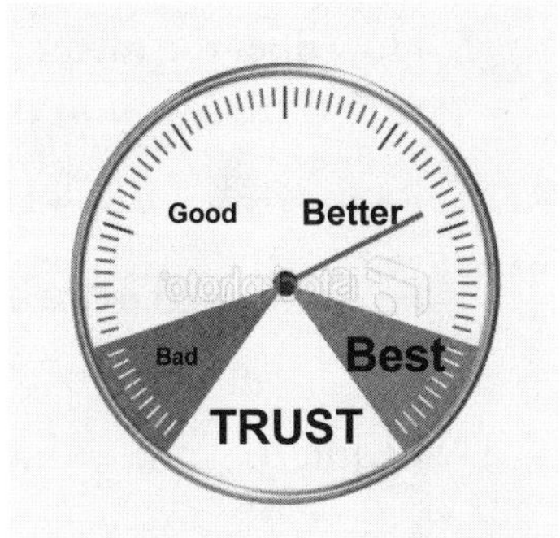

1. Assess the levels of trust in your relationships. See where The Best Meter needle is. Honestly assess where you are, and commit to do something about it.

2. As you think about your experiences with trust, one or two memories will stand out as examples worth remembering and retelling. These moments of trusting others and being trusted will inspire you. Write them in your Thoughts Book so you can later share them with others.

3. What actions can you take that will build trust in the relationships you have?

Persons with whom I will nurture positive relationships	*What actions will I take?*
1.	
2.	
3.	

With Others

1. Use the Best Meter to assess levels of trust with other departments within your organization.

2. What actions can your department take to build trust with other departments, other companies, or other countries?

In a Nutshell

1. How does the meter read on trust in the relationships you have with others? Is it in the red? Is it time to take positive action?
2. Be trustworthy and loyal, especially to those who are absent.
3. Be committed to excellence and be among the best at what you do.
4. Be fun to work with.
5. The ultimate measure of trust transcends legal documents and agreements. Trust is a matter of character and commitment to the well-being of everyone in balance with becoming your best. Be a person of your word. What you say is what you do.
6. Trust is a commitment to:
   - Being dependable
   - Giving feedback
   - Showing respect
   - Giving honor
   - Demonstrating humility
   - Removing hostility and anger
   - Being thoughtful
   - Making and keeping psychological agreements
   - Listening to understand
   - Building character
   - Demonstrating competence
   - Saying "I'm sorry"
   - Being able to be counted upon
   - Performing random acts of kindness
7. Keep the trust meter in the good, better, or best zone and out of the fair and bad zones.

Guiding Constant 8
Quick to Listen, Slow to Wrath, Quick to Understand

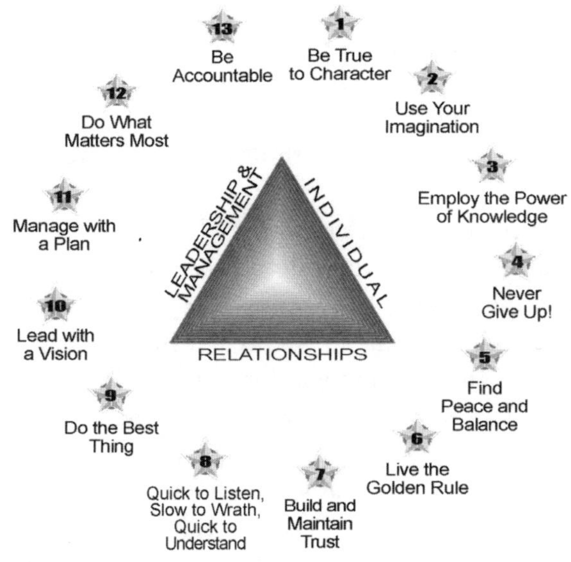

Getting to Our Best
"I have never been more discouraged in my whole life!"

Some years ago—when we had four boys under the age of nine—my wife, Roxanne, told me she wanted to run a marathon. Even though I had promised my body that I would never put it through such punishment, without thinking, I said, "I would be happy to run it with you." I really didn't know what I was getting into. However, it turned out to be one of the greatest experiences of our lives.

To prepare for the marathon, we started a sixteen-week training program. Not only did it help both of us get more physically fit, it became a wonderful time for us to visit.

One particular morning we began a training run and I asked Roxanne how she was doing. She replied evenly but unconvincingly, "Fine." Normally, I would have said, "Great," and moved on to the next subject. However, I had been teaching about the power of listening, and I sensed there was something more to the *Fine* she had replied with. I said, "That didn't sound like a very convincing 'fine.'"

Her next comment about knocked me over. She replied, "Actually, I have never been more discouraged in my whole life." I thought to myself, *Whoa! There's a big difference between "fine" and "I have never been more discouraged in my entire life."* I considered giving her a list of things she could do to feel better but I instinctively knew I should just listen. Besides, I figured she might knock me into the ditch if I started making suggestions.

Instead, I said, "It sounds like things are really weighing heavily on you."

"I'm not sure where to turn or exactly what to do," she said. And then she expressed her thoughts and concerns nonstop for the next twenty minutes. I tried to simply listen.

When we returned home about twenty-five minutes later, she stopped at our front porch and said, "Thank you for just listening. I didn't really need any advice but I needed to better understand my own feelings. It was so helpful to just get things out and to be able to verbalize things. Thank you." And then she went into the house. I was left on the front porch to reflect on our very important interchange. What was especially amazing was that Roxanne felt much better, and this issue really never came up again.

The pace of life and the drive to "get things done" can be a barrier to really listening. *Listening accurately and with empathy is one of the greatest gifts you can give yourself and others.* Connecting with others through listening not only helps you *become* your best but to *feel* your best. Being quick to listen creates an opportunity to learn and grow, for both the listener and the speaker. Even though listening is vitally important to your success and happiness, few have ever been taught how to do it.

I am always disappointed in myself when I am slow to listen, quick to wrath, and slow to understand. That particular combination never really seems to help me in any situation. To the contrary, when I am quick to listen, slow to wrath, and quick to understand, things *always* seem to work out better. It's a practice that makes a great difference in almost every interaction that I have, whether personal or professional.

Listening and the Right Frame of Mind

As I mentioned, one of the greatest gifts you can give yourself and others is the gift of being quick to listen, slow to wrath, and quick to understand.

That might sound simple, but listening is not always easy. John Robert McCloskey describes how complicated it can get: "I know that you believe you understand what you think I said, but I'm not sure you realize that what you heard is not what I meant." In addition, listening can be complicated by attitudes and emotions.

Think about what's going on in your heart and mind every time you start to communicate. You have feelings—probably some concerns or insecurities—about yourself and your worth. You are dealing with the many things that are happening in your life at the time. *You are trying to process and determine whether the communication is highly emotional or more informational.* Incidentally, this is where some of the other Guiding Constants enter the picture; for example, you will listen more effectively when you remember that your character and respect for others—living the Golden Rule—is the most effective context for listening.

Being quick to listen and slow to wrath involves the kind of listening that lifts the listener and the speaker and signals the beginning of wisdom. Listening in the right way builds positive relationships; once you have fully understood, you are able to apply judgment, reason, and wisdom. But when you think you already know what's going on, or you don't care how the other person is feeling, your communication will be laced with frustration and anger instead of understanding.

Do you wonder how important this really is? Consider this: you can become better in living all of the Guiding Constants as you apply being quick to listen and slow to wrath. Why? Because being quick to listen is one of the best ways to demonstrate your commitment to all of the other principles. Let's explore how you can more effectively master this Guiding Constant.

Being Quick to Listen Is a Power

Being quick to listen brings stability and strength into each situation, crisis, opportunity, or interaction you face. Listening—really listening—is one of the most productive ways to maximize the success of every circumstance, conversation, or interaction.

Your objective is to make the very best of every situation and to make each relationship better. The way to achieve that objective is by being quick to listen, slow to wrath, and quick to understand.

Training in Listening Skills

No matter how badly you want to achieve this objective, there may be a hurdle: if you're like many other people, you've had little or no training in how to listen. It's like parenting—you have to pick it up somehow, and there are no required classes.

Listening can be further complicated by us as individuals. If we are indifferent, impatient, selfish, or insincere, we may not even try to listen (or we might *appear* to listen but we don't actually hear).

If you're feeling overwhelmed, you lack confidence, or you're not true to character, you might not be able to genuinely listen—even though you know it's important—because of all the "noise" you're already processing.

As I reviewed the principles and processes of listening, I discovered hundreds of lists offering advice on how to listen—and we'll review some of what I learned. But I kept thinking about our desire and ability to listen. Why do I occasionally get angry or defensive when I'm talking to someone? How can I avoid communicating anger or reacting harshly? How do I help others know that I am ready and willing to listen? The answers don't involve learning listening skills alone. There is an important prerequisite to effective listening and avoiding wrath: internalizing the thirteen Constants for becoming your best. A person who is true to character, who works to fill reservoirs of trust, and who lives the Golden Rule will be a more effective listener. A person who does not align with these principles will be much less effective as a listener. Living the principles needs to be balanced with listening—really hearing what is said.

The Best Self Is Quick to Listen

People who are quick to listen, slow to wrath, and quick to understand are often seen as being reasonable and equitable. Not only are they cautious, patient, and enduring, they also possess a profound analytical power. They are able to execute the principles for becoming their best with clarity, force, and directness.

This Guiding Constant—one that is strong, powerful, and compassionate—has been demonstrated throughout history in some of our nation's most esteemed leaders.

In speaking of President Abraham Lincoln, Union officer William E. Doster recalled: "In conversation, he was a patient, attentive listener, looking for the opinion of others rather than hazarding his own, and trying to view a matter in all of its phases before coming to a conclusion."

But when the conversation dealt with more serious topics, Lincoln "disclosed a mind singularly free from the delusions of vanity, which turn people's heads in high places, and a level head, incapable of fooling itself, or being fooled by others." With character, peace, and balance, and a desire to do the best thing, Lincoln listened with great effect. As demonstrated by Lincoln, one person practicing this Guiding Constant can make all the difference in the world.

Listening deeply requires your best. It's especially important to guard against listening just so you can "argue out the other person's feelings." Being quick to listen—to genuinely listen—is especially vital with those you love most, including family and friends and those with whom you work most closely.

When You Are Squeezed

Listening is an outward manifestation of the person you are inside. To become a better listener—a sincere, interested, positive listener—you begin with what's inside of you.

What comes out when you're squeezed? When you internalize the Golden Rule, out comes kindness, empathy for the needs of those around you, and the kind of service that helps ease burdens. When you are worthy of trust, out comes integrity, a true interest in supporting others, and a commitment to stand as one with them. When you are true to character, out comes the capacity and competence to do the right thing regardless of the external pressures.

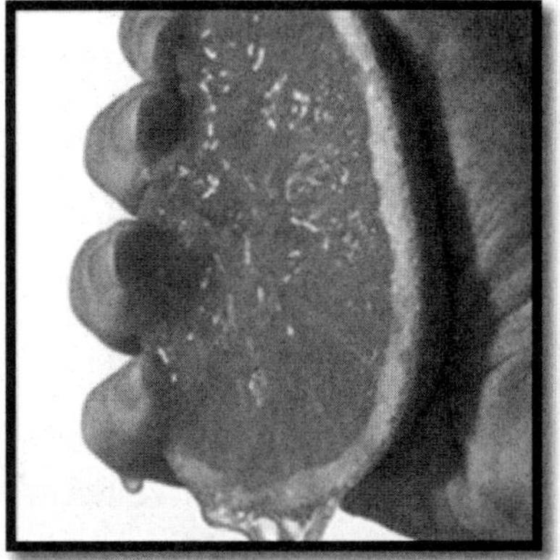

Everyone gets squeezed from time to time. When you get squeezed, slow down long enough to apply the Guiding Constants, and you'll love what comes out: the will and skill to maintain open, positive communication. Remember: you get what you give.

Wrath Is the Enemy of Listening

Wrath is defined as anger and arrogance; it rears its head when you're being opinionated, biased, prejudiced, emotional, hurt, offended, or just plain ticked off. Rather than succumbing to wrath, focus on seeking understanding.

Einstein said, "If A equals success, then the formula is A equals X plus Y and Z, with X being work, Y play, and Z keeping your mouth shut."

When an imbalance between your behavior and your principles causes you to lose your temper and composure, the result can be devastating. A hot temper—even if only for a moment and only once in awhile—sets the long-term tone for a relationship. Trust is essential to communication; being quick to listen, slow to wrath, and quick to understand strengthens your reservoirs of trust.

In a post to the *Harvard Business Review* blog, Peter Bregman describes two executives who confided in him that they had shocked themselves by acting in anger. He speaks of John (not his real name), who by all accounts is successful at work, at home, and in the community. John is described as reasonable in discussions, well-informed on the issues, and likeable. Yet he threw a phone in anger during a meeting. He was appalled. "That's not who I am," he told Peter.

Jane (not her real name) is also a successful executive—at a different company, in a different city—someone who is likeable, trusted, and admired. She has heard feedback that she's rude, abrupt, uncommunicative, and harsh. She said the same thing John did: "That's not who I am."

But when John and Jane were squeezed—when they encountered circumstances that triggered their inner wrath—that's who they became in the moment. Maybe there have been times when you've been more quick to wrath than you'd like to admit—and you've regretted it.

A Way to Remove the Wrath

How do you elminate these flash points, moments of anger, and unpleasant reactions? You learn to regularly, almost systematically, ask yourself, "What is the best thing?" If you're prone to wrath, you need a way to remind yourself that getting angry is not who you are and does not result in your best.

Affirming who you are in order to avoid reacting angrily to others is vital. Structure time to ask yourself, "What is the best thing?" Bergman suggests saying to yourself, "That's not who I am." You might anticipate the possibility of losing your temper or composure and remind yourself that it's best *not* to do so.

You're most effective when you put aside your own prejudice, anger, offense, emotion, or perspective until you have fully listened. Doing so will bring out your best and enable you to become your very best in your interactions with others.

The Best Self Is Slow to Wrath

Why is being quick to listen and quick to understand grouped with the quality of being slow to wrath? Because being quick to listen isn't the whole story.

Quickness isn't really the point; the important thing is *understanding*. Understanding displaces things like anger, indifference, jealousy, or betrayal. Wrath—anger—is too often the most automatic reaction. If you are quick to listen and quick to understand with your inner as well as your outer ears—with your character—you will more easily become slow to wrath.

You know what it's like: When you become angry, you get into trouble. And it's a serious thing; wrath is the underlying cause of a range of poor choices and harmful actions.

Look at the effect of wrath on marriage, as reported in one newspaper article: "More than half the Americans who might have celebrated their 25th wedding anniversaries since 2000 were divorced, separated, or widowed before reaching that milestone." What does that have to do with wrath? Divorce is often a result of wrath—of not listening, of letting small things turn into criticism, faultfinding, and bitter feelings. When listening stops, so does communication.

So many make a big deal out of things of no consequence. A man who had been slandered by a newspaper was extremely angry and sought help in plotting his response. When he went to Edward Everett for advice, Everett told him, "Do nothing! Half the people who bought the paper never saw the article. Half of those who saw it, did not read it. Half of those who read it, did not understand it. Half of those who understood it, did not believe it. Half of those who believed it are of no account anyway." Seeing things in the best light and refusing to get caught up in the emotion of the thing will empower you to become your best.

There is a story of an old man who was asked by a newspaper reporter the secret of his long life. His answer? "When my wife and I were married, we determined that if we ever got in a quarrel, one of us would leave the house. I attribute my longevity to the fact that I have breathed good fresh air throughout my married life." We can all benefit from some fresh air.

A story is told of a man named Charles Penrose, who loaned furniture from his home to the church where he served as a volunteer almost full-time for ten years. As the church accumulated resources, it began to buy its own furniture. Seeing Penrose subsequently removing his own household furniture from the church, members of the congregation accused him of taking church property.

It has been said that Penrose had a quick temper and was easily ignited to anger. He was deeply offended by these accusations and must have wanted to retaliate; he may have even felt justified by righteous indignation. After all, his church associates had judged him and now mistrusted him.

Resisting his instincts, Penrose spent that evening writing a verse he titled "School Thy Feelings." Two of the stanzas are quoted here:

School thy feelings; there is power
In the cool, collected mind.
Passion shatters reason's tower,
Makes the clearest vision blind.
Wound not willfully another,
Conquer haste with reason's might;
School thy feelings, sister, brother;
Train them in the path of right.

— *"School Thy Feelings," Charles W. Penrose*

Conditions of Effective Listening

You probably spend more time using your listening skills than any other kind of skill. And like other skills, listening takes practice.

What does it mean to really listen? You need to know why you are listening. You'll find out as soon as the other person starts talking. If the other person is highly emotional, your purpose in being quick to listen is to support and empathically understand that person. If what the other person is saying is heavy in facts and details, on the other hand, your job is to understand and to capture those things accurately. No matter what, as a good listener, you want to help the other person become his or her best. You can be a key facilitator toward that goal.

The Skill of Listening

There are three main skills involved in being an effective listener.

First, the purpose of listening is to understand. Until you understand, you can't be in a position to help things "get to a better place."

You can improve your ability to understand by learning and applying these powerful listening skills:

- to hear, to really listen to the *words*;
- to see, to look at body language and other cues for meaning; and
- to feel, to empathize with the feelings of the speaker.

These key roles of the listener are defined best in the four-decade discussion of active listening by Thomas Gordon.

Gordon reemphasizes the need people have to be listened to and understood. I was surprised at first, then, to read that he discourages asking questions, giving advice, or trying to reassure someone when they have a problem—I assumed those things would lead to understanding. Instead, Gordon maintains that such efforts actually cause the person to *stop* talking about the problem—which ultimately prevents understanding and finding a resolution.

To see what he means, take a look at this example from Thomas Gordon:

Let's say a coworker sighs, looks dejected, and says to you: "I'll never make it! These new quotas are ridiculous!" This is a clear signal that this person is upset, distressed, has a problem, and needs to be listened to and understood.

Most of us probably would react by reassuring our coworker, "You're a pro. I wouldn't worry about it," or by suggesting, "I think it would be a good idea to talk to your supervisor about this," or by asking "How high are they?" Responses such as these, well-intentioned as they may be, generally do more harm than good. None does anything to help the other person get relief from distress; none communicates understanding. Instead, they cause him/her to feel frustrated, misunderstood, patronized, and unaccepted. In effect, these responses communicate: "It's not OK for you to feel this way" or "I'm not comfortable hearing that you're upset, so here's how to get over it."

As defined by Gordon, active listening is a way to tell your coworker that you understand and accept his feelings. When you stop to really hear what others are saying, you give them the respect and time to fully understand for themselves what is upsetting to them. Once they come to this kind of understanding, they can resolve the issues and refocus on their tasks.

Active listening involves skills that can be learned with practice. The first skill is to *be able to tune into the need people have to say something about what they are feeling and experiencing.* Rarely will someone just walk up to you, grab you by the ears, put their forehead against yours, and say, "Listen to my problem!" Since that's not likely to happen, you must be alert to the ongoing possibility that a person needs to be heard. Once you see that someone needs to talk, be "slow to speak." Resist the urge to insert yourself into the other person's communication of his or her feelings.

Active listening means "hearing" what is meant—but maybe not said. It means being patient until the person finishes saying everything that needs to be said. It means communicating understanding by reflecting on what you heard—for example, you might say something like, "Correct me if I'm wrong, but you feel that you could be more effective if you had more feedback from your direct reports."

Voicing that kind of reflection periodically is a good checkup—it helps you determine whether you're accurately understanding what you are hearing. An important part of active listening is picking up the meaning of what is being said.

Your role as a listener will help you determine how to respond. Here are some simple suggestions:

Purpose of Active Listening	*Possible Things to Say*
What to say to check understanding when you don't think you understand.	*Let me see if I'm understanding you. You feel that …*
	What I see happening here is that …
	I'm not sure I'm getting it, but are you saying that …?
What to say when you think you understand.	*So, from your point of view …*
	Where you're coming from is …
	So, you believe that …

The second skill is to *avoid creating roadblocks to communication.* You may create roadblocks while actually trying to be helpful—for example, when you try to reassure or give an answer. You may also create roadbloacks by inadvertently asserting power or by being unsensitive or even unaware.

Gordon has identified twelve roadblocks to communication. As you read the summary of each, you'll see 1) the roadblock, 2) an example of how the roadblock is stated, and 3) a comment on the roadblock.

Roadblocks to Communication

—Ordering, directing, commanding—"You will do this or I'll find someone who will." Misused power is a serious roadblock to getting at the information that would solve the real problem. People will emotionally resist—they know that what they may need from you is not coming anytime soon.

—Warning, admonishing, threatening—"If you miss that quota once more . . ." Have you ever been warned, then done the exact opposite of what you were warned about? It's natural to respond to threats by saying to yourself, "I'll show you."

—Moralizing, preaching, imploring—"You, of all people, should have known better." This blocks communication because you seem to feel superior and believe the other person is inferior. The other person will no longer have any interest at all in talking *or* in making changes.

—Advising, giving suggestions or solutions—"You really should consider . . ." You come across as believing you're an expert, which prevents you from hearing the full story and limits consideration of all of the creative possiblities for solutions.

—Persuading with logic, lecturing, arguing—"You don't know what you're talking about, you need to be reminded that . . ." How would you react to someone who said this to you? If you're like most others, you'll defend youself from the attack.

—Judging, criticizing, disagreeing, blaming—"How could you be so thoughtless?" If the person is already feeling inferior, criticizing and judging will shut off future communication. It undermines confidence and the will to tell you how she is feeling.

—Praising, agreeing, evaluating positively, buttering up—"Nice job." This sounds like praise, doesn't it? But you have set yourself up, perhaps without realizing it, as the judge of what is good. You could be taken as insincere.

—Name-calling, ridiculing, shaming—"Don't be stupid." This can make people feel that you're not fair. People will probably call you names behind your back to reclaim a sense of control and dignity.

—Interpreting, analyzing, diagnosing—"The reason you're failing is that . . ." This kind of communication is a block to listening because you have already assumed and presumed. You've blocked the person from putting it all out where you can see the full picture.

—Reassuring, sympathizing, consoling, supporting—"It's not as bad as it could have been." It is patronizing to try to smooth over something when you both know that you probably don't really feel that way.

—Probing, questioning, interrogating—"When did you know . . ." or "Why didn't you . . ." These questions are more like an interview at the police station and don't create openness. As a result, you'll learn very little about what is really happening.

—Distracting, diverting, kidding—"When that happened to me . . ." Talking about your own history with this problem diverts attention from letting the person unload and keeps you from learning their needs.

The third skill is *the capacity to attend so completely to the person that you can accurately reflect what you heard.* This says you want to understand—and the person will help you.

When the other person feels that you understand, that you are fully involved and listening, a solution will often be reached. Once you really understand, then you can determine what it means to do the best thing.

The Legend of the Talking Stick

Our family has learned the power of effective communication in a tangible way through the legend of the talking stick. Through this legend, we discovered that real communication is possible as each person is fully heard.

As our family discussions often became energetic and occasionally heated, we found we all started talking at once, each one getting louder in an attempt to be the one that was heard. To help us ensure that each family member is heard in our discussions, we adopted the Native American tradition of the Talking Stick, which was introduced to us by Stephen R. Covey.

The Talking Stick is passed from one person to another. When the person with the Talking Stick is speaking, everyone else remains quiet. When the person with the Talking Stick is finished, he or she holds it out and whoever wishes to speak takes it. This process continues until everyone has spoken his or her peace on the matter being discussed.

The Talking Stick isn't an ordinary stick—it's carefully constructed from symbols pertaining to listening and understanding. An eagle feather tied to the Talking Stick symbolizes courage and wisdom and reminds the speaker to speak truthfully and wisely. Rabbit fur on the end of the stick symbolizes speaking softly from the heart. A blue stone is a reminder that the Great Spirit also listens to the speaker's heart. The shell changes color in different light, signifying that all creation changes and that people and their circumstances also change. Four

The Talking Stick

beads, each a different color, stand for the sunrise (yellow), the sunset (red), the earth (green), and the snow (white). Each color also represents a direction on the compass. Strands of buffalo hair signify power and strength. These symbols represent the powers of the universe the speaker has when communicating what is in his or her heart.

Rating Things on a Scale of 1 to 10

It's helpful to have good tools for successful communication. One way to improve communication was taught to us by a friend early in our marriage. The tool is to ask how strongly that you feel about something on a scale of 1 to 10. A 10 means you are *really excited*! A 1, on the other hand, means *no way*.

For example, throw out the question, "How much do you want to go to a movie?" If one person says 7 and another says 1, you've got valuable information to use in moving toward a decision that works well for both parties. If my wife ever rates her interest from at 6 or below, I listen carefully—and her response has an important impact on what we end up doing.

If you really care, this process actually allows you to *show* that you care!

One of the best ways to connect with someone else is to be quick to listen—to *really* listen. Once you've heard what the other person is saying, resist the impulse to get angry or impatient; instead, place yourself in his or her position and do as much as you can to understand. The tools and techniques described in this section will help you do exactly that. As you use them in the ways they are intended, you will leave every situation better than you found it—and you will dramatically enhance your efforts to become your best.

INSPIRATIONAL QUOTES

Quick to Listen, Slow to Wrath, Quick to Understand

"Listening is a magnetic and strange thing, a creative force. The friends who listen to us are the ones we move toward. When we are listened to, it creates us, makes us unfold and expand."

— *Brenda Ueland.*

"Courage is what it takes to stand up and speak; courage is also what it takes to sit down and listen."

— *Winston Churchill*

"The ear of the leader must ring with the voices of the people."

— *Woodrow Wilson*

"What comes out of you when you are squeezed is what is inside of you."

— *Wayne Dyer*

"You do not really understand something unless you can explain it to your grandmother."

— *Albert Einstein*

"Be patient and calm—for no one can catch fish in anger."

— *Herbert Hoover*

"The wise old owl lived in an oak; The more he saw the less he spoke; The less he spoke the more he heard: Why can't we all be like that bird?"

— *Edward H. Richards*

"The saddest part about being human is not paying attention. Presence is the gift of life."

— *Stephen Levine*

"Deep listening is miraculous for both listener and speaker. When someone receives us with open-hearted, non-judging, intensely interested listening, our spirits expand."

— *Sue Patton Thoele*

"You cannot truly listen to anyone and do anything else at the same time."

— *M. Scott Peck*

"So practice listening, rather than waiting for your turn to speak. Let the person finish, let them get the concept out, give them your full attention. They'll appreciate the courtesy, you'll look more intelligent, and you both may find the right answer to the problem."

— *Buck Woody*

"In some South Pacific cultures, a speaker holds a conch shell as a symbol of temporary position of authority. Leaders must understand who holds the conch—that is, who should be listened to and when."

— *Max De Pree*

"Envision a conversation in which each person is listened to with respect, even those whose views are different from yours. This is all possible in conversations of the heart."

— *Kay Lindahl*

Application

I invite you to live this constant: be quick to listen, slow to wrath, and quick to understand.

Individual

1. Affirm to yourself regularly that you deeply desire to become your best by being quick to listen, slow to wrath, and quick to understand.

2. What can you do to ensure you listen actively?

3. Write down the names of those who most depend on your disposition to listen effectively. List the key things you will do to listen well during your next discussion.

4. Record your plan and inspirations in your Thoughts Book.

With Others

1. Discuss with others the principles and benefits of effective listening.

2. What things can you do together to improve your ability to listen and understand?

3. Discuss the impact on your organization, customers, and clients—as well as your overall effectiveness—when you are quick to listen, slow to wrath, and quick to understand.

In a Nutshell

1. One of the greatest gifts you can give to others is to really listen to them, to be fully with them as they talk to you.

2. When you are balanced, with your life tuned to the Thirteen Guiding Constants, you have greater capacity to be quick to listen, slow to wrath, and quick to understand.

3. Remember: "What comes out of you when you are squeezed is what is inside of you."

4. Einstein said, "If A equals success, then the formula is A = X + Y + Z, with X being work, Y play, and Z keeping your mouth shut."

5. Listen with all of your faculties: use your ears to listen to the words, your eyes to read body language, and your heart to listen to feelings.

6. Put a "check" on your wrath while seeking only to listen, understand, and fully capture *the other person's* point of view. Control your anger, opinions, pride, emotional baggage, tendency to take offense, and prejudice, and focus instead on true listening.

7. Listen actively by avoiding the twelve roadblocks to communication. Carefully reflect what you hear.

8. Remember the description of the Talking Stick legend, and use the principles in your communication.

9. Use a scale of 1 to 10 to help improve the precision of your understanding.

Guiding Constant 9

Do the Best Thing

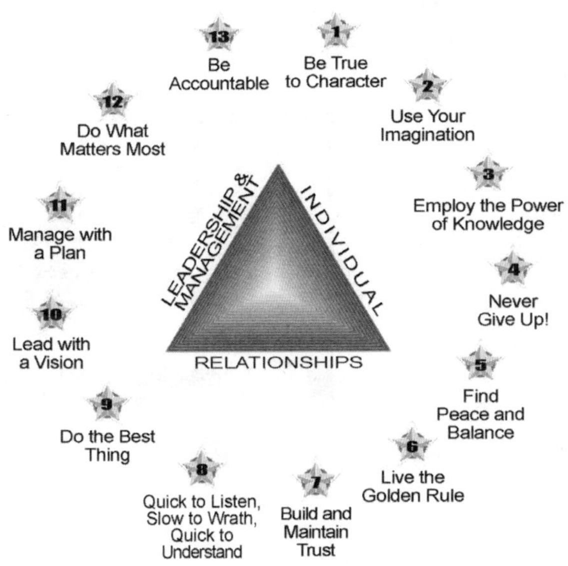

Getting to Our Best
It Is Worth It

Some of the most poignant examples of doing the best thing occur during war; these incidents involve both the courageous men and women who give their all and a nation that both rejoices and grieves over their sacrifice. One of those was Butch O'Hare, a man willing to pay the ultimate price to do the best thing when he entered the US Naval Academy and became a naval aviator. Lt. Commander

"Butch" O'Hare was presented with the Congressional Medal of Honor for his actions defending the aircraft carrier USS *Lexington* as a naval aviator during World War II.

O'Hare and his wingman were the only two who were not already engaging the enemy over the Pacific Ocean when another squadron of eight enemy planes appeared. His wingman's guns jammed, so O'Hare fought the eight twin-engine Japanese bombers alone, one against eight. He shot down three of them and damaged two others by diving into them before other American fighters arrived and chased the bombers off. No enemy bombs made it to the *Lexington*. The Medal of Honor citation calls it "one of the most daring, if not the most daring, single action in the history of combat aviation."

Chicago's O'Hare airport was named after Butch O'Hare in 1949; a Grumman F4F-3 aircraft, restored as closely as possible to the one O'Hare flew, is on display in terminal 2. His commitment to do the best thing is used as a lesson in the service academies and has been retold countless times as an example of the courage to do the very best thing even under the most treacherous circumstances.

Another story of a very different kind of heroism involves a lawyer nicknamed "Easy Eddie." Easy Eddie made a fortune as Al Capone's lawyer, keeping Capone out of jail in Chicago during the 1920s. He lived on a large estate and wielded influence in the highest government and business circles of Chicago. In the midst of his prosperity and influence, Eddie for some reason sensed he was not doing the best thing. He took a hard look at what his choices were doing to his family. Divorced from his wife, Selma, Eddie had one son—and he knew that his indulgent lifestyle and support of Al Capone was not a convincing example of good character for young Edward. It is reported that because of his son's laziness, Eddie sent him to the Western Military Academy in Alton, Illinois.

Many believe it was Eddie's desire to change his image, clean up his name, and set an example of character that led him to begin cooperating with the US Internal Revenue Service and agent Frank J. Wilson in the 1930s. Agent Wilson was also trying to do the best thing—to destroy Ca-

Artwork depticting Easy Eddie and Capone found at http://www.strangetrueus.com/strange/highlights.action

pone's empire of racketeering, prostitution, and murder. Because Eddie provided evidence of the only charge the government could prove against Capone—tax evasion—Capone was convicted and sent to Alcatraz for eleven years. But Eddie paid the ultimate price for doing the right thing. Just before Capone was released from Alcatraz, Eddie was murdered while driving in Cicero, Illinois, by two gunmen.

Easy Eddie did the best thing by taking down Al Capone. Doing so required Eddie to change his loyalties from the crime family to the government and the law—and to risk his life. He paid the ultimate price for doing the best thing, but in the process he became an example of character for his son and others.

The stories of decorated fighter pilot Butch O'Hare and crime family lawyer Easy Eddie are related by more than topic. "Easy Eddie" is Edward J. O'Hare, the father of Edward Henry "Butch" O'Hare, the Congressional Medal of Honor recipient fighter pilot. Following young Edward's secondary education at Western Military, he was appointed to the Naval Academy by U. S. Congressman John J. Cochran, a friend of his father. Edward graduated from the academy as a naval aviator in 1937. Doing the best thing can be contagious—and when one person demonstrates the energy and commitment to do the best thing, it can light a fire under others.

Guiding Constant 9, Do the Best Thing, reviews suggestions on how we can learn to see and do the best thing in our own lives.

What Is Doing the Best Thing?

Our lives are filled with good things as well as things that are better. But as we look at those things, we need to determine if each is the best thing or the best use of our time.

Doing the best thing involves an action that results in the greatest good. It is an event or act that has *good* and *better* aspects to it. It is a combination of seeing the best thing—a vision—and committing to do the best thing—a goal.

Stories about people doing the best thing can come from all walks of life, including the most unexpected places. Take cab drivers, for example: Day in and day out, these drivers get ordered around by a largely ungrateful public. Many give back to their customers what they receive from those customers: grief.

That may be the "norm," but it's not the case with every cab driver. Harvey Mackay tells a wonderful story about a very different cab driver who made the choice to do the best thing. Harvey was waiting in line at the airport cab stand when an unusual cab pulled up. The first thing Harvey noticed was that the taxi was polished and clean. The driver—dressed in a white shirt, black tie, and freshly pressed slacks—moved quickly around the cab to open the door for Harvey.

He handed Harvey a laminated card and said, "I'm Wally, your driver. While I'm loading your bags in the trunk, I'd like you to read my mission statement."

Taken back, Harvey read the card. It said: *Wally's Mission Statement: To get my customers to their destination in the quickest, safest, and cheapest way possible in a friendly environment.*

Harvey was blown away—especially when he noticed that the inside of the cab matched the outside. Both were spotlessly clean. As he slid behind the wheel, Wally said, "Would you like a cup of coffee? I have a thermos of regular and one of decaf."

My friend said jokingly, "No, I'd prefer a soft drink."

Wally smiled and said, "No problem—I have a cooler with regular and diet soda, water, and orange juice."

Almost stuttering, Harvey said, "I'll take a diet soda."

Handing him his drink, Wally said, "If you'd like something to read, I have *The Wall Street Journal*, *Time*, *Sports Illustrated*, and *USA Today*."

As they pulled away from the curb, Wally handed my friend another laminated card and said, "These are the stations I get and the music they play if you'd like to listen to the radio."

And as if that weren't enough, Wally told Harvey that he had the air conditioning on and asked if the temperature was comfortable. Then he advised Harvey of the best route to his destination for that time of day. He also let him know that he'd be happy to chat and tell him about some of the sights or, if Harvey preferred, would be happy to leave him in silence with his own thoughts.

"Tell me, Wally," an amazed Harvey Mackay asked the driver, "have you always served customers like this?"

Wally smiled into the rearview mirror. "No; in fact, I've only done so for the last two years. My first five years driving, I spent most of my time complaining like all the rest of the cabbies do. Then I heard the personal growth guru, Wayne Dyer, on the radio one day.

"He had just written a book called *You'll See It When You Believe It.* Dyer said that if you get up in the morning expecting to have a bad day, you'd rarely disappoint yourself. He said, 'Stop complaining! Differentiate yourself from your competition. Don't be a duck. Be an eagle. Ducks quack and complain. Eagles soar above the crowd.'

"That hit me right between the eyes," said Wally. "Dyer was really talking about me. I was always quacking and complaining, so I decided to change my attitude. I looked around at the other cabs and their drivers. The cabs were dirty, the drivers were unfriendly, and the customers were unhappy. So I decided to make some changes. I implemented a few at a time. When my customers responded well, I made a few more."

"I take it your approach has paid off for you," Harvey said.

"It sure has," Wally replied. "My first year as an eagle, I doubled my income from the previous year. This year, I'll probably quadruple it. You were lucky to get me today. I don't sit at cab stands anymore. My customers call me for appointments. If I can't pick them up myself, I get a reliable cabbie friend to do it and I take a piece of the action." Wally was phenomenal. He was running a limo service out of a yellow cab.

Harvey Mackay says that he probably told the story about Wally to more than fifty cab drivers over the years, and only two took the idea and ran with it. "Whenever I go to their cities, I give them a call," continues Harvey. "The rest of the drivers quacked like ducks, and told me all the reasons they couldn't do any of the things I was suggesting."

Wally chose to do the best thing, and it made all the difference to him and to his customers.

Why Doesn't Everyone Choose to Do the Best Thing?

So, couldn't every cab driver provide the same service as Wally? Yes.

A few additional examples explain how simple it can be.

Why do people go back to Disneyland again and again to see the same Main Street and ride the same rides? It is because Disneyland is committed to relentlessly doing the very best thing.

It doesn't happen only in the business world. Plenty of people also give their very best, no matter what. Johnny, a grocery bagger, shows that anyone can figure out a way to become their best by doing the best thing. Barbara Glanz, author of this "Simple Truths" story, tells what happened when Johnny—a teen with Down Syndrome—attended a seminar she presented on customer service.

"A few years ago, I was hired by a large supermarket chain to lead a customer service program—to build customer loyalty. During my speech, I said, 'Every one of you can make a difference and create memories for your customers that will motivate them to come back. How? Put your personal signature on the job. Think about something special you can do for your customer to make them feel special—a memory that will make them come back.'

"About a month after I had spoken, I received a call from a nineteen-year-old bagger named Johnny. He proudly informed me that he was a Down Syndrome individual and told me his story.

"'I like what you talked about!' he said, 'but at first I didn't think I could do anything special for our customers. After all, I'm just a bagger. Then I had an idea! Every night I would come home and find a thought for each day. If I can't find a saying I like,' he added, 'I would just think one up!'

"When Johnny had a good 'Thought for the Day,' his dad helped him set it up on the computer and print multiple copies. Johnny cut out each quote and signed his name on the back. Then he'd bring them to work the next day.

"'When I finish bagging someone's groceries, I put my Thought For The Day in their bag and say, 'thanks for shopping with us.'"

"It touched me to think that this young man—with a job most people would say is unimportant—had made it important by creating precious memories for all his customers.

"A month later the store manager called me. . . .

"'You won't believe what happened. When I was making my rounds today, I found Johnny's checkout line was three times longer than anyone else's! It went all the way down the frozen food aisle. So I quickly announced, 'We need more cashiers; get more lanes open!' I tried to get people to change lanes. But no one would move.

"'They said, "No, it's OK—we want to be in Johnny's lane; we want his Thought for the Day."'

"The store manager said, 'It was a joy to watch Johnny delight the customers. I got a lump in my throat when one woman said, "I used to shop at your store once a week, but now I come in every time I go by, because I want to get Johnny's Thought for the Day."'

"A few months later, the manager called me again.

"'Johnny has transformed our store. Now when the floral department has a broken flower or unused corsage, they find an elderly lady or a little girl and pin it on them. Everyone is having a lot of fun creating memories. A wonderful spirit of service spread throughout the entire store . . . and, all because Johnny chose to make a difference!'"

You can think of something you can do to make a memory for a co-worker, a family member, a friend—even a stranger—that will make that person feel like coming back for more. All it requires is being conscious of and doing the best thing.

The best thing to do may not be obvious at first. You probably need to experience many good things and a few better things to finally figure out the best thing—and to realize that sometimes the best thing may not be the grandest thing. One father took his family on several summer vacation trips to cultural and historic places, spending a significant amount of time and money on those trips. At the end of that summer, he asked his son what his favorite activity had been. The son's favorite summer activity had been lying on the lawn with his dad looking at the stars and talking (Dallin H. Oaks, 2007).

Doing the Best Thing May Grow Out of Making Mistakes

It's important to realize that doing the best thing often results from having done less than your best at first. Making mistakes—even big ones—in your personal or business life provides a time to learn and recommit. Examine what happened, choose to improve, and then improve some more. Remember Wally, the cab driver? He didn't do the best thing at first. He tried some things—some worked, some didn't. He gave up the things that didn't work and capitalized on those that did. Then he tried some more. As Henry Ford said, "Failure is only the opportunity to begin again, only this time more wisely."

Doing the Best Thing May Involve Doing Less

It's natural to assume that a lot of good things added together will make the best thing. But the best thing is often the one that makes things less complicated—for you and for the people around you. In his book *The Hurried Child*, David Elkind maintains that it is possible to involve children in too many lessons and too many sports activities too early. Children need free time to play and explore, create, invent their own games, make believe, and run and laugh. You've likely given a toddler an expensive toy and then watched her play all afternoon with the box the toy came in. In the same way, doing the best thing may be doing less.

Doing the best thing does involve action, though. If love is the best thing, then giving love is doing the best thing. If positive relationships with those around you are the best things, then caring deeply, communicating openly, and serving others is doing the best thing.

Doing the best thing means building a bond of total trust and unconditional love. Doing the best thing is listening when someone needs a listening ear. Doing the best thing is living by all of the Constants for becoming your best that you've learned so far in this book.

Living Guiding Constant 9

Is doing the best thing always easy or fun? No. Albert Gray said, "The common denominator of success—the secret of success of every man who has ever been successful—lies in the fact that he formed the habit of doing things that failures don't like to do." You may not always like doing what the best thing requires, at least at first. You just do those things. And you reap a reward—emotional, monetary, or both—that many never feel or realize.

Living Guiding Constant 9, Doing the Best Thing, is the result of a consciousness and interest in becoming your best. It is being true to character, building reservoirs of trust, and living the Golden Rule. It is never giving up. Doing the best thing is consciously choosing to live by and incorporate the Thirteen Constants for becoming your best every day. Once you've made that choice, you can learn to engage the highest within you by nourishing five keys:

> ***First Key:*** *Cultivate a desire for doing the best thing. You inspire yourself toward this desire by living each of the Thirteen Guiding Constants.*
>
> ***Second Key:*** *Learn to see the best thing among alternatives. The best will be accompanied by good and better things to do.*
>
> ***Third Key:*** *Commit to doing the best thing. You will be drawn into doing the best thing by the potential for great outcomes; you'll experience energy, excitement, peak effectiveness, and great satisfaction.*
>
> ***Fourth Key:*** *Choose Point A wisely, because Point B will follow.*
>
> ***Fifth Key:*** *Know what bad looks like.*

First Key: Cultivate a Desire for Doing the Best Thing

Richard Bach's *Jonathan Livingston Seagull* taught, "You are never given a dream without also being given the power to make it true." Once you've dreamed it, you long to achieve the very best thing. Dare to dream that there is much more you can achieve.

When you do the best thing you are thinking about, planning for, and deeply desiring to become your best. "The greatest achievement was at first, and for a time, a dream. The oak sleeps in the acorn, the bird waits in the egg, and in the highest vision of the soul, a waking angel stirs," wrote James Allen, author of *As a Man Thinketh.*

Cultivating a desire for doing the best thing is a choice. Wendy Farley said that desire "holds open the infinity of possibility"—and possibility lifts you to action instead of settling for a lesser outcome. The story is told of two shoe salespeople who are sent to Africa. After seeing the situation, the first salesperson sends a message: "Situation hopeless. They have no shoes!" The second salesperson surveys the same situation, and sends a different message: "Situation is glorious, huge sales imminent. They have no shoes!" Desire begins with the ability to see possibility.

"Desire is the key to motivation," said Indy 500 champion Mario Andretti, "but it's determination and commitment to an unrelenting pursuit of a goal—a commitment to excellence—that will enable you attain the success you seek." Desire becomes motivation when you make doing the best thing your vision and goal. Until you can "see" yourself doing the best thing, your desire is dormant.

Just the *idea* of doing the best thing can provide the temporary desire to do it. As it grows, said Napoleon Hill, a deep "desire is the starting point of all achievement, not a hope, not a wish, but a keen pulsating desire which transcends everything."

The desire to do the best thing grows out of a combined attitude of "want to" and "can." A negative approach will prevent you from acting; you may find yourself saying, "What I do doesn't matter. It is what it is."

You must avoid the trap of thinking you are powerless. "Everything you are against weakens you. Everything you are for empowers you," says Wayne Dyer. You must fight indifference and the tendency to compare yourself to others rather than to the very best thing. Kahlil Gibran warns, "Desire is half of life. Indifference," he continues, "is half of death." What prevents you from choosing to do the best thing is simply not caring whether you achieve it.

Second Key: Learn to See the Best Thing among Alternatives

Perspective is needed. Maybe doing the best thing is a new idea for you. You never really considered, at least in a sustained way, that doing the best thing was good or possible. Your schedule fills up with good things, sometimes better things, but you haven't made a conscious assessment of what would be best in this moment for this situation.

A desire to do the best thing is only useful if you can figure out what is best in each situation. *Best* is a comparative term, and in order to see the best thing, you also look for what is good or better. While *good* can be judged on its own, *better* and *best* are measured against good. This means that doing the best thing requires an assessment of each of the three conditions.

To do the best, you need to look for excellence and resist simply "getting by" with good or better. Dave Thomas, the founder of Wendy's, experienced bad on his own way to good, better, and best.

Dave was born to a young unmarried woman he never knew and was adopted at the age of six weeks by Rex and Auleva Thomas. Tragically, Dave's adopted mother died when he was five, and he was subsequently partially raised by his grandmother in Michigan. He dropped out of high school to work for a family who owned several KFC restaurants. Four of the restaurants were struggling, and Dave turned them around then sold them. Using his newly acquired expertise, he translated his successes into a hamburger drive-through chain with revenues totaling $2.6 billion.

A desire to have a high school diploma drove Dave Thomas, at the age of sixty, to return to high school and earn his general educational development (GED) certificate. The students embraced him. He and his wife even attended the prom and were named king and queen. In an act both poignant and hilarious, the students voted him most likely to succeed. Building on that experience, he founded the Dave Thomas Education Center in Coconut Creek, Florida, to help young adults earn their GED. The financial success Dave achieved with Wendy's was good, but he leveraged that success to do the best thing.

The best thing is often hidden in a pile of really good things to accomplish. The key is to desire to find and do the best thing, not just the good or better thing. This desire alone creates a focus that will guide your thinking and planning.

A friend reported that after learning Guiding Constant 9, he became conscious of trying to identify and do the best thing in situations as varied as talking with his wife, e-mailing a son or daughter, meeting with colleagues, requesting repairs from a mechanic, offering service to a discouraged acquaintance, or choosing between business alternatives. *Once that consciousness is turned on, the desire to do the best thing becomes a filter for almost everything.*

Everyone is pressed for time, and you may find that you have to forgo some good things in order to choose others that are better or best. Do you have more to do than you can accomplish? Then you're already conscious of the need to ignore—or at least delay—doing some very good things in order to do the best things with your time.

Here's an example of forgoing the good to focus on the best. You might spend an afternoon watching a football game on television; that's a good thing. You might decide to coach a football team made up of neighborhood boys; that may be better. Or you might decide to play football each Saturday with your grandsons; that may be best.

As with football, doing the best thing requires comparing alternatives. You have to have something to measure your choice against. For there to be a best, there should also be a better and a good.

Third Key: Commit to Doing the Best Thing

A desire to do the best thing is fueled by commitment. How committed are you to doing the best thing? What would cause you to settle for something less? Under what conditions would you give up?

What if your desire to do the best thing was so strong that you could say with absolute assurance that you would never abandon it? When your desire becomes that strong, you have gone from desire to commitment. When your commitment is absolute, you will succeed. You will find a way to do the best thing, no matter what.

This level of commitment is illustrated by the story of a pit boss in a Las Vegas casino. He was so committed to quitting smoking that he asked the community to help him in an unorthodox way: He bought a billboard that said, "If you catch me smoking, I'll pay you $100,000." His desire was so compelling that it resulted in a commitment that creatively removed any possible escape routes.

A commitment to do the best thing will result in a focus and consciousness that will spill over into every area of your life.

Doing the Best Thing at Home

Doing the best thing at home can have far-reaching consequences for good, but it's often the hardest thing to do. After all, your paycheck isn't coming from home, so you can justify overlooking doing the best thing in your family. You might feel justified working long hours because it helps your family in important ways. But those attitudes get in the way of so much potential good.

Doing the best thing in your family is usually very simple. It can be something as uncomplicated as listening—really listening—to another person, but in the rush of life, even taking time to listen can get lost. It might be something as straightforward as eating dinner together as a family. How can family dinner be the best thing to do? Here's just one reason: It's reported that the time a family spends together "eating meals at home [is] the strongest predictor of children's academic achievement and psychological adjustment." Family mealtimes have also been shown to correlate with a reduction in children smoking, drinking, or using drugs. It's not a simple matter to schedule the family for dinner each day, or even three times a week. But is it the best thing? The research says it is.

Sometimes the best thing at home is to simply be attentive—be present and available when you are with your family.

A recent experience caused me to think about this concept in a new way. As I was carefully maneuvering the winding roads through a local canyon one morning, I passed a group of hundreds of people running a marathon. It occurred to me that each one was trying to become his or her best in a contest that would not publicly recognize more than the top two or three runners in that particular race. That made me realize that too often we measure our success by a certain position or status we have obtained—when it is far more important to measure our success by our determined efforts to become our best, regardless of how we measure up to those around us. Especially important are those pivotal moments that determine how we treat our family at home. Those very private efforts at becoming our best are perhaps the most important of all, even though they will not likely ever be recognized with a prestigious title, trophy, or award.

Doing the Best Thing at Work

Doing the best thing at work may begin with stopping some things and starting others—stop procrastinating, stop taking shortcuts, and instead start "going the distance" to achieve excellence. William James counseled us to start "acting as if what you do makes a difference. It does."

Win Borden said, "Demand the best from yourself, because others will demand the best from you. . . . Successful people don't simply give a project hard work. They give it their best work." In his 1982 book, *In Search of Excellence*, Tom Peters told of Joe Girard, who sends thirteen thousand cards each month to people who purchased cars from him. He told of Frito-Lay salespeople who visit every client store *every day*, helping with more than keeping potato chips on the shelf. The people who do the best thing consistently do things that others refuse to do.

Giving the best service often results in greater revenue. People want the best—as you can see from the following ad:

Another way to determine whether you are focusing on the best thing at work is to examine your calendar and to-do lists. Do the items you find there reflect doing the best thing?

Doing the Best Thing in the Community

Making your community better can make your own life better. In our community, we have a tradition of a grand Fourth of July celebration we call "America's Freedom Festival." The thirty events that make up the festival involve hundreds of thousands of people and help our community more deeply feel patriotism and gratitude for our nation. I have had the privilege of being one of those who is fully involved in the festival and have enjoyed the opportunity to create something of value for the community.

I was always looking for ways to make our festival the best it could be, and as I was driving out of the canyon one morning in 1984, I had an unusual vista of the valley in which we live. As I saw that view of the valley, my mind's eye suddenly reflected on pictures I had seen of hot air balloons floating over Albuquerque, New Mexico, as part of their renowned festival.

It was a stunning sight. I could see the sky in our own valley studded with colorful hot air balloons as part of our Freedom Festival.

Our Freedom Festival was well established and successful but I knew there were always ways to improve on a great tradition. Inspired with this vision of hot air balloons filling the sky over our valley, I called Bill Talbot, a man who had provided years of visionary leadership to one of our area's largest banks. I asked Bill if he would like to head up a balloon event as part of our annual Freedom Festival. He took it on and made it the best. That was twenty-eight years ago, and every year since, he has managed the launch of dozens of hot air balloons with thousands of people gathered to watch. This vision, coupled with his dedicated work, is a great example of how people can work together to accomplish the best.

Fourth Key: Choose Point A Wisely, Because Point B Will Follow

It's critical to think about the choices you make and to connect each choice to the consequences that follow.

Not long ago, I attended the funeral of an inspirational mentor of mine. Arv lived a full and colorful life, and I was especially touched by one of the stories from his youth. Arv was raised in Idaho in a home surrounded by a nice garden and ten chickens. One day he and a friend found some firecrackers, and they decided to have some fun. They lit one of the firecrackers and tossed it into the henhouse to see what the chickens would do. But something happened that neither of them had anticipated: One of the chickens gobbled up the firecracker and it exploded, blowing the chicken's head off. Mortified and shocked, they secretly disposed of the chicken. Over the next couple of days, Arv's mother kept saying, "I just can't figure out what happened to one of the chickens. We used to have ten, but now there are only nine." Arv finally came clean many years later and told his mother what happened. Never in their wildest dreams did Arv and his friend think a chicken would pluck up the firecracker. Never did they anticipate losing one of their prize hens. In other words, when they initiated Point A by tossing the firecracker into the henhouse, it didn't occur to them that the result would be Point B—one less chicken.

As another example, our good neighbor took our son and his son to the supermarket; both boys were twelve. As Wynn walked out of the store, he saw his son Jon rapidly pushing a shopping cart across the parking lot—with our son Steven inside the cart. Suddenly Jon let go of the cart. As the shopping cart quickly headed directly toward a parked car, it dawned on both boys that there was no way to stop the cart—and that something bad was going to happen. Sure enough, the cart crashed into the car. Fortunately, Steven was not hurt but they had to square things up with the car owner to pay for the damage.

That experience gave Wynn the chance to teach the principle of Point A–Point B. When you let go on one end, something else is going to happen on the other end. You should do only those things at Point A that will have a good outcome at Point B.

Don't smoke that first cigarette; there is a devastating Point B. Don't do insider trading; it has wrecked the lives of more than one good person. Don't lie, cheat, or take things that aren't yours; Point B will catch up with you and it isn't worth the cost. Don't abuse others physically, mentally, or emotionally; the Point B of abuse is one of the saddest things in our culture.

Choose well your Point As. And if by chance some of the Point Bs don't work out as well as you had hoped, give it another shot. Try to improve and do better.

Fifth Key: Understand What *Bad* Looks Like

As you try to do the best thing, you will run into what *bad* looks like. Good things pay off for us and others; bad things cost us and cost others, and not just in terms of money. You probably know a lot about what bad looks like. What's bad is to scream and yell at another person (unless there is a fire). What's bad is to hit someone else. What's bad is to break your word or betray someone through unfaithfulness in all its varieties. What's bad is to abuse another person emotionally. Bad may rob you of doing the best.

Decisions and behaviors run the spectrum from bad to best, with everything in between. A good example can be seen in terms of celebrating a birthday. To do the bad is to forget the birthday entirely—especially if the person is your partner or someone else close to you. To do good is to remember the birthday and wish the person a happy birthday. To do better is to provide a nice card, a cake, and a gift. The best thing is to put up signs, banners, and balloons; provide a cake and a special gift; and help the person feel extraordinarily special.

You can see a similar progression in the workplace. A manager who is oblivious to the needs and productivity of his employees is doing a bad thing. To acknowledge the employee and to let him know he is important is good. To be aware of the productivity of the employee, to acknowledge his contribution, and to give guidance is better. To provide the employee with the vision of the organization, to help him see how he can be part of that vision, to set up the desired results of his efforts, to provide feedback on how things are going, and to understand and help him realize his goals is the best.

It's always important to anticipate the bad and do whatever you can to avoid it. Our company had a misunderstanding with a competitor who was also a customer. In a very delicate situation, we agreed to avoid the bad through some compromises that restored our confidence in each other and allowed us to continue doing a significant amount of business together.

We avoided a disaster because we did our homework and saw what was taking place in the external environment with respect to federal regulations. We prepared and planned for an internal response to what was happening in the external environment, which significantly helped us instead of hurting us. Looking for potential bad can be good; in fact, it can be best.

It's important to know what's bad so you can plan for it and avoid it. But the bad shouldn't dominate your thoughts. We are most successful when we focus relentlessly on the best and what the best looks like.

A good example of this is found on a plaque on the wall of an old church in Leicester, England, which reads, "In the year 1654 when all things were, throughout this nation, either demolished or profaned, Sir Robert Shirley, Baronet, founded and built this church. He it is whose singular praise it is to have done the best things in the worst times, and to have hoped them in the most calamitous."

Frequently, the best options come into focus when you combine other guiding principles of character, imagination, knowledge and wisdom, and living the Golden Rule.

Ultimately, each of us is judged by the body of our work as a whole—but bad things can cost us dearly. They can even become a mortal threat. It takes only a few bad things to shift the way in which people regard us and all the things we have done and contributed; instead of remembering the best and the inspired, they tend to focus on the bad. When you feel the pressure to be less than you ought or to do less than you can, think *I want to do the best thing*. Then let that thought give life to an action that changes everything—that places you on the path to becoming better, doing better, and changing the world in the best way possible. Do as Abraham Lincoln described: "I do the best I know how, the very best I can; and I mean to keep on doing it to the end. If the end brings me out all right, what is said against me will not amount to anything."

INSPIRATIONAL QUOTES

Do the Best Thing

"When we do the best that we can, we never know what miracle is wrought in our life, or in the life of another."

— Helen Keller

"We have to do the best we can. This is our sacred human responsibility."

— Albert Einstein

"You don't want to be merely the best of the best. You want to be the only ones who do what you do."

— Jerry Garcia

"Duty makes us do things well, but love makes us do them beautifully."

— Zig Ziglar

"Everyone has inside of him a piece of good news. The good news is that you don't know how great you can be! How much you can love! What you can accomplish! And what your potential is!"

— Anne Frank

"Good, better, best. Never let it rest. Till your good is better and your better is best."

— St. Jerome

"Make the most of yourself, for that is all there is of you."

— Ralph Waldo Emerson

"Happiness does not come from doing easy work but from the afterglow of satisfaction that comes after the achievement of a difficult task that demanded our best."

— Theodore I. Rubin

"Mistakes are the portals of discovery."

— James Joyce

Application

In your Thoughts Book make columns for bad, fair, good, better, and best. Record what constitutes bad, fair, good, better, or best responses to any situation you may face in relationships or work.

Move forward toward the best. Modeling this behavior will have a powerful effect on all those you work with.

Individual

1. Affirm to yourself regularly that you desire to do the very best thing.

2. Plan ahead do to ensure that you *see* the bad, fair, good, better, and best, then work to do the best thing.

3. Write down the names of people and a description of situations where you want to avoid the bad.

4. Now write down the names of people and a description of situations where you want to do the best thing and examples of what the best thing might be.

5. Use your Thoughts Book to record your plans and inspirations.

With Others

1. Discuss with another person how you can improve the ability to see the bad, fair, good, better, and best.

2. Discuss with someone the things you can do together to realize the best thing.

In a Nutshell

Access and apply the other guiding principles as you reflect on next steps, then do the best thing. The best thing could be to do nothing at this time, or it could be to act now or get others involved in a solution.

1. **Cultivate a desire for doing the best thing.** Inspire yourself toward this desire by living each of the Thirteen Guiding Constants.

2. **Learn to see the best thing among alternatives**. There are good things, better things, and the best alternatives. Focus on the best alternatives.

3. **Commit to doing the best thing**. Doing the best thing results in energy, excitement, peak effectiveness, and great satisfaction. You are drawn into doing the best thing by the potential for great outcomes in all kinds of actions.

4. **Choose Point A Wisely, because Point B will follow**.

5. **Know what *bad* looks like.** Learn from your mistakes and the mistakes or misfortunes of others. Understanding the bad and actively avoiding it can help you improve and work toward the best.

6. **Mentally use the Best Meter.** Hold it up to all situations and circumstances to help you arrive at good decisions and to see the best alternatives.

PART THREE
LEADERSHIP & MANAGEMENT

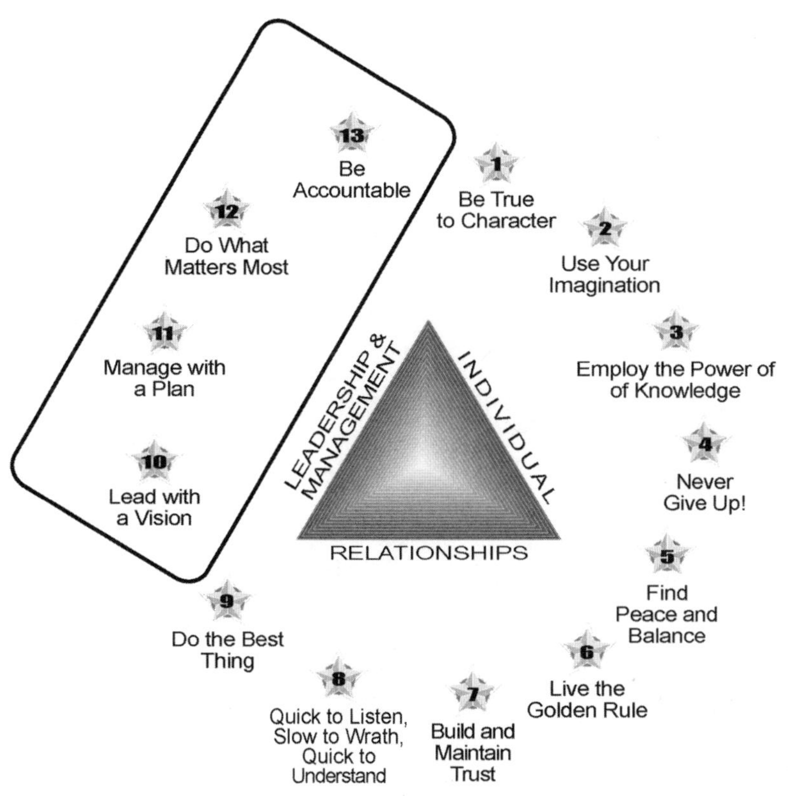

Guiding Constant 10

Lead with a Vision

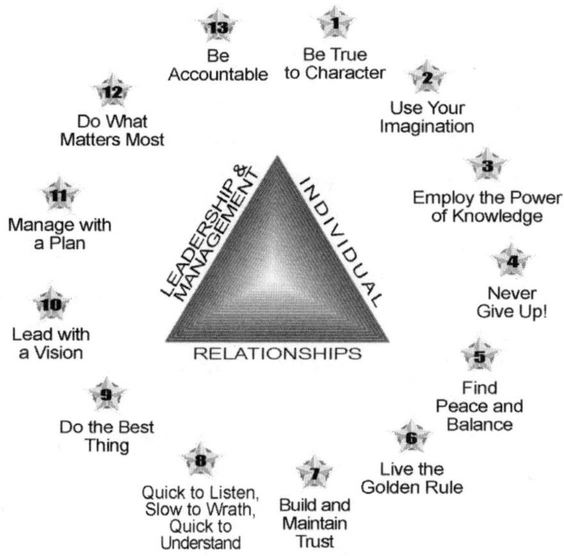

Vision Springs from Deep Within

A VISION MIGHT ALSO BE CALLED a dream, idea, mission, inspiration, calling, purpose, motto, or passion. These synonyms can often be used interchangeably with *vision* and provide a deeper richness to its meaning. But whatever word you use to describe it, the vision of one can influence many and can literally change a life, an organization, and even the world.

While deeply personal, a vision will eventually touch others. It generally germinates deep within and you can feel its power as it grows. From its beginning as a mere thought to its transformation into a physical creation and reality, something magical seems to blossom.

This growth process happens almost by nature as you ponder your own unique vision, purpose, gifts, and abilities and as you realize how they may be wonderfully manifest in your life and in the lives of others.

The same process occurs with an organization. The discovery of a vision from deep within an organization's purpose and uniqueness influences the direction of your organization in the same way it influences you.

In reality, every person is connected to an organization in some way. An *organization* may be a couple, a family, a community, a team, a business, a church, a service group, a country, or a world, to name just some examples. The best leadership often occurs when you connect your personal uniqueness to that of your organization(s).

Leadership might be aptly described as a stewardship. In other words, you—like every other person—have been given a unique set of talents and skills. The real question is how you will use those talents, circumstances, abilities, and skills to bless others—and, in the process, realize increased happiness, peace, and fulfillment in your life. You are a more effective leader when you think in terms of being a responsible and effective steward. And much of that effectiveness flows from a vision that encompasses stewardship.

Figuring out how you can use your talents to live more fully, enjoy greater abundance, and better contribute to your organizations and the world provides insight into your personal or organizational vision.

It is literally impossible to do good without impacting others or the world in which you live! The same applies if you do bad. The fact is, you make a difference, one way or another, and you should never underestimate the power of your influence.

Let's look at a few examples that illustrate the power of a personal or organizational vision.

The No. 2857 bus on which Parks was riding

No Ordinary Bus

The bus pictured here is no ordinary bus. Its first four rows of seats were reserved. This fact, combined with the vision of just one person, changed an entire country.

In 1955, more than 75 percent of the bus riders of Montgomery, Alabama, were black citizens. These individuals, because of nothing more than the color of their skin, were forced to ride in the back of the bus. Not a predetermined number of rows, the "colored" section was designated by a sign that could be moved by the driver. As more white people boarded the bus, the sign was moved back—and black riders occupying the now "white" section were forced to move. If there were no empty seats in their section, the black riders had to stand—or leave the bus!

That's not all. Black people were not allowed to board at the front of the bus if white people were already sitting there. Instead, after paying their fare, they had to leave the bus and reenter through the back door. It was not unusual for the bus to depart before the black riders could get to the back door and board the bus.

Complaints from the black community were ignored. But one member of this community had a vision—and her arrest for refusing to move to the back of the bus was an act of defiance and peaceful protest "heard around the world."

Her resistance of mistreatment on the bus actually started more than a decade earlier in 1943 as Rosa Louise McCauley Parks was heading for home one day. She paid her fare for her ride, dropped her purse, and sat down briefly on a seat reserved for whites, to retrieve the purse. When she sat in that seat, the bus driver insisted she get off the bus. He drove off without her.

Fast forward more than a decade to 1955. When Mrs. Parks boarded the Cleveland Avenue bus to go home after work, she found a seat in the first row of the colored section, halfway to the back of the bus. The white seats filled up quickly, so the driver moved the colored section sign farther back to make seats available for more whites at the front of the bus.

Years later, Mrs. Parks recounted, "When that white driver stepped back toward us, when he waved his hand and ordered us up and out of our seats, I felt a determination cover my body like a quilt on a winter night."

Mrs. Parks moved, but only from the aisle to the window. She did not comply with the driver's demand that she move to the colored section, which now began a few rows behind her.

She later said, "I only knew that, as I was being arrested, that it was the very last time that I would ever ride in humiliation of this kind." A vision of freedom, respect, and equality was born.

Her arrest was only the beginning. Mrs. Parks found allies at her church, and they organized the Montgomery Bus Boycott. They agreed to continue the boycott until changes were made in the way they were being treated on the buses. A new organization was created around the rally; members of the Montgomery Improvement Association elected as their president the newly appointed minister of the Dexter Avenue Baptist Church, Dr. Martin Luther King.

The rest of the story—or at least its impact—is widely known. The courts struck down the laws and practices related to public transportation. Mrs. Parks was accorded the highest respect the nation could give her, the Presidential Medal of Freedom, and with it the honor of lying in state in the rotunda of the US Capitol building upon her death—the first woman and only the second black person to do so. Her vision of a new world was taken up by people who committed to do the best thing and to never give up.

As it did with Rosa Parks, your vision might often arise as a result of adversity. Many times a vision starts with a "refiner's fire," which can expand your understanding of what you are capable of doing and what your *true* individual or organizational greatness may be.

To Have a Vision Is to See

How important is vision? Helen Keller believed that it is more important than sight. "The most pathetic person in the world," she said, "is someone who has sight, but has no vision." The word *pathetic* is a strong one—and why is it so appropriate in describing the lack of vision? Because, according to Earl Nightingale—considered the "dean" of personal development—you are literally what you think about. To abdicate who you are by failing to have a vision for yourself leaves you with little more than the daily grind. Look at it this way: Vision creates energy, confidence, and resolve. Lack of vision is often accompanied by fear, lack of motivation, and low self-confidence.

To have a vision is to see, with an inner eye, the very best outcome you can imagine—the wisest and most effective thing you can see yourself achieving. The inner eye is the tool that enables you to see things that have not yet become a real part of your experience. Vision helps you create that reality in your mind, and then create it in the minds of others—colleagues and coworkers, family members, people in the community, members of a team—that you enlist to bring the vision to life and reality.

In order to lead with vision you must first *have* a vision. Not every vision needs to change the world or even the community. A vision can be exciting and motivating even if it is simple and small in scope. At the other end of the spectrum, a vision may be audacious and draw on the support of millions.

Your vision may be very personal and apply only to you, or it may have enormous impact on your family, team, city, town, or country. Let's look at an inspiring example of how to lead with a vision, even when the goal seemed impossible.

The Race for Space

John F. Kennedy and the United States were in a precarious ideological battle between communism and democracy. The Soviet Union had taken control of the message of Cold War superiority with the launch of the Sputnik satellite and the manned orbital flight of Yuri Gagarin. The reasoning went something like this: If Soviet rockets can send a man into space then surely they can send a nuclear payload to America. Fearing Soviet capacity to launch nuclear weapons in their direction, America was on its heels. President Kennedy had suffered an embarrassing loss at the Bay of Pigs, and the Russians felt confident enough in their position and strength to build intercontinental ballistic missile capability in Cuba, only ninety-one miles from the United States.

Kennedy countered with a vision. In a speech to congress on May 25, 1961, Kennedy captured the minds of America and its scientists:

"These are extraordinary times. And we face an extraordinary challenge. Our strength as well as our convictions have imposed upon this nation the role of leader in freedom's cause. No role in history could be more difficult or more important. *We stand for freedom.*

"I believe we possess all the resources and talents necessary. But the facts of the matter are that we have never made the national decisions or marshaled the national resources required for such leadership. We have never specified long-range goals on an urgent time schedule, or managed our resources and our time so as to insure their fulfillment. . . .

"Space is open to us now; and our eagerness to share its meaning is not governed by the efforts of others. *We go into space because whatever mankind must undertake, free men must fully share.*"

President Kennedy then asked Congress to provide the funds to achieve a startling vision: to land a man on the moon and return him safely to earth *before the end of the decade.* He then demonstrated the power of vision when he told Congress, "But in a very real sense, it will not be one man going to the moon—if we make this judgment affirmatively, it will be an entire nation. For all of us must work to put him there. If we are to go only half way, or reduce our sights in the face of difficulty, in my judgment it would be better not to go at all."

It wasn't just money that was needed, Kennedy said—"every scientist, every engineer, every serviceman, every technician, contractor, and civil servant [must give] his personal pledge that this nation will move forward, with the full speed of freedom, in the exciting adventure of space."

The following September, Kennedy told students at Rice University, "We choose to go to the moon in this decade and do the other things, not because they are easy, but because they are hard, because that goal will serve to organize and measure the best of our energies and skills. . . ." Kennedy's organizational vision galvanized a nation to new heights that seemed almost impossible and realized the dream of a man walking on the moon.

A Knock at the Door: "I Will Be Your Top Salesman"

My company was holding its annual event for college students who were employed by our publishing company as sales representatives. Each would soon be assigned an area somewhere in the country to represent our firm in selling children's books and other educational products.

During this week of "sales school," we taught these energetic college students ethics, organization, sales skills, and product knowledge, and we also provided examples of persistence. As part of the training we also explained the many weekly incentives we had and talked about the big Hawaii trip we used to reward our top producers. Everyone who hit a certain level of sales would qualify, and the competition to be among the top sales representatives was intense.

This was a time of excitement and great energy. Hundreds of these students would work seventy-five hours a week during the summer and earn enough to pay for the upcoming academic year.

Well-recognized motivational speakers were part of the week's program; they included respected leaders like Dennis Waitley, Zig Ziglar, Norman Vincent Peale, Earl Nightingale, Ira Hayes, Charlie "Tremendous" Jones, and Doug Snarr, to name a few. Needless to say, this was a great time as individuals assessed their potential and what they could accomplish during the summer. In a sense, this experience set them on a "success pathway" for their careers.

At the end of the third of five days of training, there was a knock on my hotel room door. I answered and saw a skinny, sickly looking kid who was about six feet tall. He introduced himself to me as John. He said, "I just wanted to introduce myself and let you know that I will be your number-one salesman this summer." I thought to myself, *Yea, right!* Despite my disbelief, I gave him encouragement, adding that I would like to stay in touch with him as he gave his very best throughout the summer. He said, "OK, but don't forget: I will be your number-one salesman."

John had an inspiring, burning personal vision. It was a huge idea that entered his heart and mind from deep within and that subsequently provided his capacity for leadership and action.

He actually started off a little slow, but by the fourth and fifth week of the summer, he was among our top sales representatives. By the tenth week, he was consistently one of our best, and by the end of the summer he finished at the top. That's right—John was the number-one sales representative in the company.

Year after year, I observed that our top-performing sales representatives had a vision of what they wanted to accomplish; it was a vision that drove them on when others faltered along the way. I saw in them a deep personal vision that provided the source for successful leadership and stewardship. I understood what they were experiencing because I had felt exactly the same way, and my vision had driven *me* on!

The examples of Rosa Parks, John F. Kennedy, and these sales representatives are just a few that show the power of a vision that flows deeply from within.

As I have studied and observed outstanding individuals and organizations domestically and internationally, they definitely have one thing in common: an inspiring and deeply felt vision and idea of what they can be. I have also observed that there are typically a number of key attributes that are present in an individual or organizational vision. Some apply to an individual vision, some apply to an organizational vision, and some apply to both. Let's look at few of these attributes.

Attributes of a Transformational Vision

A vision is *transformational,* and when you have a clear, compelling vision you transform the effort, the conversation, and the results of not only your own life, but the life of your organization—whether that organization is a company, a community, a team, or a family. Almost more powerful than anything else that happens is what you and others become in the process of transformation.

A vision *sets a positive and meaningful direction with a purpose and cause.* It rallies support that results in commitments and new levels of contribution.

When a vision *aligns with the Guiding Constants*, the vision is empowered. Using your imagination, the power of knowledge, never giving up, and building and maintaining trust will all work together to instill power into your vision.

A vision *carries a sense of urgency and mission.* When a vision is based on principles—in Kennedy's case, the foundational principle was freedom—the sense of urgency encompasses more than revenue and return on investment. The ultimate virtue of the mission or cause invites unusual effort and commitment.

The right vision is *inspiring.* It can make your efforts noble and meaningful. You are inspired to fully give your best in cooperation with your colleagues and together you achieve the best.

A vision *is clear, simple, and easy to remember.* Many remember Kennedy's clear, simple statement: "Our strength as well as our convictions have imposed upon this nation the role of leader in freedom's cause. We choose to go to the moon."

A vision *provides the desired direction, purpose, and inspiration in the absence of supervision.* Kennedy was clear about what was required when he said, "Unless every scientist, every engineer, every serviceman, and every

The vision statement should be a bit more inspiring than the one on the wall in this cartoon.

technician, contractor, and civil servant gives his personal pledge, the goal will not be realized."

A vision *encourages alignment of Guiding Constants, people, and effort around the vision*. People feel encouraged and empowered by it. They willingly subscribe to it and join their commitment with your conviction as the leader.

A vision *represents the heart and soul of an individual or the group* it leads. It embodies the values and personal needs for contributing to something bigger than the people who embrace it. The vision generates passion and energy.

A vision is *developed through individual and shared leadership*. Each participant in the vision is a "leader" as he or she contributes uniqueness to the whole.

A vision is *long term and should be modified with care*. The vision holds people together. It does not change quickly. Kennedy's vision was a nine-year push—his goal was to put a man on the moon before the decade was out.

A vision is clearly *communicated through centers of influence* to all members of the team or community. The vision is lived, modeled, and taught over and over again by key stakeholders and to one another.

A vision becomes *anchored in the individual or organizational culture.* It becomes part of the conscience of each person touched by the vision. A test of the organizational vision is how well each person understands it, is influenced by it, and can explain it to another.

A vision comes in all forms, shapes, and sizes. I have seen it in art, writing, prose, song, and in mind-mapping sketches. I have seen some visions that can be stated in just a few words and some that require an entire page. The vision is expressed in a way that works best for you and your organization. The value of the vision is what it communicates to you and others. What does it mean? If it is clear and helps to set the direction of leadership, then it ensures that you will head in the right direction.

To better help you identify a way to describe your vision, below are some samples of effective individual and organizational vision statements. Remember the alternate words that describe vision, including *dream, idea, mission, inspiration, calling, purpose,* or *passion.* Just as when you climb from peak to peak, you gain whole new scenic views when you identify an inspiring vision; your initial vision helps you climb to see an expanded vision or a new set of possibilities. Frequently one vision inspires another. Let's look first at a few personal visions and then move to some organizational visions.

Personal Vision Statements

Nelson Mandela: "I am the captain of my soul." A vision of a free South Africa for all made the rock piles of Robben Island Prison more endurable during the twenty-seven years of Nelson Mandela's incarceration. The poem that kept Mandela focused and that burned deeply within his soul as a vision was *Invictus*, words that inspired him to be "the master of his fate, and the captain of his soul."

Leonardo da Vinci: "I am a man of 'unquenchable curiosity' and 'feverishly inventive imagination.'" Some twenty years after da Vinci's death, goldsmith and sculptor Benvenuto Cellini was reported as saying, "There had never been another man born in the world who knew as much as Leonardo, not so much about painting, sculptures, and architecture, as that he was a very great philosopher."

Orville and Wilbur Wright: "Flight is possible, and we believe we can develop the first heavier-than-air aircraft." It was vision, quiet resolve, and the application of scientific methodology that enabled Orville and Wilbur to carry the human race skyward.

Mahatma Gandhi: Let the first act of every morning be to make the following resolve for the day:

- I shall not fear anyone on earth.
- I shall fear only God.
- I shall not bear ill toward anyone.
- I shall not submit to injustice from anyone.
- I shall conquer untruth by truth.
- And, in resisting untruth, I shall put up with all suffering.

Gardner H. Russell: "To achieve the seemingly impossible." An international consultant, Gardner maintained a reputation of solving what appeared to be impossible situations by helping to inspire possible solutions. His positive attitude and approach to finding best solutions was extraordinary and was impacted by his vision statement.

Henry Ford: "A car that is affordable for every American that wants one." Henry Ford's vision was exceptional, because before that time, it wasn't the case in America. Cars took a long time to build and were expensive for the few who could afford them. Ford's vision—his mental creation—paved the way to the physical reality. People had cars, which meant they had more freedom to travel, which ultimately opened the roadways of a nation and created increased commerce. The impact of Ford's vision went on and on, demonstrating that a personal vision can affect many.

Just as a personal vision can affect many, so can an organizational vision have profound impact on countless numbers of people.

Organizational Vision Statements and Their Impact

Following are a number of vision statements from outstanding organizations that are leaders in their field and industry. While some are more recent organizations that have had enormous impact in their industries and on the world, others are seasoned organizations that have performed year after year, decade after decade, sustaining success.

The primary objective of an effective vision statement, whether individual or organizational, is to describe what is in your heart and mind; you should be more concerned with intent rather than trying to follow some sort of etiquette. You'll find that this intent will often provide the form for your vision.

The real test is to ask yourself if your vision statement describes your purpose and influences the desired behavior in the absence of supervision. Does your vision statement keep the organization focused on what matters most?

Let's get on with some examples. It's impossible to include every organization worthy of recognition, and there are many excellent examples, so I hope these few examples will be useful.

Apple

"Apple is committed to bringing the best personal computing experience to students, educators, creative professionals and consumers around the world through its innovative hardware, software and Internet offerings."

Avon

"To be the company that best understands and satisfies the product, service, and self-fulfillment needs of women—globally."

Boeing

"People working together as one global company for aerospace leadership."

Chevron

"At the heart of the Chevron way is our vision . . . to be the global energy company most admired for its people, partnership, and performance."

Delta Airlines

"We—Delta's employees, customers, and community partners—together form a force for positive local and global change, dedicated to bettering standards of living and the environment where we and our customers live and work."

Facebook

"To make the world better through transparency of information and increased sharing of thoughts and ideas."

Google

"To develop a perfect search engine."

Microsoft

"Create experiences that combine the magic of software with the power of Internet services across a world of devices."

Nike

"To carry on his legacy of innovative thinking, whether to develop products that help athletes of every level of ability reach their potential, or to create business opportunities that set Nike apart from the competition and provide value for our shareholders."

Ritz-Carlton

"We are Ladies and Gentlemen serving Ladies and Gentlemen."

The United States Air Force

One key part of the Air Force vision: "We do not lie, cheat or steal; nor tolerate any among us that do."

Southwest Airlines

"Dedication to the highest quality of customer service delivered with a sense of warmth, friendliness, individual pride, and company spirit."

Walmart

"Help people to save money so that they can live better."

Westin Hotels

"Year after year, Westin and its people will be regarded as the best and most sought-after hotel and resort management group in North America."

Points to Discover and Write Your Personal or Organizational Vision

Work first at the personal level then apply the practice of discovery to some of the organizations in your life. Use your Thoughts Book as a place to go through the exercises and to capture your impressions from each exercise. Take your time. There is no rush.

- What are your deepest values, built upon correct principles, by which you lead your life? Your organization?

- What are your unique skills, talents, and abilities from which you can build and benefit others for good? List your unique skills or talents.

- As you reflect on your life, now and for the days or years to come, how do you hope others will describe you when you are at the senior part of your life? How do you hope others will describe your organization?

- What is the best that can be for you individually? Organizationally?

- Build on your notes and the inspiration of other's examples; take some time and dedicate yourself to writing or revising your vision.

- Just let the ideas flow and see what comes from deep within you.

- The result is your vision! While you may improve the format with some refinements over time, don't forget the substance of your vision.

- Refine, adjust, and polish it over time as you respond to your deep inner feelings, impressions, and inspiration. Allow this vision to create a direction in your life or organization and to impact all you do.

In describing the power of vision, Ralph Waldo Emerson wrote, "What lies behind us and what lies before us are tiny matters as compared to what lies within us."

I Can Do Hard Things

A powerful example of this principle was Brenda Clark Sederberg. While she never achieved fame or fortune, her example is one that inspires and empowers.

After receiving a bachelor's and master's degree in elementary education, she devoted her teaching skills to her own family before being diagnosed with primary progressive multiple sclerosis—a progressively debilitating and ultimately fatal disease. While steadily weakening over a period of seventeen years, she continued to be as active as possible, volunteering regularly at her children's schools and attending church services every week. She was known for her generosity, thirst for knowledge, perennially positive attitude, and zest for life because of a vision statement that transcended her physical disability: "I can do hard things."

All of us, like Brenda, can do hard things and inspiring things if we capture a transformational vision.

The impact of your vision, while quiet and ever present, will be astounding over time as it becomes a reality.

INSPIRATIONAL QUOTES

Lead with a Vision

"Make no little plans; they have no magic to stir men's blood and probably themselves will not be realized. Make big plans; aim high in hope and work."

— *Daniel Hudson Burnham*

"A rock pile ceases to be a rock pile the moment a single man contemplates it, bearing within him the image of a cathedral."

— *Antoine De Saint-Exupery*

"A vision is not just a picture of what could be; it is an appeal to our better selves, a call to become something more."

— *Rosabeth Moss Katner*

"Cherish your visions and your dreams, as they are the children of your soul, the blueprints of your ultimate achievements."

— *Napoleon Hill*

"Every age needs men who will redeem the time by living with a vision of the things that are to be."

— *Adlai E. Stevenson*

"Vision without action is a dream. Action without vision is simply passing the time. Action with Vision is making a positive difference."

— *Joel Barker*

"Vision is the art of seeing what is invisible to others."

— *Jonathan Swift*

"I skate to where the puck is going to be, not where it has been."

— *Wayne Gretzky*

Application

Define, refine, and discuss the vision you have for yourself as an individual and for key organizations you are associated with.

Individual

1. Complete the vision exercise. Use your Thoughts Book as a place to capture your answers and the draft of your vision.

2. Think deeply about what your best looks like, and consider it as part of your vision. You should consider what the best looks like in your personal life, in your work, in your family, or in your community life.

With Others

1. Review with those in your key organizations what the organizational vision looks like.

2. If a vision does not currently exist for your organization or team, go to work to help create one, inviting the participation and ideas of all key stakeholders.

3. If a vision does exist, what can you do to better live, implement, and teach it to others? What is the history and spirit of the vision or mission?

In a Nutshell

1. The vision of one can influence many.
2. The vision springs from deep within as you reflect on your own uniqueness and how you can contribute to a better organization and world.
3. The mental creation precedes the physical creation and future reality.
4. Consider leadership as a stewardship. What can you do with the opportunity, position, gifts, talents, and skills that you have to contribute?
5. When you do good, you influence your organization, community, and world for good. You can uniquely make a difference. Never give up working toward good and to realize the best that can be.
6. Frequently, your best vision is discovered through hardship and adversity. Through these experiences, you discover who you really are and develop a great capacity to give to others.
7. Use the vision, mission, purpose, cause, and passion that you have to lead your life and your organization.
8. A vision, dream, idea, mission, inspiration, calling, purpose, or passion can literally change a life, an organization, and even the world.

Guiding Constant 11

Manage with a Plan

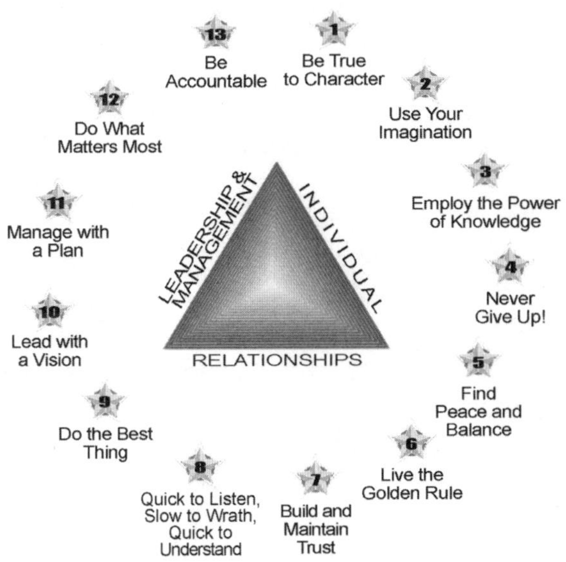

Achieving Your Vision

Angela Wolf is blind. Her blindness was triggered by a high dose of vitamin A administered by her doctor when she was twelve years old. The resulting *pseudo tumor cerebri*—literally translated, "false brain tumor"—caused a reaction in her body that rendered her blind.

But with a vision of her future that would stagger a person without this disability, Angela chose to be a school teacher. In May 2005 Angela completed her student-teaching apprenticeship and received her teaching certificate. It was for herself and the Angela Wolfs of the world that Helen Keller said, "While they were saying among themselves it cannot be done, it was done."

Teach a typically active class of second-graders without sight? How could it happen? The excerpts below from an article about Angela make it clear that her goal to be a teacher required a "vision" and a plan. Angela managed her plan with a deep commitment to realize her vision.

"I recall thinking almost from the beginning that regardless of my blindness, I could do whatever I want to do in life," Angela remembers. Her physical disability rendered her sightless but made her vision of being a teacher all the more clear.

"Whatever I want to do, whether it's finding my way through a building or learning to be a teacher, I just have to figure out the 'how,'" says Angela. "I have to do things a bit differently, but, in the end, I get it done."

Angela managed the achievement of her vision with a plan consisting of small goals that led to big ones. Her plan included small steps at first; as those were mastered, she added more goals. She started by learning Braille and how to use a cane, and gradually learned more complex tasks.

To make her work with her students go more smoothly, she starts the first day with each new class helping them understand her blindness and what it will mean to both her and them. There are always a lot of questions. The students are generally puzzled by simple things, like how she chooses her outfit in the morning.

Kay Randall explains in the article that "if a student wants to know how she finds the milk and cereal in order to make breakfast, she tells them. If they want to know if blind people get married (Angela's husband is an accomplished musician and is blind), she tells them.

"Every time a new problem arises, Angela stops and thinks, 'OK, so this is the situation as it stands now—what am I going to do to make it work?' And she immediately begins to generate solutions. If you can even vaguely imagine what it would be like to monitor and teach a room full of young children, you get some idea of how many obstacles someone who's blind has to overcome to do this."

No Title Necessary

You don't need the title of *manager* in order to be one. A person like Angela Wolf is a manager but her title is *teacher*. Your vision may be about making things better at work or at home, making you a manager in that place whether your title is *warehouseman*, *salesperson*, *mom*, or *dad*.

You are a manager when you have a vision and goals for achieving that vision. For a person with a vision, the goals are part of the plan. Perhaps you are a nurse, a technician, or a construction worker. You can lead with a vision by "seeing" yourself doing something more effectively or in a better way. Your vision is to do the best thing—to realize the best for your work, your family, wherever achieving the best matters to you. You manage with a plan by setting goals to achieve your best.

In the case of a vision that is limited in scope but of high value, you may be the person you manage. Your vision may be a never-to-be-forgotten family trip or a deeper, more satisfying relationship with your spouse. The first step is to define what the best looks like for you.

I *Am* a Manager!

Managers with the title of manager realize their vision just like others do. Angela had a goal to teach school, and she had to define what her best looked like. In the same way, the manager of an organization must first establish what the best looks like.

People to Help

As you work to implement your best, others are an integral part in implementing your vision. Even if you don't have the title of manager, you may need to enlist the help of others, such as key stakeholders, coworkers, or family members, to help achieve your vision.

Angela Wolf, for example, drew her students into her vision by making them her partners. She fully explained what their relationship would look like, she was kind to them, and they committed to return kindness of their own by not taking advantage of her. They became comanagers of the plan. Together they achieved their best.

Managers must also attract people to the vision. Once managers attract the people, they establish systems and structures to ensure those people adopt the vision and produce high-quality and high-quantity work toward achievement of their best. Even if the people are required to assist by virtue of their employment, the high quality and high quantity of their commitment and work is vital to realizing the sustainable best.

Attracting People to the Vision

Whether you're hiring people or recruiting current employees to the vision, it is very difficult to manage with a plan unless you have the right people standing with you. Management's task, explains Drucker, is "to make people capable of joint performance, to make their strengths effective and their weaknesses irrelevant." Your first question as manager is, "Who will help me?"

As a manager you'll harness a variety of resources to achieve your vision, but none is as important as people. People are the ones who develop the systems and structures that help you realize a vision and a plan. Effective management means that you lead, guide, inspire, and empower people to stand with you and help you achieve your vision and your best. People do the work of achieving the vision.

For larger-scale visions, attracting and inspiring people to your vision and defining the systems and structures that will help the people achieve institutional and organizational goals is vital.

Attracting the Right People

Would a person risk his own life to be around someone who is deeply committed to living Guiding Constants? That's exactly what happened when an ad was run in a British newspaper to recruit a crew for an Antarctic crossing led by Ernest Shackleton, the British explorer.

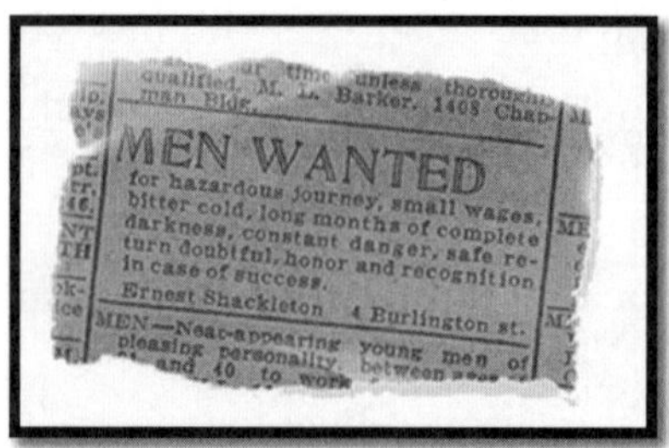

qualified. M. L. Barker. 1408 Chapman Bldg.

MEN WANTED
for hazardous journey, small wages, bitter cold, long months of complete darkness, constant danger, safe return doubtful, honor and recognition in case of success.
Ernest Shackleton 4 Burlington st.

MEN—Neat-appearing young men of pleasing personality between ages of 21 and 40 to work

Men wanted for hazardous journey. Small wages. Bitter cold. Long months of complete darkness. Constant danger. Safe return doubtful. Honor and recognition in case of success.

Would you answer that ad? Five thousand people *did*, according to Robert Mill, one of Shackleton's friends. From that pool of willing adventurers, Shackelton chose twenty-eight crewmen, including sailors, scientists, surgeons, and other specialists, all of whom were elated and honored that they had been chosen to risk their lives in the Antarctic.

Why would thousands of men try to join an expedition so dangerous that, as the ad warned, "Safe return doubtful"?

These men tried to join the expedition because they had been recruited to the vision. More to the point, they were attracted to Shackleton. They wanted what Shackleton wanted: to be the first to do something that appeared impossible. They wanted to be with him when he became the first person to travel from the Weddell Sea to the Ross Sea overland via the South Pole. If anyone could accomplish that feat, it was Shackleton. These men wanted to stand with one of the most inspiring leaders of the past two centuries because they knew he expected them to be leaders, too. Everyone had to contribute or all would fail. They wouldn't just fail—they would die.

True to the warning in the newspaper's classified ad, Shackleton's ship and crew never reached the shore of Antarctica in the Weddell Sea. Unseasonably cold weather trapped them in the ice pack just miles from land. The story of Shackleton's leadership and single-minded dedication to the survival and safe return of his men is an epic story of leadership and management. Shackleton's men claim their survival was due to one thing: Ernest Shackleton.

How Did Shackleton Do It?

What could Shackelton have said or done that would cause these men to revere him, even when the expedition failed?

The early freezing of the ice pack forced Shackleton and his crew to formulate and adopt a new vision: to return every man safely home. With that vision in hand, the intermediate goals became clear.

To turn the seemingly insurmountable obstacles into stepping stones, Shackleton and his men anticipated and planned for those obstacles. They managed day by day using a plan that combined high quality and high quantity effort, character, and will.

The Software of Effective Management

We're talking here about the "software"—what's inside that makes the difference in individuals and that ultimately leads to the best in every endeavor.

Together, Shackleton and his team prepared for the worst, planned every move, implemented processes and systems, and collected all the information possible to give them the best chance for sailing to and crossing the Antarctic. Yet management tools and the hard sciences are not what we talk about when describing his success.

The will of Shackleton and his men—their character and commitment to the survival of each man—led them to the decisions they made and the effort they expended to achieve the vision. These attributes are the Guiding Constants.

"He who is plenteously provided for from within," said Goethe, "needs but little from without." Who are the people "plenteously provided for from within"? They know who they are, and they want to invest in something important. When Jim Collins, author of *Good to Great*, speaks of getting the right people on the bus, what are those people like? What makes them the "right" people? Collins might be describing people like Shackleton and his crew when he postulates that humility plus will equals true greatness. Shackleton's will, his unwillingness to give up, and his humility in submitting to the forces of the external environment was matched by the will and humility of his men to submit to leadership and merge their will with his.

Business schools, textbooks, and magazine articles on management rightly point out the need for, and describe the tools and methods of, effective management, such as project management methods and applications, financial reports, measures of productivity, time accounting, and so on. But the stories of great achievement tell of skills founded on core values—the "software" of moving a vision, and its people, forward. Shackleton's unusual drive and conviction reflected how he was taught to think

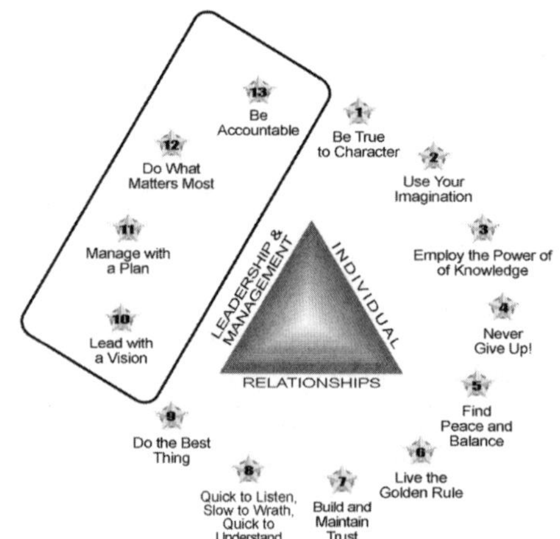

as he grew up. It's how he was wired. It was a developed talent that combined his mind and heart.

So much of the last four Guiding Constants in our list of thirteen—Lead with a Vision (10), Manage with a Plan (11), Do What Matters Most (12), and Be Accountable (13)—has to do with the mind and the internal values and character of the individual. Yes, managers must employ tools to gather and analyze information. Information is indispensible, and tools are necessary. But the mind and heart together are the software that makes the ultimate difference in your success.

"Houston, We've had a Problem"

One of the greatest adventures in the history of space exploration was, by all measures, a failure. It was also an example of applying the software of the Guiding Constants to achieving a vision.

Apollo 13 did not achieve the planned goal of landing on the moon. But a team of managers and scientists came together to create a historic victory out of a near catastrophe.

Apollo 13 astronauts Jack Swigert, James Lovell, and Fred Haize were on their way to the moon, anticipating an orbit and lunar landing, when a large bang followed by oxygen venting from the command module prompted a simple but profound report: "Houston, we've had a problem here."

In the moment it took to say those words, the goal of landing on the moon was abandoned in favor of a goal of getting the three astronauts safely home. *Apollo 13* became a modern-day Shackleton story.

The biggest concern—the loss of power in the command module, *Odyssey*—meant that battery backup power had to be turned off and preserved for reentry. The lunar module, *Aquarius,* would serve as a lifeboat but it was only designed to support two men for two days; now it would be needed to support the crew of three for four days or longer. How could they do it? Was it possible? What was the solution?

Getting the crew home alive meant defining and flying the fastest route to earth and conserving oxygen, water, and power at a volume that seemed impossible. It also meant filtering the carbon dioxide the astronauts were exhaling into the lunar module. But, the filters in *Aquarius* were not designed for three men. All of the problems facing the astronauts became the problems of the *Apollo 13* support team on the ground in Houston. The team assembled all available materials on the spacecraft and began to rig a filter.

As depicted in the movie *Apollo 13*, there were points along the path where the hope of success waned to the point that the team felt no solution could be found. NASA's director was said to have expressed his fear by saying, "This could be the worst disaster NASA has ever faced."

Operations director Gene Kranz is reported to have responded with, "With all due respect, sir, I believe this is going to be our finest hour." The will to succeed, the character to never give up and to do everything required to succeed—in other words—the software, is the difference-maker for successful managers. The movie portrayed Gene Kranz committing himself and everyone around him to victory when he said, "We've never lost an American in space, and we're sure as hell not gonna lose one on my watch! Failure is not an option." Technical skills of all varieties were in the room—but what kept them working was the conviction that they could find a solution.

Gene Kranz and the NASA engineers used some very basic principles to solve the problems and bring the astronauts to earth. These principles are founded in character and the commitment to never abandon the goal. They are about changing the goal to the highest and best outcome when the original goal must be abandoned. It is all about internalizing Guiding Constants in your life for those moments when you can and should be at your very best. And those moments come often in your relationships with those around you who are working to help achieve the vision.

Living Guiding Constant 11
Envision Yourself as a Manager

You may not be "the boss," but you are still the manager of something—your own time and resources, for one. As a manager of an organization—such as a family, a sports team, a nonprofit, a community organization, or a work group in a business—what is the most significant contribution you can make? How can you communicate that contribution so enough resources will be committed to make the vision into a plan and the plan into a result, a real outcome?

This is the principle of taking the vision and determining *how* you will make the vision a reality. The ability to manage effectively is to make decisions to achieve what matters most rather than jumping to one problem after another. The effective executive "starves the problems and feeds the opportunities."

If you're not careful with your thoughts, it is so easy to get into the habit of feeding the problems and starving the opportunities. To help avoid this and to plan effectively, you need a plan to guide you in the realization of your vision. But first, I invite you to see yourself as a manager, beginning with the management of your own time and effort.

Henry Ford Knew the Keys to Achieving a Vision

What could Henry Ford do to ensure the success of the automobile? First, he had a vision of a world at peace because people were able to live well. This vision included giving people both the desire and the capability of owning his Model T. But he knew he couldn't supply every American with a car if he could make only one car a day; that would be high quality but low quantity, a vision that was not sustainable. And even his own workers couldn't afford a car on the two-dollars-per-day wages he was paying.

Ford had to create inventory and a market at the same time. To achieve this, he envisioned how to lower the cost by speeding up production. Then he created a franchised network of dealers that made the cars immediately available in every city around the country. He organized local motor clubs where people were trained and encouraged to explore their world by "taking a drive." The story of how Ford accomplished his vision is American legend.

Every schoolchild has read about the invention of the assembly line. It was a supply problem, trying to move the parts to the assembly point for each car, that was keeping production time and costs high. Ford envisioned moving the cars to the parts along a line and having each worker specialize in just one aspect of assembly as the car passed his station on the line. The result was that Henry Ford's plant could produce a Model T chassis in ninety-three minutes instead of the more than thirteen hours originally required.

But it was another decision that may have been even bolder and more brilliant. What isn't often reported in American history texts is that Ford more than doubled wages from two dollars per day to five dollars per day for the average assembly line worker. He also reduced the workday from nine hours to eight hours. With this move, Ford reduced worker turnover due to the monotony of the work on the assembly line, created an instant labor pool as people flocked to Michigan, and increased production time by making it possible to run three shifts. He also made it possible for thousands of his own employees to purchase Model Ts and created a flood of newspaper reports about how he stood for the American worker. Ford not only transformed manufacturing, he also helped create the middle class.

Glimpses of Ford's character—his inner best—can be seen as he encouraged veterans and people with disabilities by providing opportunities to work and be self-sufficient. Specially designed equipment was fabricated to enable people without a limb to work on the line. In 1937, Ford Motor Company's newsletter stated that "11,632 workers in various stages of disability" were employed at Ford.

Solving problems is at the heart of Manage with a Plan. Sometimes the original plan must give way to an emergency contingency plan, as happened in the cases of Shackleton and *Apollo 13*. At other times, the survival of an idea depends on the vision to more economically produce something, while at the same time making it possible for people to afford the product, as happened to Ford.

The software of management, the Guiding Constants, guide us to greater effectiveness. If you're wondering what your thought process should be if you're confronted with a dilemma in the management of your vision, the key is to rely on the inner strength, the software of management, to do the best thing.

How to Manage with a Plan: Four Keys

Decisions are made and actions are taken at every step of your life—in your relationships, in your work, and in your business. Either consciously or subconsciously, you break your visions and plans into tasks or actions. To be the most effective you can be, to achieve your best, you plan. You ask yourself: What is to be done? Hosw will it be done? How will it be measured? When will it be done? Who will do it?

To answer these questions, I've listed four key actions that will help you focus on the things that matter most in achieving your goal.

Key 1: Set Your Goals

Begin by thinking specifically about what you would like to do this year (short-term) and in the future (more than twelve months from now) in the key areas of your life.

Goals should be specific, measurable, achievable, relevant, and time-driven (SMART). A relatively simple way to make an effective goal is to ask yourself what you *specifically* want to accomplish and what date you want to accomplish it by.

Possible Categories of Goals at the Personal or Individual Level

Personal

You may choose a goal to play the piano or take signing lessons by the end of the year. You may set a goal to stay physically fit or to get into shape. You may set a goal to have a healthy diet or to get out of debt. Be specific and set a goal that is measurable.

Family/Friends

You may set a goal to visit your children's home if they live at a distance or to hold a reunion of family or friends. You may set a goal to stay close to a spouse, companion, or loved one.

Professional/Work/Education

Consider setting a goal to be among the best at what you do professionally or to obtain a degree in some specialized field.

Service/Community/World/Church

You may set a goal to serve in a soup kitchen, to do some humanitarian service, or to contribute to your church or community in some way.

Reflect upon each area in your life and ask yourself, "What are the most important things that I can do to realize my vision within each area this year?" Listen to the inspiration and impressions that come to you. Write down your goal for each area. This literally represents the steps of how to realize your vision and your best during the upcoming year. Step by step, you will turn your vision into a reality through this process.

My Personal Vision and Goals for ____________
Year

Confidential

Name ______________________________

1. Personal: Spiritual, Physical, Emotional, Mental

2. Family and Friends: Relationships, Fun, Time

3. Work and Professional: Accomplishments, Contribution, Growth

4. Service: Religious, Community, Individual

5. Accountability: I will share my goals with ______________________________

At the Organizational Level

What things matter most organizationally—for your family, team, company, organization, community, or country?

Once again, it's good to set goals for a year at a time so there are easy accountability points of reference and so you can evaluate your progress toward those goals.

If you lead an organization, you may have revenue goals, financial goals, market share goals, or customer-satisfaction goals.

If you lead an athletic team, you may have goals about where you hope to place at the end of the season or about the development and strength of the team.

If you are at the head of an organizational team, you may have a goal of contributing to the whole in an extraordinary manner.

If you lead a community or country, what do you desire to accomplish that serves the community well and leaves the community in better shape for the future?

Whether you are setting personal or organizational goals, it's always best to start by asking what your best looks like. Setting a goal is not a one-time process, but something you will refine and repeat many times throughout your life.

Key 2: Develop a Plan to Achieve Your Goals

A plan is the result of careful thought about *how* best to achieve your goals, and it contains the things you must do to achieve the vision you've decided on. Formulating the plan creates the outcome in your mind; in other words, it's the mental creation of achieving your best. When you write it down on paper and follow the steps you've created, you then achieve your vision.

A plan of action takes into account what is happening in the external environment. It gives direction and, when followed, gives you the highest probability of reaching your goals.

Cornelius Fitcher said, "Planning without action is futile; action without planning is fatal."

What specific things can you do to realize your goals?

At the Personal Level

Generally, simply setting your goal helps you move a long way down the road to accomplishment.

Next, figure out when and how you will achieve your goal. If one of your goals is to be physically fit, *specifically* what does that look like? One year I made a physical fitness goal to walk or run one thousand miles. I broke it down into pieces and determined that I had to walk or run a little more than eighty miles a month, or twenty miles a week.

I figured that sounded like a pretty good goal and that I could accomplish quite a few others things at the same time; for example, I figured I could listen to soundtracks and learn or be edified along the way. Regardless of whether I listened to something, this became a special time for me that affected the rest of the day. It infused my day with more energy. In fact, I came up with many ideas for this book while out walking or running.

At the Organizational Level

An effective plan begins with a detailed description of the vision, values, and goals—in short, a detailed picture of what you hope to achieve. Then you can work to be sure that the end aligns with your vision, goals, and values.

The vision statement in our firm is "We treat people right." This drives our goals and plans by causing us to reflect on whether shareholders, customers, colleagues, and the families of our associates are all being treated right.

With a clear description of the vision and goals, you can define the required work in objectives and tasks with timelines. You can also organize the components of the project into manageable pieces that could be called deliverables or project milestones. The project milestones can define work to be done across a number of people or teams in parallel and can also describe the sequence of work to be performed by a single team.

Organizationally, the following components are helpful as you set up your management plan:

- What are your organizational (team, family, community) goals? Be sure the goals are clear and can be easily communicated to the team, since team members will be engaged in the goal process.

- What is your strategy? In other words, how do you expect to realize your goals?

- What systems are needed to realize your goals? You might need accounting systems, reward and compensation systems, training systems, administration systems, marketing systems, communication systems, financial systems, or IT systems, among others.

- What structure is needed? Consider people, assignments, buildings, vehicles, equipment, and other infrastructure.
- What are the key metrics that will help you know whether you're on track? What are the specific metrics, and how will you measure the best?

The most basic components of your plan will be organized around what you need and are able to do. The specifics include a clear picture of the desired results and the resources you need to accomplish those results.

One of the greatest helps in this process will be mastering the core of the Thirteen Constants as you go through this process. Each one of the Thirteen Constants can have a significant influence on your ability to develop an effective plan from which to manage the realization of your goals.

Key 3: Work the Plan

The vision for achievement of an important result cannot usually be realized in a few moments of effort. You are generally most effective as you focus on doing what matters most.

A weekly and daily plan establishes the pathway to successfully realizing your vision and goals—but you can't just write it down. You have to "work" the plan. Whether the goal is to make money, improve family life, or complete a community project, using a plan to manage your own effort or the efforts of others is essential to success.

The Chinese philosopher Lao Tzu wisely said, "A journey of a thousand miles begins with a single step." Whether you are traveling a thousand miles or just taking one step, you need to do it according to plan. The details of the plan become the milestones, and achievement of the milestones becomes the measure of your progress. "If there is one secret of success," says Drucker, "it is concentration. Effective executives do first things first, and they do one thing at a time." In other words, if you want to achieve your vision or goal, concentrate your energy on the most important thing now.

Another important part of this key is to never take your eye off of the external environment.

When the *Endurance* got trapped in the ice, the first stage in Ernest Shackleton's plan for saving his men was to reach Elephant Island. The external environment provided ice flows on which he could travel in the direction of Elephant Island. When the external environment changed and the ice flows became unstable, Shackleton adjusted to meet the change. He and his crew launched the lifeboat they had been pulling across the ice and began to sail and row toward Elephant Island. While the external environment changed, the focus remained the same—and the goal remained intact.

Once Shackleton and his crew reached the island, he analyzed the current situation and reformulated his strategy. The new strategy was to send a small rescue crew to Georgia Island, leaving the remainder of the men on Elephant Island with a promise that the rescuers would return for them.

When the vision and goals are clear, the thinking required to produce a plan and strategy for achieving them can be effective. When the plan is effective, the vision can be achieved. Effectiveness depends on organizing resources into a plan of action and then working the plan.

Key 4: Measure Results

It's important to ask how you're doing. The quality of your effort increases when you (as a manager, parent, employee, or other role) know when the work you're doing is moving you closer to achieving your goals. That requires measuring your progress.

A firm grasp on key indicators of success enables managers to properly reward and motivate employees. People will be most productive if systems for measuring quality performance are in place.

In our company, one set of metrics we've employed is to call 20 percent of our customers and ask them questions about their experience with our company. We link everything we learn from them about the quality of our service to the managers, engineers, and associates who contributed to the customer's experience.

We then analyze that information from customers to determine what we can do for our associates and employees so they can be more effective; we want to make sure that each person has the tools required to do his or her best. Customer feedback is a key indicator of performance for our employees—and it becomes thse measure for determining whether employee performance lines up with the company vision and our goal to treat people right.

Once the goals are set for the year, we set up the key metrics and indicators by day, month, quarter, and year in four basic categories:

Economic engine (revenue, number of jobs completed, number of widgets sold or installed—in other words, quantity)

Quality (by individual, by day, call 20 percent of customers, cross-tabulation, number of inspections and results per pay period)

Safety (safety training that takes place and the number of accidents or workmen's compensation claims)

Customer satisfaction (customer surveys and satisfaction levels)

Rock Band Teaches Measurement Lesson

The rock band Van Halen clearly understood the role of measurement in management. The band insisted on a unique key indicator in its touring concert contract: Section 126 of the contract required the stage crew and electricians setting up the arena for the concert to provide a bowl of M&Ms—with all the brown M&Ms removed.

Those who overlooked or ignored the requirement to provide M&Ms with the brown ones removed risked being fired and having to make up the financial guarantees for the show.

At first glance, that sounds like a ridiculous demand by an overindulged rock diva. Why was Van Halen so meticulous with the M&M demand?

The electrical power requirements for the band to produce a successful concert were precise. The contract called for amplifiers and speakers specified as "15 amperage voltage sockets at 20-foot spaces, evenly, providing 19 amperes." With dozens of cities on the schedule and eight eighteen-wheelers of equipment to set up in a short time frame, there was no time to make sure all of the power outlets were up to specifications. For the concert to be a success, the power supply had to work.

Because the concert scheduling left no time to check the work, Van Halen vocalist and songwriter David Lee Roth created a "key indicator." In an obscure place in the contract was the M&M requirement. Roth checked for the M&M bowl first thing in every city. If he saw a brown M&M he would demand a line-by-line check of the entire electrical setup. Here's why: If Roth saw a brown M&M, he was also likely to see a technical problem in the electrical system that could threaten the show, because he knew he was dealing with a person who did not pay attention to detail. No manager has—or should spend—the time to test every element of a solution.

Remember Angela Wolf? Her false brain tumor was completely out of her control, as was the high dose of vitamin A that caused it. But instead of reacting with defeat, she adopted a staggering vision that astounded all with whom she came in contact. To those who said it couldn't be done, Angela Wolf proclaimed that it could—and then set out to *prove* that it could. Her secret: deep commitment to a plan that helped her realize her vision. The same thing is within your grasp—you can achieve a vision that inspires with a plan that will carry you to your very best.

INSPIRATIONAL QUOTES
Manage with a Plan

"Quality is never an accident; it is always the result of high intention, sincere effort, intelligent direction and skillful execution; it represents the wise choice of many alternatives."

— William Foster

"Good fortune is what happens when opportunity meets with planning."

— Thomas Edison

"There can be hope only for a society which acts as one big family, not as many separate ones."

— Anwar Sadat

"Unless you have a definite, precise, clearly set goals, you are not going to realize the maximum potential that lies within you."

— Zig Ziglar

"Good management is the art of making problems so interesting and their solutions so constructive that everyone wants to get to work and deal with them."

— Paul Hawken

"The secret of successful managing is to keep the five guys who hate you away from the four guys who haven't made up their minds."

— Casey Stengel

"When performance is measured, performance improves. When performance is measured and reported back, the rate of improvement accelerates."

— Thomas Monson

Application

To apply Guiding Constant 11, manage with a plan by reflecting on the principles and processes in this chapter.

Individual

1. Reflect on what the best looks like for you in applying Guiding Constant 11, Manage with a Plan.

2. Set individual goals. Consider using the goal sheet that helps provide greater balance in goal setting.

3. Develop a plan of action to accomplish those goals.

4. Use your Thoughts Book to record your plans and inspirations for managing with a plan.

5. Share your goals with someone you care about. Report your progress at the end of the year.

With Others

1. Schedule a time and list the people you want to engage as you teach how to manage with a plan.

2. Plan time to brainstorm with your closest associates, family members, or the other people who will assist you in setting and achieving organizational goals.

3. Set organizational goals.

4. Communicate your goals to all key stakeholders.

5. Set up a framework for accountability and for making adjustments as needed to achieve your goals.

IN A NUTSHELL

1. Your vision becomes a reality as you develop a plan of how to achieve it.

2. Being a manager has far more to do with what is inside of you and your determination to realize the goal than it does with your title. Use the "software" of management.

3. A well-thought-out plan allows for alignment at all levels to effectively optimize activity.

4. Set your goals.

5. Develop your plan.

6. Work your plan.

7. Measure results. Make adjustments as necessary.

8. Adapt your plan as necessary to accommodate change and what's coming at you from the external environment.

Guiding Constant 12
Do What Matters Most

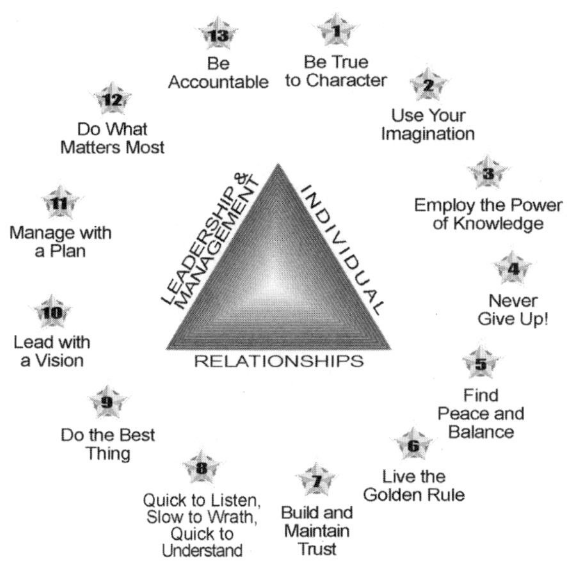

Four Chaplains and Doing What Mattered Most

In February 1943, torpedoes from a German submarine exploded in the hull of the USAT *Dorchester*. In a frantic effort to survive, the 902 soldiers aboard desperately searched for life jackets and lifeboats. Four officers—US Army chaplains and friends

despite their different religious affiliations—gave comfort and encouragement to the boys as they searched for life jackets.

The chaplains located life jackets in the storage lockers, put them on as many soldiers as they could find, and guided the soldiers to the life rafts. When the final life jackets had been found and distributed to the soldiers, something nearly unfathomable happened.

Realizing there were not enough life jackets, the four chaplains removed theirs and fastened them on four terrified soldiers. In all, 230 men were rescued. As the *Dorchester* sank, those survivors witnessed the ultimate sacrifice: four chaplains standing arm in arm on the deck, singing as the ship disappeared into the sea. Less than thirty minutes following the explosion, the USAT *Dorchester* had sunk.

As in the case of the four chaplains, doing what matters most has occasionally meant that someone has given his all. You and I probably won't be called on to make this kind of choice, but doing what matters most always requires sacrifice. Doing what matters most begins with aligning your actions with the Guiding Constants, consciously and consistently manifesting these Constants in your life.

The four chaplains did not simply muster a single act of courage and selflessness in an otherwise self-serving life. Rabbi Alexander D. Goode, Methodist reverend George L. Fox, Catholic priest John P. Washington, and Reformed Church in America reverend Clark V. Poling met and became friends at the Army Chaplains School at Harvard University. They had already committed their own lives to saving souls and redirecting lives for good.

Their characters had already been refined by choosing to do the best thing—to do what mattered most. Reverend Fox, for example, had already served as a medical corps assistant in WWI and had been awarded the Silver Star, the Purple Heart, and the French Croix de Guerre. He volunteered as an army chaplain after studying at the Boston University School of Theology and being ordained a Methodist clergyman.

While the four chaplains went far beyond what most will ever experience, their story does illustrate a key point of Guiding Constant 12: We picture ourselves doing what matters most within each of our individual roles. A chaplain's role is to save souls, and the vision the four chaplains had of their role was translated into doing what mattered most as they saved the lives of soldiers on the *Dorchester*.

Working for High Quality and High Quantity—The Sustainable Best

The best may be defined as high quality and high quantity. For Angela Wolf, the best is a positive connection with her students, who show their gratitude and respect by working hard and working together to achieve the best in the classroom, therefore achieving high *quality*.

Just one day of high quality in Angela's classroom won't be enough, though. It must be sustained—in other words, the students need to work together and achieve high quality day after day, week after week, month after month. This is an example of high *quantity*.

How would you define high quality and high quantity as you've "defined" the best outcome for yourself individually or for your family or for your organization? Let's look at an example. For your family, your vision may be for everyone to express gratitude and show kindness. It's a positive step for that to happen once—you will have achieved high quality. But if it happens often and regularly, you will have achieved high quantity.

High-quality *and* high-quantity achievement differs from one individual to another and from one organization to another; each has to define its personal best. Achieving the best always means achieving *both* high quality and high quantity—when both occur simultaneously, you achieve *sustainability*.

These examples can be better understood through the Quality and Quantity Matrix, which helps illustrate how the sustainable best is achieved. Look over the matrix for few minutes and identify where high quality and high quantity are found. Where do you want to be?

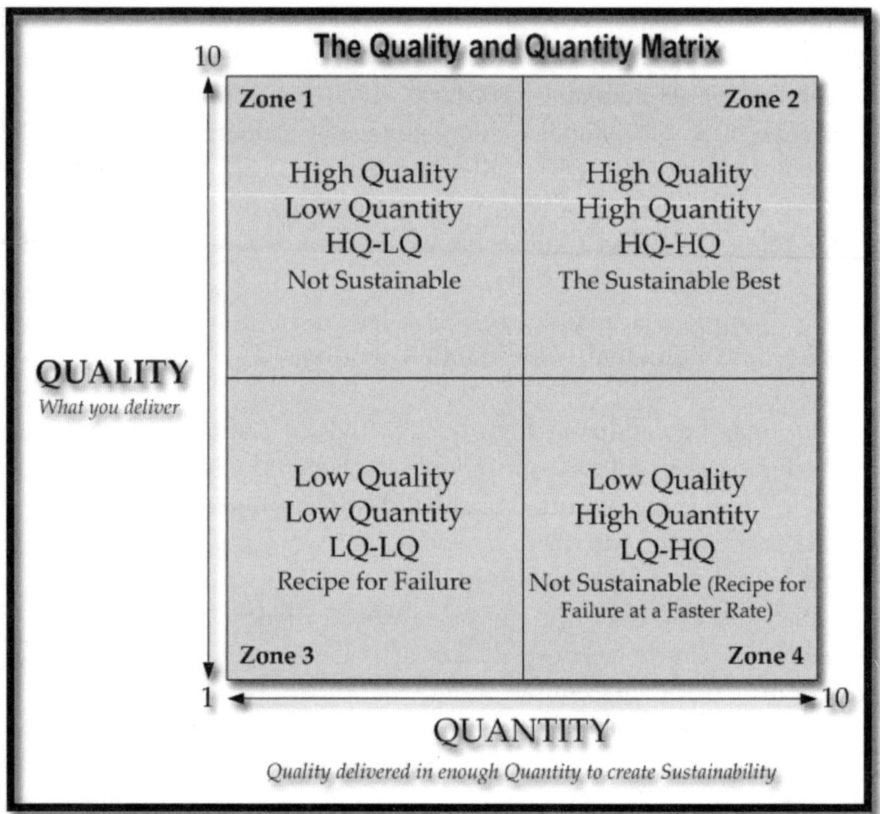

Achieving High Quality *and* High Quantity

Once you define the quality as an individual or an organization, you need to define the critical mass, or amount, of quantity needed to produce the sustainable best. The goal is for your interpersonal relationships, your products, or your services to be in Zone 2—High Quality, High Quantity—where the sustainable best is manifest.

Trying to deliver or promote a poor-quality product, service, or idea is costly and can be fatal to the ultimate success of the project, so you need to focus on quality first. It usually requires patience, testing, and training to create consistent high quality. Once established, quality may then be scaled to needed levels of quantity so that the project can be sustainable.

There are a few cases where quantity needs to come before quality. Sales prospecting is a good example. You might say to yourself, "This is just a numbers game. If I knock on enough doors, I may get the sales I want."

Even then, you can't ignore quality. How much better to add quality to your effort by finding a way to create a worthy lead out of every person to whom you talk. Unless you have a way to do that, you may not be able to locate enough qualified customers—*quantity*—to create a sustainable sales model, no matter how many doors you knock on.

What Matters Most as a Lens

Think of doing what matters most as a lens through which you see your vision for achieving what matters most. Proust wrote, "The real voyage of discovery consists not of seeking new landscapes, but in seeing through new eyes." The lens of what matters most brings into focus your vision for your relationships, your work, and your community service.

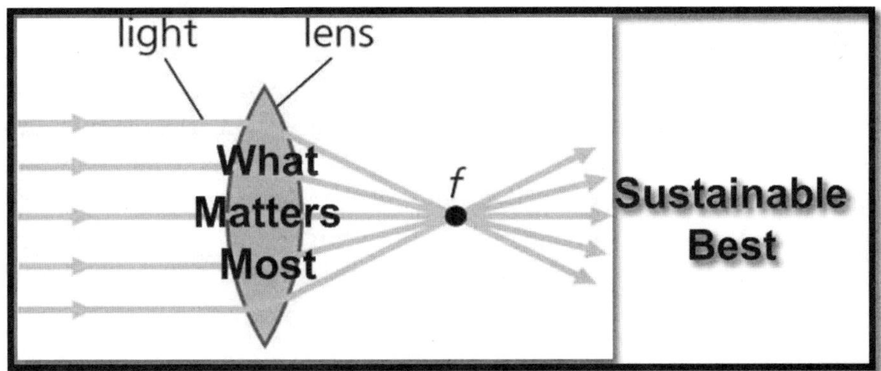

The "what matters most lens" helps you "see" and define your sustainable best—the opposite of a flash-in-the-pan best, a one-shot wonder, or a single shining moment. It is the ideal of doing and being your best self or organization. An effort that starts with a flash, can't be sustained, and burns out quickly does not necessarily qualify as doing what matters most. A few illustrations will help you see how it works.

Let's take customer service as an example. What does looking through the lens at what matters most show you about customer service? Imagine a company committed to doing the best thing with a vision and mission of serving the customer superbly well. The company's service technicians are so thorough and meticulous that they are able to perform only one service call per day. The quality of the work is high, but the quantity—one service call per day—is insufficient. The service technicians must also attend to the *quantity* of work completed—if they want to stay employed, they need to complete enough service calls each day to generate the revenue necessary to pay them and to provide an adequate return for the organization. If they don't balance quality and quantity, their work is not sustainable.

As another example, consider doing what matters most for a father who is trying to build positive relationships with his family. He takes all family members to a professional soccer game where the family's favorite team beats its rival. They eat delicious food and cheer together for their winning team. One son exclaims, "This is the funnest day ever, Dad!" It *was* a great day—but what if it was the only family time this father gave during the entire month, focusing the rest of his time on his work? Positive family relationships are difficult to sustain on "quality time" alone—there must also be "quantity time." A balance of the two results in sustained positive relationships.

As still another example, imagine that engineers invented such a precision-quality product that it is written up in business journals as the engineering breakthrough of the decade. But when it comes time to translate the product into an effective economic engine, the manufacturing division finds it cannot mass-produce the device as specified by the engineers. The precision can be duplicated by hand, but can not be mass-produced. As a result, no one can afford to buy the the product and few units are sold. Without quantity, the value of quality is limited or even nonexistent.

Reviewing High Quality and High Quantity

Clearly understanding the high quality and high quantity of Zone 2 and how they work together in your life and your organization creates the *lens* that will focus your actions and energy on what matters most—and will enable you to achieve your sustainable best.

The Magnificence of the Body, Mind, and Heart

Not long ago, we were visiting our son and his wife, west of Phoenix, Arizona, near the White Tank Mountains. It is a beautiful but rugged mountain terrain. One morning we hiked three miles up a ravine. After arriving at a waterfall and enjoying this captivating area where the American Indians made their home, we decided to jog back down the trail.

As we navigated the trail at about four miles per hour, I was utterly amazed how my mind and body, working together, knew exactly how to adjust to the ever-changing terrain—a boulder here, a dip there, a rattle snake slithering along the side of the trail, a spiny cactus—as we gradually went up and down, descending safely back to where the cars were parked.

The experience caused me to reflect on how our body systems work together as we navigate through the daily challenges of life. Just as your body adjusts to the terrain as you jog over a trail in the mountains, your mind and heart adjust to the "terrain" of your relationships, your work, and everything you face from moment to moment. The Guiding Constants merge so that your "heart and mind memory" consistently leads to achieving your sustainable best and doing what matters most.

Repetition is crucial to the development of both muscle memory and heart and mind memory. One moment of creativity, or being quick to listen once in a while, is not sustainable and will not support you "in the heat of the game." One moment of trust does not fill a reservoir of trust—but being consistently trustworthy makes trust sustainable. And when important qualities are sustainable, you do what matters most.

What Matters Most Sustained for Three Decades

While in prison for fighting against apartheid in South Africa, Nelson Mandela and his associates accomplished something remarkable, something certainly in the realm of what matters most. His accomplishment is a great example of the intangibles.

When Nelson Mandela was incarcerated at Robben Island Prison, he chose to spread to other prisoners his love for and belief in education. Robben Island became known as the Nelson Mandela University. The suffering and cruelty of prison life was made bearable for the men as they focused on study and learning. The prisoners studied together on the rock pile, at meals, and any other time they could. They learned English, geography, mathematics, political history, and philosophy. Valuing the continuous development of knowledge, the prisoners not only studied together, they earned correspondence degrees together.

Mandela converted the terrible conditions of Robben Island Prison into a place of learning and writing. He was known for saying, "Struggling is the way I live." He felt that overcoming and making the most of the barriers and obstacles placed in his pathway helped him develop his greatest strengths as a statesman. In fact, Mandela considered the twenty-seven years he spent on Robben Island and at Pollsmoor Prison his preparation to become the president of South Africa.

"There is no passion to be found playing small," said Mandela, "in settling for a life that is less than the one you are capable of living." Doing what matters most is a choice.

Looking through the lens of doing what mattered most to him, Mandela drew on Guiding Constants such as character, creativity, and never giving up to achieve the sustainable best. He aligned his life to these Constants—and, in spite of seeming insurmountable obstacles, he pursued his choice over three decades until he achieved the sustainable best outcome. His choice was about high quality and high quantity.

Choose to Do What Matters Most

Doing what matters most starts with your vision. The lens you look through to see what matters most is made sharp and clear by your vision of the best outcome you can achieve. Mandela didn't simply fill his days with things to do; he filled them with work focused on what mattered most with a vision that his work would "amount to something."

What matters most is a mindset—a way of thinking. Your mental creation of Becoming Your Best becomes a reality as you use tools to focus your time and energy on doing what matters most. Five important steps will help you to conserve time and to maximize your personal effectiveness.

1. Reflect on what matters most for each role.

2. Look ahead to see what's coming by using a twelve- to fifteen-month calendar.

3. Create a weekly plan for what matters most. This preweek (preflight) type of planning helps assure that you have highly productive weeks. Most time-management systems are just that—time managers. You don't need to manage time; *you need to manage yourself.* A lack of time is not what keeps you from being productive. If you desire to be more productive in the most important ways, you can make quality use of your time by consistently focusing on what matters most in each of your

roles. When you do this, the result will be high-quality and high-quantity achievements.

4. Make a to-do list.

5. Protect and preserve your time and energy.

1. Reflect on What Matters Most for Each Role

"We often spend so much time coping with problems along our path," says author Peter Senge, "that we forget why we are on that path in the first place. The result is that we only have a dim, or even an inaccurate, view of what's really important to us."

Doing What Matters Most

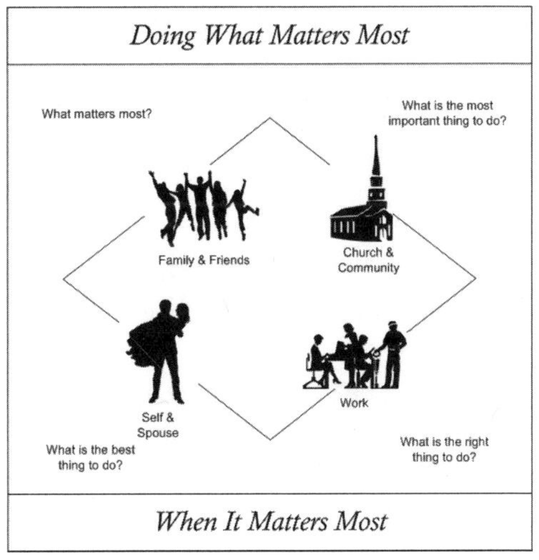

When It Matters Most

To understand what matters most to you, reflect on your various roles and the vision you have for achieving what matters most in each role. What is meant by the word *role*? For our purposes, roles are the key responsibilities and relationships you carry out on a daily basis. An example of a high-priority role is your relationship with family members as a father, husband, and grandfather—or as a mother, wife, and grandmother.

Separate your roles and responsibilities so you can ask yourself guiding questions about them: "What matters most today and this week for each of my roles?"

To decide what matters most in each of your roles, you may find listening to your feelings allows you to mentally create what the best looks like. Reflection is best done at a quiet time when your mind is at rest from pressures. "Only when the clamor of the outside world is silenced," says author Sarah Breathnach, "will you be able to hear the deeper vibration." That kind of reflection on your roles helps you identify what matters most in each one at this moment.

Most Important Roles in Life	Personal Self	Companion	Family and Friends	Knowledge Worker	Education School	Service Community
Think of actions or things that you can do that Would Matter Most under each role.						
List those actions under the appropriate heading.						

Examples of Possible Role Descriptions

The practice of reflection was powerfully portrayed in a story told earlier—one you'll certainly remember. When a customer service consultant invited the staff to make a difference in the grocery store where they worked, Johnny—the nineteen-year-old bagger with Down Syndrome—reflected on his own service and came up with an idea for doing his best within his role. He decided to write a "thought for the day" on slips of paper and put one in the grocery bag of each customer. Customers stood in long lines just to speak to Johnny and receive his thought for the day. He mentally created a vision for himself of what he could do for the customers at the store.

Taking time to reflect on what matters most gives you focus and helps you avoid being controlled by the events in your life. Choosing what matters most means choosing to be master of your own fate.

Once you have reflected on your roles and established the mindset of looking through the lens of doing what matters most, you now have actions you can take to achieve your best. You are ready to plan and carry out your mental creation of what matters most. To do this efficiently and effectively, you use tools that help you use your time wisely.

2. Look Ahead to See What's Coming Using a Twelve- to Fifteen-Month Calendar

It has been said that life is not measured by the number of breaths we take, but by the moments that take our breath away. Such moments may not impact you, though, if you don't notice them. To make sure you experience the moments that take your breath away, look ahead at what's coming at you. Lincoln maintained that the best thing about the future is that it comes one day at a time. But for those who don't anticipate the future, the seasons may come and go unnoticed.

May 11

Sunday	Monday	Tuesday	Wednesday	Thursday	Friday	Saturday
May 1	2	3	4	5	6	7
8	9	10	11	12	13	14
15	16	17	18	19	20	21
22	23	24	25	26	27	28
29	30	31	June 1	2	3	4

Recording what is coming at you on a twelve- to fifteen-month calendar allows you to plan and prepare. Some examples of things you want to see coming well in advance are important family dates, business meetings and conferences, travel plans (including vacations), and potential events in the external environment that could significantly impact your internal environment.

I use my twelve- to fifteen-month calendar to look ahead with what matters most in mind. With my to-do list and weekly planner nearby, I start by looking out one month ahead then gradually look farther ahead. At one point I noticed I had tentatively scheduled foot surgery in July—but I had also penciled in the possible wedding date of our son in early August. Since foot surgery meant I couldn't wear a shoe for two or three weeks, I rescheduled the surgery in favor of what mattered most: being healthy for our son's big day. Seeing what was coming at me helped me avert a disaster of my own making.

3. Create a Weekly Plan

Every achievement is the result of a mental creation. As you "see" that achievement in your mind's eye, you can also envision what it will take to

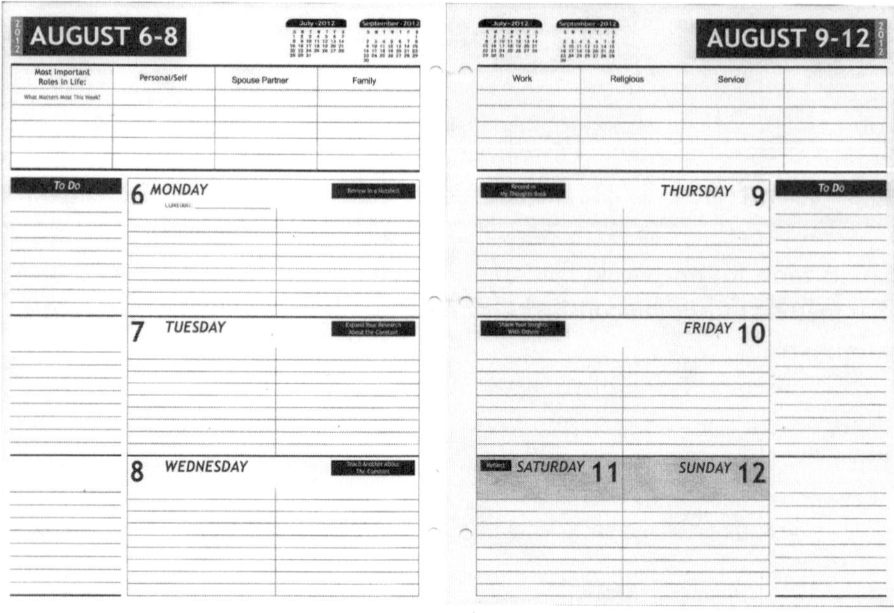

Pre-Flight or Pre-Week Planning Worksheet

achieve what matters most. Author Robert Collier, who wrote *The Law of the Higher Potential*, said, "Visualize this thing that you want, see it, feel it, believe in it. Make your mental blue print, and begin to build."

We have two sons who are fighter pilots; both have flown the F-16. They've described the level of detail that goes into their mission planning, briefs, and debriefs, and it's absolutely amazing!

A fighter pilot wouldn't dare go into a mission without a plan. There are so many things to consider and account for: surface-to-air missiles, enemy aircraft, air refueling at the correct time and place, turbulence from other aircraft, weapons impact timing, and so on. Pilots also generally have primary objectives (the absolute most important parts of the mission) and secondary objectives (those things that would be nice to accomplish in addition to the primary objectives). A pilot typically calls this *preflight planning* or *mission planning*. It's the process through which they determine what matters most and then develop the plan to help them accomplish what matters most.

Just as a pilot does preflight planning, I believe it's critical to do *pre-week planning*. Such planning consists of determining what matters most in the upcoming week in each of your roles (parent, spouse, friend, employee, and so on) and specifying an actual time during the week when you'll do what you've identified.

If it's critical to the success of a pilot to fly with a detailed plan, wouldn't it also be critical and essential to your success to have a weekly plan?

Use a worksheet like the one illustrated to plan out the week in advance around your key roles, responsibilities, and goals. This weekly planning sheet becomes your guide—your lens—as you move through the week. It doesn't have to be paper; you can also use an electronic calendar.

Set a time each week to reflect on what is coming and to plan what matters most for one week. Few things will have a greater impact on doing what matters most than consistently doing pre-flight planning and creating a weekly plan.

Begin with a review of your roles and what matters most. The bottom of the weekly planning tool provides space where you can note what you want to focus on in each of your roles.

Next, decide when you will accomplish each goal and write it on your weekly calendar. The weekly plan is not only a record of what matters most in each role, but is also a record of when you will accomplish those things. You now know what matters most in each of your roles and when you will do the tasks that will result in high-quality and high-quantity outcomes.

Remember: You don't need to manage time. You need to manage *yourself.* If we want to be more productive in the most important ways, we are most effective when we make quality use of our time by focusing consistently on doing what matters most.

4. Make a To-Do List

Keep your priorities in front of you by building a to-do list of the most important things you need to do today and in the near future.

During the week, things will come up that need to get done at some point but that don't necessarily need to be on your calendar. That's a great use of the to-do list—it's important but there's no specific time in which it needs to be accomplished.

Once you have seen in your mind's eye what matters most and you have recorded it in your weekly plan, break your vision down by creating a to-do list of the high-priority tasks. This will align your plan with what matters most in your various roles.

The main idea is to have a reminder of important tasks in front of you. When you recognize something important that needs to be done, write it down. Whether you use daily sheets or a rolling to-do list (either electronic

What Matters Most-To Do List

or paper-based), make sure the important things are in front of you—then make choices based on what's important right now.

Be careful not to fall into the trap of writing your lists on scraps of paper; they can get lost or quickly overwhelm you. A to-do list allows you to have "what matters most" notes in a predictable place where you can easily find them, saving even more time.

Remember, action today can prevent a crisis tomorrow. What should you do today to prevent a crisis tomorrow—or two months from now?

David Allen, productivity author and consultant, explains that breaking things down on a to-do list helps remove barriers to achieving them. He recommends creating a detailed to-do list. He uses a great example: imagine that your mother's birthday is coming. Now imagine that you write nothing but "Mom" on your to-do list. You may find yourself ignoring the reminder on your to-do list and putting off buying her a gift because you aren't sure what to buy. You're stuck. Writing "Mom" on your to-do list hasn't really helped you "complete it."

A better option, he says, is to write "Call sister re: Mom's birthday." Now you've attacked the big task you've been delaying by breaking it down into an action. Telephoning your sister is something you can do. And since you know that your sister will have a great idea for a gift, you've created a pathway to achieving what matters most in your role as a son.

I find that taking just a few minutes to organize each task with a telephone number or a few possible ways to solve a problem helps me get that important item done.

As you reflect on what matters most, mentally create a vision of your best, and use your weekly plan and to-do list to achieve those things, you'll experience peace and a sense of accomplishment. You'll fulfill each of your roles with actions that matter most to you and those around you.

Now that you have a proven pathway of mentally creating and doing what matters most, you must be alert to the distractions that can rob you of the time and energy needed to achieve your best.

5. Protect and Conserve Your Time and Energy

The sheer speed at which all of us are moving can spin you away from what matters most to you. In a world where everything seems urgent, it's easy to feel hammered from every side by things that are not always important.

There is instant communication almost everywhere you go—you can even be reached in the wilderness in many places—so you need to exert yourself to avoid being pushed around by the sheer force of activity. Creating an internal guide to help you stay focused on the most important things in life increases your effectiveness.

Activity trap is an apt way to describe what sometimes happens to your time. You get trapped in activities that matter little at the expense of things that matter most. Those things that occupy your mind and time must be put into their proper place by focusing on what matters most.

- **Ways to Protect Your Time**

Choose to spend your time on what matters most. Preserve and protect your time. There are plenty of good ways to spend your time—but even "good" things can keep you from doing what matters most. You may find that the following practices will help protect your energy and time, both of which are critical to effectively doing what matters most.

- **Effectively Manage E-mail and Other Electronic Media**

This doesn't mean you should ignore electronic media: E-mail is an extraordinary communication tool when used correctly. You simply need to leverage it to help you achieve what matters most.

You may be in a profession where it's critical to respond to e-mail or voice mail in a timely way. If so, you need to find a way to stay on top of things—something that requires effort, push, and a good plan. As technology improves, you will be able to be more effective in the use of these tools.

In order to optimize the use of e-mail, voice mail, and other electronic media, consider the following:

- Know when to use e-mail or voice mail. If an item is emotionally charged, hard to communicate, a key negotiation, or would be better handled in person, simply pick up the phone or go see the individual in person. E-mails and voice mails are best used for transactional communication or for the exchange of information.

- For important communications, call regarding an e-mail that is going to be sent to minimize any misunderstanding.

- Use screens or blocks on your e-mail to filter out junk e-mails.

- To prevent e-mail or voice mail from controlling you, plan time to read or listen and then respond to it. You might consider silencing or turning off your e-mail or voice mail notification tool then setting aside two or three blocks of time during the day to handle it.

You might also consider setting up e-mail-monitoring tools or filters. You can designate organizational messages or messages merely copied to be stored in a folder where you can review them later. E-mail from highly important senders can be filtered to folders you check more regularly so it won't get lost in the volume of incoming messages.

The following will help you more effectively manage e-mail and other electronic media:

- Answer promptly.

- Be precise, complete, and as brief as possible, but make sure all relevant details are included.

- Double-check spelling, grammar, dates, and times before clicking Send.

- Give people as much notice as possible when you need something from them.

- If you're going to be away, leave a message so they'll know not to expect an answer until you return.

If you consciously work to strike a balance between controlling the time you spend on e-mail and ensuring that you communicate in an effective, timely way, you'll control electronic media instead of letting it control you.

- **Ineffective Meetings Are Deadly**

Don't meet unless you really need to! If communication is informational—in other words, one way—don't meet; send an e-mail instead. In fact, if the information can be communicated in any way other than in a meeting—in an e-mail or by telephone, for example—try that first.

When conference calls or meetings *are* necessary for collaboration purposes and to maximize communication, consider the following ideas:

- Invite the right people.
- Have an objective and meaningful purpose for the meeting.
- Start on time and be on time (or preferably a few minutes early).
- Have a clear agenda and provide any supporting documents or reports ahead of time.
- Make a record of issues and decisions.
- Invite participation—if participation is unnecessary, you should not be meeting; send the information another way.
- Create a "parking lot" for items that surface but are not meant for the current meeting. Put these items on a future agenda or handle at another time/place.
- Handle individual items off-line.
- Prevent any single discussion from taking too much time.
- Close with a review of any action items for individuals or the group.

- Schedule when and where the next meeting will be.

- End on time or early.

Always take your calendar and weekly planning pages (electronic or hard copy) with you. Then if you find yourself stuck in an ineffective meeting, you can use the time to reflect on what matters most, record ideas for each of your roles, and plan for the future actions that will help you achieve your goals.

- **Avoid Negative, Draining Interactions with Others**

Recently, a close friend—a very capable individual—called and wanted to know if he could come over and visit about an important matter. He had just had a "run-in" with a neighbor, a local church leader, and wanted to discuss what to do. As my friend and I visited, a plan was developed to help resolve the issue and restore good feelings. When my friend returned home, the neighbor was on his doorstep; both were prepared to apologize and get back on the right foot. They had a nice forty-five-minute visit during which they resolved things and restored a high level of trust.

The initial negative interaction that started the whole thing probably took only about forty-five seconds—then they each went their separate ways, stewing over the unpleasant interaction and unresolved issue. It took about three hours to resolve and restore good feelings; together, they figured out how to resolve the issue that caused the problem in the first place, all ill was forgotten, and they both moved forward with good feelings.

I have certainly had similar experiences. How much better would it be to completely sidestep these types of events in the first place? It would save valuable time and emotional upset.

Remember: Negative interactions, confrontations, and altercations with others can sap your energy and strength. To help you diffuse negativity, try the following:

- Avoid negative interactions in the first place. Anticipate possible conflicts and figure out how to eliminate them before they come up.

- Take a deep breath and be determined that you will take the high road and help the situation to end in a more positive way.

- Keep things in perspective. Do you really have to solve the problem right then? Can you tell a humorous story to break the ice and then assure the other person that you can solve the problem?

- If the situation *is* a big deal, be quick to listen and slow to wrath. A person who is upset usually persists because he feels he is not being heard. Once you understand another person's point of view, you are usually much better able to contribute to a more productive outcome.

- Be a catalyst for getting to a better place. Sometimes listening is all that is needed. Other times, collaborating to find positive solutions is helpful. You may be able to help resolve the issue then and there, or it may be necessary to follow up at a better time.

- Figure out a way to communicate better and to solve issues before they become a challenge.

- Try to avoid individuals that are chronically negative or cause regular "blowouts." Life is too short.

- You can't really change or control others; don't allow them to throw you off. Draw upon your strong inner core for your own peace, happiness, and direction.

Your positive and peaceful energy and effective use of time are two of your most precious resources. Be a master at conserving them carefully.

- **Keep Current Projects in Front of You**

Time is lost trying to remember where you put something or answering questions about whatever you've misplaced. Taking time to endlessly shuffle through papers can be a huge drain on your time.

One of the most effective ways to keep what matters most in front of you is to have a simple system for locating things. Use a simple method to store current projects where they can be seen. This helps maintain the focus on those high-priority projects that must receive your highest and best effort.

In summary, go for high quality and high quantity in each of your roles in life as you strive for your best. The consistent application of doing what matters most and weekly planning will help you to conserve time, to maximize your effectiveness consistently, and to do those things that matter most.

INSPIRATIONAL QUOTES

Do What Matters Most

"Speed is irrelevant if you are going in the wrong direction."

— *Mahatma Gandhi*

"You live longer when you realize that any time spent being unhappy is wasted."

— *Ruth E. Renkl*

"Vision—It reaches beyond the thing that is, into the conception of what can be. Imagination gives you the picture. Vision gives you the impulse to make the picture your own."

— *Collier*

"Every day I remind myself that my inner and outer life are based on the labors of other men, living and dead, and that I must exert myself in order to give in the same measure as I have received and am still receiving."

— *Albert Einstein*

"It is not living that matters, but living rightly."

— *Socrates*

"They key is not to prioritize what's on your schedule, but to schedule your priorities."

— *Stephen R. Covey*

"If life and its rushed pace and many stresses have made it difficult for you to feel like rejoicing, then perhaps now is a good time to refocus on what matters most."

— *Dieter F. Uchtdorf*

Application

To apply Guiding Constant 12, begin by reflecting on your roles and what matters most to you within each one.

Individual

1. Define and write down your key roles in life.
2. Reflect on what matters most in each role. Write in your Thoughts Book as you reflect on your roles and what matters most in each one.
3. Keep a twelve- to fifteen-month calendar so you will know what is coming.
4. Plan weekly by recording what you will do in each role and when.
5. Create a to-do list to track high-priority tasks.

With Others

1. Schedule a time to discuss the key parts of this chapter with individuals or a team within your organization.
2. Discuss how weekly "preflight" planning is going and what you can do to make it a consistent practice.
3. Discuss how you can more effectively use e-mail, voice mail, or other electronic media.
4. Discuss how you can make your meetings more effective.
5. Discuss how you can avoid emotional blowups or negative interactions.

6. Reflect on what matters most in the organization.
7. Discuss what matters most as an organization.

In a Nutshell

Define what matters most for each of your roles. Next, use tools to focus your energy on doing what matters most, ensuring that you achieve your sustainable best.

1. Develop a "what matters most" mindset.

2. Work to achieve sustainability by balancing high quality and high quantity.

3. Take time each week to go through a "mental creation" or "pre-flight planning" of your vision by reflecting on your life's roles and by setting goals for each one to be achieved this week.

4. Keep yourself ahead of the curve by regularly scanning your long-term calendar, weekly worksheet, and your to-do list. Remember: Action today can prevent a crisis tomorrow.

5. Protect and conserve your time and positive energy through good organization and a clear lens of what matters most.

6. Use e-mail, voice mail, and other communication devices effectively and wisely.

7. If you hold a meeting at all, make it productive and worthwhile. Don't waste others' time!

8. Avoid negative interactions and blowouts. Maintain a healthy sense of humor.

9. Have fun!

Guiding Constant 13

Be Accountable

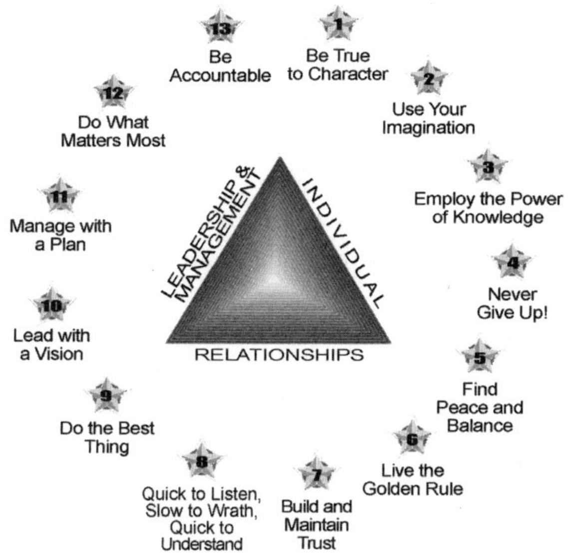

The Meaning of Accountability: The Thrill of Victory!

WHENEVER YOU STEP UP AND TAKE RESPONSIBILITY, the result can be both obvious and subtle. The obvious result is that the work is done, the deadline is reached, or the need is met. But consider the more subtle results, too: Energy levels change. People around you feel momentum beginning to build. A spirit of possibility takes over. You see a positive alternative to any downward spiral, to any seemingly insurmountable obstacle, and even to the fear that the current opportunity may slip out of your grasp unrealized.

The choice to step up and take responsibility produces an inescapable type of synergy. The power of the Guiding Constants contributes to that synergy—a synergy not of only of minds or effort, but of principles. When your will and the power of the Guiding Constants come together in a commitment to be accountable, you have started down a pathway that leads to the thrill of victory!

You may find this to be one of the most exciting Guiding Constants. In fact, there are *no* Guiding Constants without being accountable, because accountability commits you to becoming your best. Consider the example of being true to character: you set a target for a deeper, more meaningful character, and you hold yourself accountable by increasing your integrity.

You steadily become your best as you choose to be accountable and accept responsibility for continuous improvement. Character, imagination, persistence, vision, planning, and measuring results are the cause and the result of accountability. The Guiding Constants are brought together in a synergy of action with the decision to commit and to seize the chance to remove the obstacles and grab the opportunities.

To Act or Not to Act: That is the Question

Embedded in the commitment to be accountable is a commitment to act—not just until the going gets tough or until you are distracted by one thing or another. Not just until it inconveniences you or demands too much. You commit to your core to achieve your best. As the mythical figure Yoda from *Star Wars* so sagely put it, there is no "try"—there is only "do."

Character enables you to make a commitment that goes beyond trying and on to achieving. Can any person give up after making a commitment to never give up? Sure; it happens all the time. But if it stops happening for you today—if you resolve right now to hold yourself accountable for results—you take a big step forward in becoming your best. There are few thrills like the thrill of victory over self. You can almost feel the excitement as you contemplate making that kind of commitment.

Committing to Be Accountable

Someone once said it is easy to tell the difference between just being "involved" and truly being "committed." It is like an eggs and ham breakfast—the chicken was involved but the pig was fully committed.

William H. Murray, the Scottish mountaineer and explorer, exhibited this kind of daily triumph in the most demanding environment. As a prisoner of war during WWII, he occupied his mind by writing a book, *Mountaineering in Scotland*. He wrote the draft on toilet paper; when the Gestapo discovered his "manuscript," they destroyed it. His prison companions couldn't believe it when Murray simply began to write the book all over again. His second draft was published after the war, was widely read, and inspired the revitalization of mountain climbing in Scotland and elsewhere.

"Providence Moves Too"

Committing to be accountable can have surprising effects. Occasionally I'll make a commitment and start to work on something when suddenly a person or other resource important to my success comes along. I am convinced that the act of deeply committing and making the commitment public attracts others with like minds.

William H. Murray, who scrawled out his first draft on toilet paper, wrote in his book *The Scottish Himalayan Expedition* about what can happen when we commit and then act:

> *But when I said that nothing had been done I erred in one important matter. We had definitely committed ourselves and were halfway out of our ruts. We had put down our passage money—booked a sailing to Bombay. This may sound too simple, but is great in consequence. Until one is committed, there is hesitancy, the chance to draw back, always ineffectiveness. Concerning all acts of initiative (and creation), there is one elementary truth the ignorance of which kills countless ideas and splendid plans: that the moment one definitely commits oneself,* the providence moves too. *A whole stream of events issues from the decision, raising in one's favor all manner of unforeseen incidents, meetings and material assistance, which no man could have dreamt would have come his way. I learned a deep respect for one of Goethe's couplets:*
>
> Whatever you can do or dream you can, begin it.
> Boldness has genius, power and magic in it!

Six Ways to Be Accountable

Although there are many ways to be accountable, I would like to describe six important elements that you may find helpful. As you incorporate these six ways to be accountable into your own life, you'll find they will provide energy, focus, and success.

As you review each of these six ways, consider how you can apply them to become your best through accountability:

1. Take responsibility for your actions and situations.
2. Eliminate procrastination. Do it! Do it right! Do it right now!
3. Don't criticize, condemn, blame, and complain.
4. Be accountable to principles and the Guiding Constants.
5. Utilize the power of relationship agreements.
6. Report back on your assignment or goals.

1. Take Responsibility for Your Actions and Situations
Bread Crumbs Accountability

After making toast or whatever, please wipe the crumbs up with a wet cloth.
The test is to wipe your hand across the counter, and if the crumbs are all gone, yippee! It's clean! Thank you!!!
P.S. And PLEASE don't wipe the crumbs onto the floor ☺

Thank you for the feedback and training.
Well done. Nice smooth "crumbless" counters.
☺

One day not long ago, I got up early, made some toast with jam, grabbed a quick glass of orange juice, and headed out to exercise. When I returned, my wife, Roxanne, had gone out on some errands and the note you see here was taped to the toaster.

This was my opportunity for "choice." I could take responsibility or I could blame it on something else—the toast, my being in a hurry, my mother, or just being a man. What would *you* do?

Here's what I did: Fortunately, I made a wise decision and accepted positive responsibility. I cleaned up the mess, leaving a smooth, clean countertop and making sure no crumbs fell on the floor. I left the note you see here in place of Roxanne's note. Then I went to work in my office, which is near the kitchen.

Awhile later, Roxanne returned home. I listened carefully; when I heard her begin to laugh I knew she had read my note. I was grateful that she had written such a positive, upbeat note to offer feedback and help me see a better way. I was also grateful that I chose to be responsible. I suppose I'll never leave crumbs on the counter or floor again.

Fess Up and Own the Problem

It happens to everyone: we fall short or make a mistake. An important part of being accountable is to take your medicine and admit it. You may be surprised at the reaction you get. When there is a misunderstanding, confusion, a missed meeting, something not going right, or a mistake, simply "fess up"—take responsibility and move on. When it's all over, take stock of what went right and wrong. Evaluate what you could have done better, jot down your thoughts, and then put it behind you. Go to bed, get some rest, and get ready for a fresh day tomorrow.

If you make a mistake, confess it before anyone else can. I remember a situation in my own life where things could have gone badly but didn't because I took a chance and just "fessed up." I was taking four individuals to the airport and almost missed the turnoff. We were talking, and I was distracted until it was almost too late to make the exit. I crossed several lanes of traffic and hit the exit just right!

It would have ended there except for the highway patrolman who was right behind me. Of course, he immediately pulled me over. When the patrolman walked up to the window, I asked, "Is there a problem, officer?" (Quick to listen ☺) He said, "You crossed over three lanes to exit the highway."

He was right. I was wrong.

Normally I would have pled my case and explained my problem. This time, I decided not to try to explain my predicament and the tight airplane schedule facing my colleagues. I just took it on the chin. I told the officer that I really blew it. I admitted that it was totally my fault. I explained that we were all talking, and I just did something really dumb.

The officer looked at me and said, "May I see your insurance card, license, and registration?" I thought I was sunk! He took my documents to his car and came back within a few minutes. He looked at me with a smile, handed my documents back, and said, "Mr. Shallenberger, please be more careful and have a nice day!" With that he returned to his car, and I was on my way.

In this case, taking responsibility for my actions had an immediate positive response. I took responsibility for my actions and the trooper was kind enough to not give me a ticket. His simple suggestion that I be more careful had an impact on me, and I have tried to be more careful ever since.

Your particular situation may not involve crumbs on the counter or admitting that you made a mistake to a police officer—it's the principle that counts. There is an important distinction between "it's not finished" and "I haven't finished it." The difference is in the willingness to be accountable—to fess up—for what you do and what you fail or refuse to do. The willingness to fess up is a sign of character that signals to others that you keep your commitments.

People who do not take accountability—who refuse to fess up—can be found putting things off or blaming others. Some even engage in deeply psychological "games," such as acting helpless and incapable of completing the task. Others may say they were not aware of what was required or that other people did not step up. None of these behaviors take you any closer to the victory. Fessing up does.

You may be tempted to offer any one of the classic copouts: *I didn't know* or *I wasn't there* or *I didn't have time* or *It's not my job*. But using those excuses creates more anxiety and doesn't take you toward personal or institutional success. Fess up and win.

Put Yourself in Her Shoes

One day I tried to apply this same idea—taking responsibility for my actions—to all of my weaknesses. I thought of the criticisms my wife might have of me and wrote them all down. It was an interesting analysis. I came up with about seven doozies. I shared my list with Roxanne to see how close I was and we had a great laugh over the list.

Something interesting happened. My commitment to take responsibility and to improve had a positive effect on both me and Roxanne. Getting those "sources of possible irritation" out on the table somehow made it easier for me to keep working on them and made them less of a concern for her. That small exercise demonstrated how taking responsibility can have immediate positive effects in our families.

2. Overcome Blaming, Criticizing, and Complaining
Any Fool Can Complain

When I was twenty I read a powerful passage from Dale Carnegie's *How to Win Friends and Influence People* that I've never forgotten: "Any fool can criticize, condemn, and complain—and most fools do. But it takes character and self-control to be understanding." Thomas Carlyle said, "A great man shows his greatness by the way he treats little men. Instead of condemning people, let's try to understand them. Let's try to figure out why they do what they do. That's a lot more profitable and intriguing than criticism, and it breeds sympathy, tolerance, and kindness. 'To know all is to forgive all.'"

One Man's War on Complaining

I can imagine how Dale Carnegie would feel about the Reverend Will Bowen of Christ Church Unity in Kansas City, Missouri. NBC television correspondent George Lewis reported in 2007 that the Reverend Bowen and his church have a vision of ridding the world of complaining.

"The one thing we can agree on," said the Reverend Bowen, "is there's too much complaining." As his own private stand against it, the Reverend Bowen committed his congregation to refrain from complaining, criticizing, using sarcasm, and gossiping for twenty-one days—just three short weeks. To remind and motivate his congregation, everyone who pledged to accept the challenge was given a purple bracelet embossed with *Complaint-Free World*. Anyone who slipped up had to change the bracelet to the other wrist and start counting the days all over again.

It took the Reverend Bowen himself three and a half months to achieve twenty-one consecutive complaint-free days. Some members of his congregation took as long as seven months to reach the goal. It's obviously not easy—but it's an idea that has resonated with millions since that humble beginning five years ago. Poet Laureate Maya Angelou's bracelet was number 6 million, and the website reports distributing more than 9.8 million bracelets worldwide as of this writing.

The Reverend Bowen's vision is for that website—acomplaintfreeworld.org—to lead the charge in eradicating whining, gossiping, complaining, and criticizing for the entire world. Look at the hard numbers: The Reverend Bowen figures that if the average person complains 20 times a day for

30 days, 9 million bracelets have stopped almost 5.5 billion complaints just this month alone.

Complaining functions for us. The Reverend Bowen explains that people complain for the same reason a baby cries: They want their circumstances to change and they are unable to say so in a constructive way. Dr. Robert Anthony said, "When you blame others, you give up your power to change." The Reverend Bowen suggests that whenever someone complains to you, you should ask how he or she would like to see the situation resolved. If the person continues to criticize or whine, ask again, "How would you like to see that situation resolved in the best possible way?" Such an approach has the potential to change the time and energy invested in complaining into a productive discussion about possibilities. If the issue is important to the complainer, he or she will be happy to make that switch. If the issue is unimportant, he or she will be motivated to move on to a more relevant topic. Reporter George Lewis reflects on his own experience by saying, "I'm still waiting for those negative thoughts to dry up. As of this writing, I've had eight relapses, with my longest complaint-free period lasting five days. I'm continuing the effort as I head off to Israel on assignment and will keep you posted if and when I make it to the twenty-one-day mark." Lewis's premise and goal is supported by Gene Bedley, who says, "Responsibility finds a way. Irresponsibility makes excuses." In fact, he says, those who blame or criticize may be revealing themselves to be the responsible parties. "The [person] who complains about the way the ball bounces," says football coach and announcer Lou Holtz, "is likely to be the one who dropped it."

As we take more responsibility, the obvious benefit is that complaining will slow down and eventually stop. The less obvious but even great benefit is that you will save time and will focus your thoughts and communications on positive topics and outcomes. The time spent complaining will become time spent achieving good things.

3. Eliminate Procrastination. Do it! Do it Right! Do it Right Now!
I'll Read This Section Later

Procrastination often occurs when you are up against a barrier. You can become "high-centered" and in need of help. When that happens, you need to talk to someone immediately who can help you back off the rock and get things going again. Saying "I'll do it tomorrow" can't be that bad, can it? Yes, it can. Procrastination can become a debilitating habit and must be avoided.

At the low end, your procrastination may seem like a simple inconvenience to those you affect. You'll get it done—just not right now. The problem is that procrastination is a breach of a commitment to act—a breach of trust. At the high end, procrastination could have a truly damaging effect. How many have put off a colonoscopy or even a dental checkup only to face greater difficulties as a result? Abraham Lincoln said it well: "You cannot escape the responsibility of tomorrow by evading it today."

Which of the Guiding Constants is affected by procrastination? All of them! Procrastination reduces trust and undermines character. When you procrastinate, you appear to be a person who is not choosing to do the best thing or what matters most. You may even be violating the Golden Rule—after all, you wouldn't want someone else to delay action on something important to you, would you? "Until you value yourself," says Scott Peck, "you will not value your time. Until you value your time, you will not do anything with it."

"But," the procrastinator will say, "I am not doing *nothing*—I'm simply going to do it later." To the person who is waiting for the commitment to be kept, that looks very much like nothing. Theodore Roosevelt said, "In a moment of decision the best thing to do is the right thing to do. The worst thing you can do is nothing." When you chronically procrastinate, you damage your character, sending a message that you can't be counted on. At its worst, procrastination could damage or destroy a relationship you intended to value but just didn't get around to. More than one person has said, "I wanted to tell him that I love him, but the accident took him from me before I could say it." Delaying action can have consequences for your life. You may delay a phone call, put off reroofing the house, fail to check the oil level in the car, forget to purchase a birthday card, wait to sell the car, or put off writing to a sick friend until it is too late. These decisions to procrastinate not only fail to avert a problem but they prevent an opportunity to do something good.

So what do you do when confronted with your own procrastination? Lee Iacocca had a great answer: "Anything. Something. So long as we just don't sit there. If we screw up, start over. Try something else. If we wait until we've satisfied all the uncertainties, it may be too late."

Is anyone perfect at avoiding procrastination? Of course not. Some of the most common causes of procrastination can be fairly easily managed. Eliminate bookmarks in your browser to news or other Internet sites that distract you. Turn off the notification that sounds whenever an e-mail hits your inbox. There are many other ways. As you discipline yourself to avoid distractions, you increase the time you can dedicate to achievement, thereby decreasing procrastination. As Olin Miller said, "If you want to make an easy job seem mighty hard, just keep putting off doing it."

To truly overcome procrastination, the first step is to understand the vision—begin by seeing yourself doing the job right, and right now. I like to envision myself with someone I've completed a task for and hearing them say, "I knew I could count on you" (even if those words come from your own lips after you finally complete a project you've been putting off).

4. Be Accountable to Principles and the Guiding Constants

Be loyal to principles and Guiding Constants; never be blindly loyal to individuals or organizations. When you are loyal to principles, it is much easier to not compromise.

What happens if someone asks you to do something that you know or feel is wrong? Simple: Be led by timeless Guiding Constants and principles.

One of the best examples of failing to stand up for principle occurred when Hitler and a small handful of misguided individuals ordered the extermination of the Jews. This atrocity and crime against humanity was finally stopped only because entire nations that were committed to freedom and liberty stood in his way in a war that eventually involved the entire world. Millions of unnecessary deaths—both among the Jews and the people who were engaged in war—occurred because of Hitler's unprincipled decisions. Just think of those around Hitler who might have stood up against these atrocities. There were alternatives.

People and organizations that stand up for correct principles and Constants, that do the right and best things, result in stronger individuals, stronger relationships, and stronger organizations. Einstein wrote, "Man must cease attributing his problems to his environment, and learn again to exercise his will, his personal responsibility."

A "Radio" Is Embraced in South Carolina

The coach at T. L. Hanna succeeded in turning a football team from a bunch of bullies into a group of mentors and friends to James Robert Kennedy, a disabled boy who became the best-known figure in South Carolina high school football history. As told in an article by *Sports Illustrated* writer

Gary Smith, the story of the boy who could barely talk—a boy with the nickname of "Radio"—is the story of a football coach who felt accountable to teach his team more than football.

The bullying inflicted by the team was serious. On one occasion team members insisted that Radio pull the fire alarm and then kept quiet as he was taken to jail. Another time, the boys pulled down Radio's pants and painted his backside with paint thinner, causing severe burns.

Gary Smith wrote, "When we speak of the power of sports today, it's always in terms of their grip on the national marketplace, their headlock on the American psyche. It's so easy to forget all about their other powers. Radio turned 50 two months ago, but you might not have read about it. He bounded through the corridors of T. L. Hanna High collecting his birthday gifts, waving and slapping fives and hugging kids and wiggling his rear end as the students chanted, 'Go, Radio, you got it!' It took the whole bed of head football coach Harold Jones's pickup truck to get all the gifts home, just as it has on the other birthdays and the Christmases that Radio has celebrated at the school for the last 32 years."

So what happened? It was simple, really. Radio was accepted by the coach—first as a manager, then as a mascot/manager—and, eventually, he was accepted by the entire team. A coach felt a twinge of responsibility and exemplified the caring and friendship a boy desperately needed. Eighty football players and a whole high school took the challenge to be accountable. Now the team and school have created a legacy of responsibility to do the best thing for more than thirty years.

"Radio never saw the inside of an institution. He became one instead." Just before his last birthday, recounts Smith, "folks in Anderson were remarking on all the speckles of white on his head and in his whiskers. 'When Radio dies, it'll be the biggest funeral in the history of Anderson,' said Herb Phillips, an assistant football coach at Hanna. 'It'll be like a senator's or a governor's funeral.'"

As is usually the case, this example of accountability became like a rock thrown into a pond; the ripples of good touched neighboring communities. As Smith recounted, "In just the small circle of schools against which Hanna competes, there is one-eyed and slow-witted Lonnie McGee racing onto the field with the football team at Greer High each Friday night, and before him there was Housecat, whose mission in life, until he died not so long ago, was to chase down every foul ball and home run hit at Greer games, even if he had to barge into someone's home to do so, and hurry that ball right back to the umpire. There is Marlee Gambrell, born with heart and hearing and vision defects, hooting 'Don't worry 'bout it!' in the darkest moments at Belton-Honea Path High. And up until recently, there was wild-eyed Doris, taking care of the water bottles and ringing that half-ton bell on the sidelines at Easley High. Thrilled, every one of them, to take on the title—team manager—that most teenagers smirk at."

Accountability—taking responsibility by choice—multiplied itself a thousand times as it always does when people do the best thing. Character and trust come from a genuine commitment to being accountable. George L. Bell said, "You can pretend to care, but you can't pretend to show up." The coaches at T. L. Hanna showed up and cared.

5. Utilize the Power of Relationship Agreements

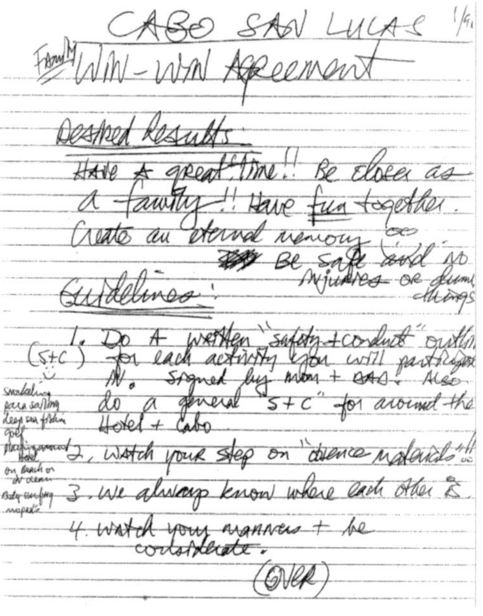

CABO SAN LUCAS 1/91

Family Win-Win Agreement

Desired Results:

Have a great time!! Be closer as a family!! Have fun together. Create an eternal memory. Be safe and no injuries or dumb things

Guidelines:

1. Do a written "safety + conduct" outline (S+C) for each activity you will participate in. Signed by Mom + Dad. Also do a general "S+C" for around the Hotel + Cabo
2. Watch your step on "dance materials"!!
3. We always know where each other is.
4. Watch your manners + be considerate.

(OVER)

When asking others to be accountable, make an agreement. Relationship agreements are known by a variety of names, including psychological contracts, social contracts, and win-win agreements; I like to call them relationship agreements. Regardless of what you call them, the principles that govern relationship agreements are similar. They provide clarity and empowerment that increase the likelihood of success. They embody the application of the Guiding Constants. They define what the supervisor, commander, or boss expects, but they also define what the person receiving the responsibility can expect from the manager.

What is a *relationship agreement*? A relationship agreement (RA) is a tool that can be used in any relationship, partnership, project, or responsibility to set clear expectations right from the beginning. The RA is used to establish the vision, goals, and objectives, which in turn lead to establishing accountability to the vision, plan, and principles.

The Shallenberger Win-Win Agreement in Cabo San Lucas

In January 1991, we held our annual company retreat in Cabo San Lucas, Mexico, and I brought three of our very active young teenage boys to the retreat. I realized that the next morning I would be in a three-hour company meeting while our boys were on the loose. I was seriously worried for them. I arose early and knew the answer was a relationship agreement—an agreement about how we would relate to each other and the environment that day. I sketched out the agreement, woke up the boys, and went over it with them. I informed them that they could not take in any activities until they had agreed and responded to our relationship agreement.

The purpose of this agreement was to ensure safety, security, and enjoyment for each family member. I needed the peace of mind of knowing that, as long as they followed the agreement, the boys would be okay. Making an agreement to follow rules that would result in a safer, more enjoyable vacation helped each family member understand and then commit to these rules.

We had a safe and fun vacation in Mexico. We didn't run over any locals or skin any noses by face-planting on the beach while boogey-boarding!

Another agreement, pictured here, proved incredibly valuable. In 1996, our son Steven wanted to become a pilot while he was still in high school. As his father, I wanted him to be successful but not only in his quest for his pilot's license. There were other characteristics and qualities (Guiding Constants) I wanted him to acquire; you'll see them detailed in this agreement. He made the agreement and succeeded; today he is an Air Force fighter pilot, so his dream was realized.

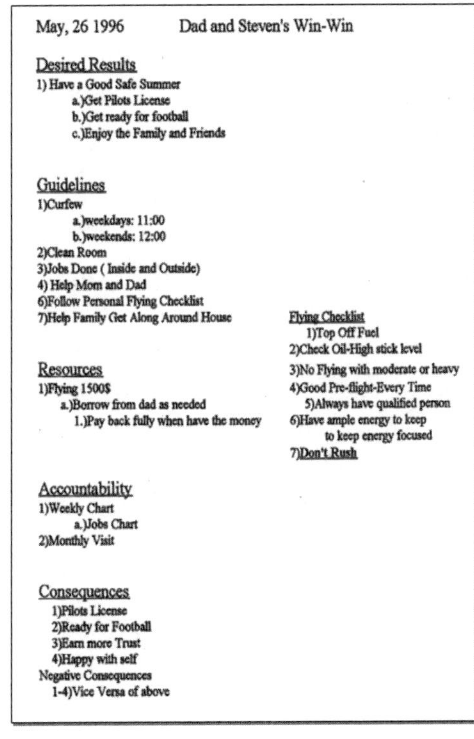
May, 26 1996 Dad and Steven's Win-Win

Desired Results
1) Have a Good Safe Summer
a.)Get Pilots License
b.)Get ready for football
c.)Enjoy the Family and Friends

Guidelines
1)Curfew
a.)weekdays: 11:00
b.)weekends: 12:00
2)Clean Room
3)Jobs Done (Inside and Outside)
4) Help Mom and Dad
6)Follow Personal Flying Checklist
7)Help Family Get Along Around House

Flying Checklist
1)Top Off Fuel
2)Check Oil-High stick level
3)No Flying with moderate or heavy
4)Good Pre-flight-Every Time
5)Always have qualified person
6)Have ample energy to keep
to keep energy focused
7)Don't Rush

Resources
1)Flying 1500$
a.)Borrow from dad as needed
1.)Pay back fully when have the money

Accountability
1)Weekly Chart
a.)Jobs Chart
2)Monthly Visit

Consequences
1)Pilots License
2)Ready for Football
3)Earn more Trust
4)Happy with self
Negative Consequences
1-4)Vice Versa of above

The "legacy" for me and Steven in our relationship agreement is that all aspects of the agreement were met. With the fulfilling of this and other agreements, Steven fulfilled his dream to be a fighter pilot, and I fulfilled my dream to see him become a responsible, contributing influence for good in the world.

6. Report Back on Your Assignment or Goals

The relationship agreement is about taking the initiative to track progress and report back on results, along with your plan of how to proceed in the future. Set an agreed-upon time to report back and maintain a high degree of accountability and communication.

In our company, we formally make and track agreements in this way, and we report on goals quarterly and annually. At each quarterly meeting with our board, our executives report how they did on their goals for the last quarter and what their plans are for the next quarter. The same routine takes place at our annual retreat, where the executives report on the previous year's goals and preview their plans for the coming year. We have consistently done this for thirty years, and it has helped our firm be one of the leading companies in our industry.

This ongoing program of "return and report" focuses on the progress toward our vision, goals, and objectives. It is accountability in action.

To return and report provides the mother or father, the supervisor or manager, the ability to track progress. It also provides the person who received the assignment the opportunity to show what has been accomplished. Nothing but good can result. Both sides should relish the opportunity to give and receive the progress report. "Return and report" provides the opportunity to find out what is working well and what needs additional attention as well as a review of resources and any need for more. Just the expectation that you will report your progress has a positive impact on performance.

Reporting on the completion of an agreement puts into play all of the Guiding Constants once again. Character is enhanced. Trust is extended and built up. All parties see and feel the effect of doing the best thing. There is a good feeling all around.

The "Be" in Be Accountable

We invite you now to "turn it up a notch" with Be Accountable. You may have already noticed that the title of this Guiding Constant includes the word *be*. To "be" is a state of being, an inner state of the self that is immovable and ever present. To be accountable is not only to "do" something—it is to "be" something, to be whole and balanced. It is to acquire, fully develop, and live the Thirteen Guiding Constants in a deep and meaningful pattern of living.

Don't Be Fooled

I've already emphasized that the Guiding Constants will work in your life with accountability and responsibility. Examine the examples below of people who took responsibility by living the Guiding Constants to the fullest. Note how what they did contributed significantly to others in almost every case.

Don't be fooled into thinking that these were exceptional people, notables who are so far ahead of you that you can't ever approach their achievements. Who was Galileo before he observed gravity? Who was Helen Keller before she broke through her anger and hopelessness to learn to speak and read Braille? Who were the four chaplains who courageously saved the lives of hundreds of soldiers before they surrendered their life jackets and went down with the *Dorcester*?

The "real" people living these Guiding Constants made a difference for themselves and those around them. Orville and Wilbur Wright operated a humble bicycle repair shop before showing us all that we could fly; Wally was nothing particularly exceptional before he became a wildly successful taxi driver; Angela Wolf rose out of blindness to become a public school teacher; Rosa Parks, a seamstress at the Montgomery Fair store, changed history; and the crew and support team of *Apollo 13* made themselves accountable to achieve the impossible.

These people were all "you" before they confronted their own character, decided to be accountable, and took responsibility. You can become your best by learning, internalizing, and living the Guiding Constants in your life. Truly, the best songs have not been written.

Take a moment to reflect on the Guiding Constants and the people who held themselves accountable, those who hoped for a better tomorrow as they worked to become their very best. Ponder what they did and who they were before and after. They are you and me.

As you move forward, applying the Guiding Constants, you will find that being accountable is the key that enables you to succeed in each. As you become accountable, you'll learn how it feels to effect lasting change . . . how it looks to take all the good in your life and make it the best. You too will fly on wings you never realized you had to achieve all you once thought impossible. You will, quite simply, become your best, and your journey will never again be the same.

INSPIRATIONAL QUOTES
Be Accountable

"Complaining is like bad breath; you notice it when it comes out of somebody else's mouth, but not your own."

— *Will Bowen*

"Nothing is so fatiguing as the eternal hanging on of an uncompleted task."

— *William James*

"Commitment is what transforms a promise into a reality. . . . Commitment is the stuff character is made of; the power to change the face of things. It is the daily triumph of integrity over skepticism."

— *Abraham Lincoln*

"If we screw up, start over. Try something else. If we wait until we've satisfied all the uncertainties, it may be too late."

— *Lee Iacocca*

"Freedom is the will to be responsible to ourselves."

— *Friedrich Nietzsche*

"At the end of the day we are accountable to ourselves—our success is a result of what we do."

— *Catherine Pulsifer*

"Responsibility is the price of greatness."

— *Sir Winston Churchill*

"I am free because I know that I alone am morally responsible for everything I do."

— *Robert Heinlein*

Application

Personal

1. Replace whining with gratitude, blaming with forgiveness and accepting responsibility, and procrastination with proactivity.

2. Join the war against mindless complaining.

3. Remember that accountability is an accumulation of the effect of each of the Guiding Constants in your life.

4. Accountability doesn't happen overnight, and no one is perfect, but as you strive to live each of the Guiding Constants and as you become accountable, you will improve in each of the most important qualities you can develop for your success and happiness. You will become your best.

With Others

1. Schedule a time to discuss the key parts of this chapter with individuals or a team in your organization.

2. Discuss your vision and goals with a trusted person in your organization or family.

3. With your team, choose a vision and goal regarding greater dependability and reliability for team members and team output.

4. Reflect together on how the process worked for you.

5. Discuss other areas where you can improve accountability.

Accountability is most often a team function made possible by personal commitments from each member of the team. Each person commits to accountability and each person engages. The resulting collaboration produces results.

In a Nutshell

1. Be accountable to timeless universal principles and the Guiding Constants.
2. Be principle-centered.
3. To be accountable is to be responsible.
4. To be accountable is to be worthy of trust.
5. Establish a norm of accountability and responsibility in your life, within your relationships, and in your leadership and management.
6. Refuse to blame, whine, or criticize. Take responsibility.
7. Accountability cannot exist without proper accounting practices; in other words, an absence of accounting means an absence of accountability.
8. What is your vision? What are your goals? What is your best? How do you measure the realization of your vision, your goals, and your best?
9. Accountability means to report on your progress. To whom do you report?
10. Counsel with others as you report your progress; evaluate how you can improve and move to the next step.
11. Your success or failure depends on you.

EPILOGUE

I HOPE YOU ENJOYED THE THIRTEEN GUIDING CONSTANTS and that you will see the end of this book as the beginning of your journey to Becoming Your Best.

One of my favorite quotes—another one by Ralph Waldo Emerson—tells us, "Sow a thought and you reap an action; sow an act and you reap a habit; sow a habit and you reap a character; sow a character and you reap a destiny."

Sowing the thoughts and actions of the Thirteen Guiding Constants literally does create a destiny for you and those with whom you associate.

Virtually every successful example of accomplishment or achievement throughout the history of the world, whether in a personal or professional setting, is accompanied by alignment with the Thirteen Guiding Constants. On the flip side, virtually every failure is a result of violation of the Constants.

Creating an environment where your thoughts can regularly be focused on the Thirteen Guiding Constants allows them to influence your actions, which ultimately allows them to be a powerful force of habit in your everyday life.

These habits then contribute to being a strong individual, having strong relationships, and being able to exercise strong leadership and management for good. This takes time, but the results will be sure and steady and will make a significance difference for good.

One of the most powerful examples of this in my lifetime is the creation of the Egyptian-Israeli Peace Accord that was forged by Anwar Sadat and Menachem Begin. This remarkable story is an example of complete alignment and active presence of the Thirteen Guiding Constants.

One Person Can Make a Difference; Two Together Can Make a Bigger Difference

Israel and Egypt were bitter enemies for thousands of years—and during much of that time they were literally at war. Who would think it possible that the people of these two countries—people full of hatred toward each other—could change enough to create an historic peace accord that would bring decades of peace, even respect, to their nations?

And who would think it possible that one person was the catalyst behind it all?

Could one person really make that much of a difference, especially in a situation of such massive proportion? Absolutely. In fact, one person living by the Thirteen Guiding Constants and understanding the principles of becoming your best made a huge difference in this case. That one person influenced another, and eventually two nations were at peace.

Anwar El Sadat—the third president of Egypt, who ruled from 1970 until his assassination in 1981—learned much of what he knew from Gamal Abdel Nasser, Egypt's second president, who ruled from 1956 until his death in 1970. Working with Nasser, Sadat learned the dangerous game of nation-building in a world of superpower rivalries.

Egypt eventually became the leading "nonaligned" country in the world—giving a voice, through Nasser, to the desires of undeveloped and postcolonial societies. Nasser was considered a hero because of his development and defense of the Suez Canal, but his prominence later suffered greatly as a result of the Six Day War. During the brief but intense conflict, the Israeli military completely destroyed the Egyptian air forces—which were mostly caught unaware on the ground—and swept through the Sinai Peninsula to the Suez Canal, routing the Egyptian army and killing at least three thousand soldiers. The devastation threatened to bankrupt the government. Nasser's abilities were eventually strained to their limit by internal squabbling among Arab nations and the growing Palestinian movement. Under the cumulative strain, Nasser collapsed and died on September 29, 1970.

As Nasser's successor, Sadat was completely unknown and untested. Over the next eleven years, however, Sadat demonstrated extraordinary leadership abilities. His first trial on the international scene came in the aftermath of the Six Day War when he openly offered the Israelis a peace treaty in exchange for the return of the Sinai lands taken in the attack.

As he assumed leadership of Egypt, domestic crisis and international intrigue plagued Sadat with seemingly insurmountable problems. The Egyptian economy continued to reel as a result of the war with Israel, and Egypt's relationship with the Soviet Union continued to deteriorate as the Soviets proved to be unreliable allies. When pressed for military support to replace resources lost to the devastation of the Six Day War, the Soviets simply ignored Sadat's requests. In a move characteristic of the boldness that soon became his trademark, Sadat expelled the Soviets. This grand gesture solidified internal Egyptian support at a time when the average Egyptian suffered greatly.

Behind the scenes, however, Sadat plotted to retake the Egyptian Sinai if the Israelis continued to refuse the Egyptian peace initiative. On October 6, 1973, Sadat struck. With exceptional military precision, the Egyptian army crossed the Suez back into the Sinai and began driving the Israeli army into the desert. Though short-lived, the attack created new momentum for peace both in Egypt and in Israel. These pressures coincided with continued domestic problems in Egypt.

Convinced that peace with Israel would reap an enormous "peace dividend," Sadat initiated his most important diplomatic ploy. In a 1977 speech to the Egyptian parliament, Sadat affirmed his willingness to go anywhere to negotiate peace with the Israelis. He affirmed that he would even go to the Israeli parliament to speak for peace. The Israelis responded with an invitation to do just that. Sadat's speech to the Knesset—Israel's national legislature—initiated a new momentum for peace that eventually culminated in the 1978 Camp David Accords and a final peace treaty with Israel in 1979.

For his efforts, Sadat won the Nobel Prize for Peace along with Israeli Prime Minister Menachem Begin.

Sadat's vision and determination impacted his former enemy. Almost overnight, Begin's public image—that of a seemingly irresponsible nationalist radical—was transformed to that of a statesman of historic proportions. That image was reinforced by international recognition, of course, when he was awarded the Nobel Peace Prize along with Sadat in 1978.

Despite fierce criticism of the peace treaty and blatant objection to it within Begin's own party, the treaty was ratified with an overwhelming majority in the Knesset. And even after violent clashes of soldiers during the forceful eviction of settlements in the Sinai, political support for the treaty did not diminish, and the Sinai was handed over to Egypt in 1982.

President Jimmy Carter shaking hands with Sadat and Begin at the signing of the Egyptian-Israeli Peace Treaty on the grounds of the White House, 1979.

Sadat demonstrated the strength to do what was best and to focus on what was most important even at the sacrifice of his own safety and well-being. At home in Egypt, the peace treaty with Israel and Sadat's new relationship with the West generated considerable domestic opposition, especially among fundamentalist Muslim groups. In 1980 and 1981, Sadat took desperate gambles in response to these new internal problems. Demonstrating the personal integrity to do the best thing, Sadat left a legacy of peace despite the difficult consequences: On October 6, 1981, Sadat died at the hands of fundamentalist assassins during a military review celebrating the 1973 Suez crossing.

These two countries have honored the agreement Sadat and Begin engineered for close to forty years. As long as the leaders and peoples of these nations are aligned with the Guiding Constants, they will have the capacity to preserve this peace. When they violate the principles and Constants, the peace will be threatened.

This is only one of countless inspiring examples that demonstrate the results of using correct principles in our lives.

Whether your challenge is maximizing what your best looks like or improving a relationship or leading a team of people or achieving peace in your state or nation after countless years of strife—IT IS POSSIBLE TO BE YOUR BEST IN MEETING THAT CHALLENGE.

This book is now played out in your life as you give seed to the powerful principles and Guiding Constants. Cultivate them, care for them, and they will be a mighty force for you in your life and the lives of many others.

I wish you well in that journey.

Steve Shallenberger

REFERENCES

All citations are given in order as they appear in the chapter.

Guiding Constant 1

1. The story of Gandhi and eating sugar: Craig Schindler and Gary Lapid, *The Great Turning* (Rochester, Vermont: Bear and Company, 1989) 121.
2. "Be the change in the world you want to see": Michael Potts, "Arun Gandhi Shares the Mahatma's Message," *India–West* 27, no. 13 (1 February 2002): A34; see also Carmella B'Hahn, "Be the Change You Wish to See: An Interview with Arun Gandhi," *Reclaiming Children and Youth* 10, no. 1 (Spring 2001): 6.
3. "Labor to keep alive in your breast that little spark of celestial fire, conscience," http://en.wikiquote.org/wiki/Conscience
4. Einstein quote on setting an example: Robert N. Lussier and Christopher F. Achua, *Leadership: Theory, Application & Skill Development* (Mason, OH: South-Western, Cengage Learning, 2007), 70.
5. Pineaar on Mandela: Francois Pienaar and Edward Griffiths, *Rainbow Warrior* (London: CollinsWillow, 1999).
6. Helen Keller quote on character: John C. Maxwell, *Beyond Talent: Become Someone Who Gets Extraordinary Results* (Nashville, TN: Thomas Nelson, 2011), 205.
7. Father to Laertes: *Hamlet*, Act 1, Scene 3, in *The Complete Works of Shakespeare* 11–12 (Philadelphia, PA: George Barrie and Sons, 1899), 166.
8. Quote by Polonius: *Hamlet*, Act 1, Scene 3, in Lewis M. Andrews, *To Thine Own Self Be True* (New York: Doubleday, 1989), 3.
9. Aristotle quote: Will Durant, *The Story of Philosophy* (Bremen, Germany: Erscheinungsort, 2012), 87.
10. O'Neill quote on Reagan: Stephen F. Knott and Jeffrey L. Chidester, *At Reagan's Side: Insiders' Recollections From Sacramento to the White House* (Lanham, MD: Rowman & Littlefield, 2009), 140.
11. Mathilda's "almost" lie: William H. Herndon and Jesse W. Wik, *Herndon's Lincoln* (Champaign, IL: University of Illinois Press, 2006), 34.
12. Reputation is the shadow: Abraham Lincoln, *Lincoln's Own Stories*, http://www.quotationspage.com/quotes/Abraham_Lincoln/
13. Strength of character quote: Henry Drummond, *famouspoetsandpoems.com/thematic_quotes/strength_quotes.html.*
14. John Wooden quote: Brian D. Biro and John Wooden, *Beyond Success: The 15 Secrets of Effective Leadership and Life* (New York: Penguin Putnam, 2001), 38.

15. "I think you're going to break the school record": Victor L. Brown, "Make Yourself an Honest Man," *Speeches* (Provo, UT: Brigham Young University, 1973).
16. Quote on character: Eugene Garver, *Aristotle's Rhetoric: An Art of Character* (Chicago: University of Chicago Press, 1994), 90.
17. N. Eldon Tanner story: Told by N. Eldon Tanner to a group that included Steven R. Shallenberger.
18. Henry Ford quote on experience: Carol Bettino, *Directions: Your Roadmap to Happiness* (Indianapolis: Dogear Publishing, 2009), 120.
19. Honor Code of the United States Air Force Academy: http://www.usafa.af.mil/information/factsheets/factsheet.asp?id=9427.
20. Jon M. Huntsman quote: Jon M. Huntsman, *Winners Never Cheat: Everyday Values We Learned as Children (But May Have Forgotten)* (Saddle River, NJ: Pearson Education/Prentice Hall, 2005), xii.
21. Good men finish first: Jon M. Huntsman, *Winners Never Cheat: Everyday Values We Learned as Children (But May Have Forgotten)* (Saddle River, NJ: Pearson Education/Prentice Hall, 2005). See also http://knowledge.wharton.upenn.edu/article.cfm?articleid=1207.
22. Ronald Reagan quote: Ronald Reagan, "Remarks on Signing the Intermediate-Range Nuclear Forces Treaty," December 8, 1987. *Encyclopedia of the Reagan-Bush Years,* 1996, ed. Peter B. Levy, (Greenwood Press, Westport, CT), 204.
23. George Washington's Rules of Civility: http://www.history.org/almanack/life/manners/rules2.cfm.
24. George Washington the most recognized leader: http://en.wikipedia.org/wiki/George_Washington.
25. George Washington was the unanimous choice as president: Joseph M. Bessette and John J. Pitney Jr., *American Government and Politics: Deliberation, Democracy and Citizenship* (Independence, KY: Wadsworth, Cengage Learning, 2011), 50.
26. Washington quote after Cornwallis surrender: Robert W. Lincoln, *Lives of the Presidents of the United States* (New York: Watson & Co., 1833), 45.
27. Washington story about punctuality: Robert Haven Schauffler, ed., *Washington's Birthday: Its History, Observance, Spirit and Significance* (Berkeley, CA: University of California Libraries, 1913), 240.
28. Washington's letter to his sister, Betty: Robert Haven Schauffler, ed., *Washington's Birthday: Its History, Observance, Spirit and Significance* (Berkeley, CA: University of California Libraries, 1913), 240.
29. Washington's incorruptible integrity: David Ramsay, *The Life of George Washington*, Chapter 13, Part 2: Reflections on Washington's Life and Death, http://www.earlyamerica.com/lives/gwlife/chapt13/indexb.html.
30. Washington quote on firmness and virtue: Jay A. Parry and Andrew M. Allison, *The Real George Washington* (Malta, ID: National Center for Constitutional Studies, 1991).
31. Washington quote on virtues eclipsed by vices: David Ramsay, *The Life of George Washington, Commander in Chief of the Armies of the Unite States of America* (New York, NY: Hopkins and Seymour, 1807), 331.
32. Washington forming soldiers of freemen: David Ramsay, *The Life of George Washington, Commander in Chief of the Armies of the Unite States of America*, http://www.earlyamerica.com/lives/gwlife/chapt13/indexb.html.

33. Washington's equanimity: David Ramsay, *The Life of George Washington, Commander in Chief of the Armies of the Unite States of America* (Washington: 1807), at http://www.earlyamerica.com/lives/gwlife/chapt13/indexb.html.
34. The patriotism of Washington: *The Life of George Washington, Commander in Chief of the Armies of the Unite States of America*, http://www.earlyamerica.com/lives/gwlife/chapt13/indexb.html.

Guiding Constant 2

1. Walt Disney's imagination: http://disney.go.com/disneyinsider/history
2. The greatest picture is not yet painted: Lincoln Steffens, *Bits and Pieces* (Virginia Beach, VA: Regent University School of Divinity: 1994), 17.
3. Bernard Baruch on Sir Isaac Newton's curiosity: Mike Hughes, *Lessons Are for Learning* (Stafford, U.K.: Network Education Press, 2000), 31.
4. Einstein quote on curiosity: Richard Alan Krieger, *Civilization's Quotations: Life's Ideal* (New York, NY: Algora Publishing, 2002), 139.
5. Number of inventions and patents: Thomas Alva Edison in *Movers & Shakers: The 100 Most Influential Figures in Modern Business* (New York: Basic Books, 2003), 169–171.
6. Edison's inquisitive childhood. Neil Baldwin, *Edison: Inventing the Century* (Chicago: University of Chicago Press, 2001); see also Matthew Josephson, *Edison* (New York: McGraw Hill, 1959).
7. "One of the best informed men in the world on scientific subjects."
8. Quote about Edison's deafness—http://www.u-s-history.com/pages/h1608.html.
9. Marie Curie's history: from http://inventors.about.com/library/inventors/blMarie-Curie.htm; see also http://departments.kings.edu/womens_history/mariecurie.html ; Susan Quinn, *Marie Curie: A Life* (New York: Perseus Publishing, 1996); Rosalyn Pflaum, *Grand Obsession—Madame Curie and Her World* (New York: Bantam, Dell, Doubleday, 1989).
10. De Bono's vertical thinking theories: Edward De Bono, *Lateral thinking: Creativity Step by Step* (New York: Harper & Row, 1970); Edward De Bono, *Serious Creativity: Using the Power of Lateral Thinking to Create New Ideas* (New York: Harper Business, 1992).
11. History and description of mind-mapping: http://www.mind-mapping.org/mind-mapping-and-you/basic-introduction-to-mindmapping.html.
12. Steven Boyley mind map: http://www.nlpmind.com/mind_mapping.htm (copyrighted).
13. Examples for the Use of Mind Mapping in Brainstorming: http://mindmapping-softwareblog.com/increase-the-visual-impact-of-your-mind-maps-with-images-and-color/.
14. Jennifer Goddard, Tree branch mind map: http://www.fuzz2buzz.com/en/mex/mind-map/software/66/laws-mind-mapping; http://www.fuzz2buzz.com/en/mind-stuff/product/how-mind-map-workbook-pa.

15. Mind map "Used to Capture and Present a Large Volume of Information in a Small Space": http://www.mindmapinspirataion.com; http://www.mindmapinspiration.com/wp-content/uploads/2009/05/the-qualities-of-leonardo-da-vinci-mindmap.jpg.
16. Mind map "Can be Used to Reinforce Behavior and Clarify Thinking" copyright Tony Buzan, www. mindmapart.com; http://www.mindmapinspiration.com/wp-content/uploads/2009/06/exercises-for-relaxation-mind-map-tony-buzan.jpg,
17. Mind map depicting the Process Used to Think About Ways to Market: http://www.mymindmap.net/images/Mind_Map_Template_Mulit_Rnd_small.jpg.
18. Mind map "Notice Bored": http://www.iso27001security.com./html/27002.html; media located at http://www.iso27001security.com./assets/images/ISO_27002_mind_map_780.gif.
19. Story of August Kekulé: Allan J. Rocke, *Image and Reality—Kekule, Kopp and the Scientific Imagination* (Chicago: The University of Chicago Press, 2010).
20. The account of a carbonized bamboo filament: http://www.creativity-portal.com/articles/michael-michalko/creative-thinking-habits-thomas-edison2.html.
21. Graham Wallas, *The Art of Thought* (New York: Harcourt, Brace and Co, 1926).
22. Da Vinci's journals and sketches, media locations: http://img.artknowledgenews.com/files2008/LeonardoDaVinciPenAndInk.jpg; http://www.zenker.se/Surprise/da_vinci.jpg; see also http://content.answcdn.com/main/content/img/oxford/Oxford_Body/019852403x.leonardo-da-vinci.2.jpg; http://2.bp.blogspot.com/_xCykdpQhXe8/TFL4qlDPuRI/AAAAAAAAM0Y/_DIPVkTEZa8/s1600/leonardo-da-vinci-+helicopter+screw+concept.jpg; http://www.dailygalaxy.com/photos/uncategorized/2008/04/28/vinciwdm2704_468x459_2.jpg.
23. Michael Kanin captures the agony and ecstasy of the writing dilemma beautifully in this poem: *Of forty-odd years in this noble profession / I've harbored a guilt and my conscience is smitten./ So here is my slightly embarrassed confession – / I don't like to write, but I love to have written.* In Lilless McPherson Shilling and Linda K. Fuller, *The Dictionary of Quotations in Communications* (Westport, CT: Greenwood Press, 1997), 264.
24. Harriet Beecher Stowe quote: Sophy Burnham, *http://www.shannonwoodward.com/quotes.html.*
25. Talmud quote: Frank L. Battisti, *On Becoming a Conductor: Lessons and Meditations on the Art of Conducting* (Meredith Music Publications, 2007), 137.
26. Discovery quote: Patti Garrett Shade and Richard Shade, *Curiosita Teaching: Integrating Creative Thinking into Your 21st Century Classroom* (Saline, MI: McNaughton & Gunn, 2011), 173.
27. Napoleon Hill's expression on the fruits of adversity: http://personalexcellence.co/blog/101-most-inspiring-quotes-part-2/ Quote 43.
28. Thomas Edison's quote about capability: John C. Maxwell, *Talent is Never Enough: Discover the Choices that Will Take You* (Nashville, TN: Thomas Nelson, 2007), 16.

Guiding Constant 3

1. Man's flight through life: Robert Kennedy, *Of Knowledge and Power: The Complexities of National Intelligence* (Westport, CT: Greenwood, Publishing Group, 2008), 7.
2. Jack Canfield quote: Steven D. Price, *The Quotable Billionaire: Advice and Reflections from and for the Real, Former, Almost, and Wanna-Be Super-Rich* (New York: Skyhorse Publishing, 2009), 121.
3. Anne Sullivan quote: Helen Keller and James Berger, *The Story Of My Life: The Restored Edition* (New York: Random House, 2004), 226.
4. Ben Carson quotes and history: Ben Carson, *Gifted Hands: The Ben Carson Story* (Grand Rapids, MI: First Sondervan, 1990).
5. Photo of Ben Carson: http://www.biography.com/imported/images/Biography/Images/Profiles/C/Ben-Carson-475422-1-402.jpg.
6. Maria Mitchell quote: Jason A. Merchey, *Building a Life of Value: Timeless Wisdom to Inspire and Empower Us* (Beverly Hills, CA: Little Moose Press, 2005), 8.
7. *U.S. News* ranking of best hospitals places Johns-Hopkins at #3 for 2011–2012.
8. Zambia story: http://www.usaid.gov/stories/zambia/fp_zm_frederick.pdf; see also http://allafrica.com/stories/201108310367.html.
9. Socrates story about knowledge: M. Littleton, *Moody Monthly* (June 1989), 29.
10. Deepak Chopra quote: Deepak Chopra, *The Spontaneous Fulfillment of Desire: Harnessing the Infinite Power of Coincidence* (New York: Crown Publishing, 2003), 84.
11. Dieter Uchtdorf story about learning: Dieter F. Uchtdorf, "Two Principles for Any Economy," *Liahona*, Nov. 2009, 55–58.
12. J.K. Rowling speaking through Albus Dumbledore: Colon Duriez, *Field Guide to Harry Potter* (Downers Grove, IL: InterVarsity Press, 2007), 133.
13. "A continuous process" quote: http://www.ncbi.nlm.nih.gov/pubmed/10264266.
14. Sullenberger information : http://topics.nytimes.com/top/reference/timestopics/subjects/a/airplane_accidents_and_incidents/us_airways_flight_1549/index.html.
15. Sullenberger image: http://news.uns.purdue.edu/images/2010/sullenberger-hudson.jpg Accessed at Purdue University News Service http://www.purdue.edu/newsroom/events/2010/100902CordovaSullenberger.html.
16. Thoreau quote: Larry Chang, *Wisdom for the Soul: Five Millennia of Prescriptions for Spiritual Healing* (Washington, DC: Gnosophia, 2006), 349.
17. Edison invents the carbon filament: Marc Rothenberg, *The History of Science in the United States— An Encyclopedia* (Garland, NY: Smithsonian Institution, 2001).
18. Edison's drawing of his patented carbon filament: http://www.invention-protection.com/pdf_patents/pat223898.pdf.
19. Orville and Wilbur Wright quote: http://www.searchquotes.com/search/Wilbur%20-Wright/.
20. Orville and Wilbur Wright photos: http://cache2.artprintimages.com/lrg/26/2693/EBTUD00Z.jpg.
21. Breakfast of Champions graphic: http://www.wheaties.com/.
22. Michael Gelb champions quote: ttp://thinkexist.com/quotation/champions_know_that_success_is_inevitable-that/262103.html.

23. Quote from *In Search of Excellence:* http://www.tompeters.com/dispatches/008106.php.
24. Continue-Start-Stop survey method: Original source not known.
25. Survey methods and applications referenced: http://www.surveymonkey.com/; http://www.surveygizmo.com/; http://www.zoomerang.com; http://www.qualtrics.com/ Survey software application; http://www.checkbox.com/ Survey Software application.
26. Air brake: The air brake was invented by George Westinghouse in 1869 (US patent No. 88929).
27. M. Russell Ballard, "Let Us Think Straight," *Speeches* (Provo, UT: Intellectual Reserve, Inc., 1983), http://speeches.byu.edu/reader/reader.php?id=6892.
28. "A little learning is a dang'rous thing": Quoted in Francis Bacon, *The Advancement of Learning*, Vol. 1 (London: Macmillan, 1905), 140.
29. Quote on danger: Bill Swainson, *Encarta Book of Quotations* (2000), 461.
30. "Sloppy, inconclusive thinking": Lord Thomson of Fleet, *After I Was Sixty* (London: Hamis Hamilton, 1975), 106.
31. Quote on common sense: http://www.firstbiz.com/manthe01.htm Also attributed to Lord Chesterfield.
32. "Failure is instructive" quote: Neil J. Salkind, *Encyclopedia of Educational Psychology*, Vol. 1 (Thousand Oaks, CA: Sage Publications, 2008), 393.
33. Ballard quote: M. Russell Ballard, "Let Us Think Straight," *Speeches* (Provo, UT: Intellectual Reserve, Inc., 1983); http://speeches.byu.edu/reader/reader.php?id=6892.
34. Quote on pursuing intellectual interests: Tom D. Crouch, *The Wright Brothers in Wings: A History of Aviation from Kites to the Space Age* (Garland, NY: Smithsonian Institution, 2004), 56.

Guiding Constant 4

1. Photo of Churchill surveying bombing of London: http://static.bbc.co.uk/history/img/ic/640/images/resources/events/germany_bombs_london.jpg.
2. Martin Gilbert, *Churchill and America* (New York, NY: Free Press, 2008), 44.
3. Goethe quote on "Magic is believing in yourself": Jack Reigle, *Silver Bullets: Strategic Intelligence for Better Design Firm Management* (Minneapolis, MN: Bascomb Hill, 2008), 21.
4. J.K. Rowling quotes and story: http://www.facebook.com/pages/J-K-Rowling/106783881197?v=info.
5. Glen Cunningham story: http://en.wikipedia.org/wiki/Glenn_Cunningham_%28athlete%29.
6. Roger Bannister record: http://en.wikipedia.org/wiki/Roger_Bannister.
7. Happiness quote (Anonymous): Ward A. Wilson, *Words for Thought* (Bloomington, IN: Xilibris, 2009), 279.
8. *New Yorker* cartoon: http://1.bp.blogspot.com/_s57ISZAyJXI/R984p2JQUAI/AAAAAAAAAvg/Ey1ZXGeQHB4/s400/Dana+Fradon+1+May+1965+tragedy+comedy+pair.jpg.

9. Patton quote on accepting challenges: Chris Davies, George S. Patton *Winning Client Trust* (Birmingham, UK: Academy Press, 2011), 25.
10. Barton quote: John Maxwell, *Becoming a Person of Influence* (Nashville, TN: Thomas Nelson, 2006), 67.
11. 2008 economic collapse: http://money.cnn.com/2008/12/01/news/economy/recession/index.htm.
12. Wendy Wasserstein quote: Randy Howe, *Here We Stand: 600 Inspiring Messages from the World's Best* (Guildford, CT: Lyons Press/Globe Pequot Press, 2009), 29.
13. Lincoln political record: www.des.emory.edu/mfp/efficacynotgiveup.html.
14. Lincoln letter to John T. Stuart: Doris Kearns Goodwin, *Team of Rivals: The Political Genius of Abraham Lincoln* (New York: Simon and Schuster, 2005), 99.
15. Michael Jordan quote on persistence: M.J. Ryan, *This Year I Will: How to Finally Change a Habit* (New York: Broadway Books/Random House, 2006), 63.
16. Sound character quote: Og Mandino, *Greatest Salesman in the World, Part II: The End of the Story* (New York: Bantam Books, 1989), http://www.quora.com/Self-Improvement/How-do-you-get-over-the-shame-of-failure.
17. John Keates quote: Larry Chang, *Wisdom for the Soul: Five Millennia of Prescriptions for Spiritual Healing* (Washington, DC: Gnosophia Publishers, 2006), 292.
18. John Abbot poem: Jacob Morton Braude, *Lifetime Speaker's Encyclopedia*, Vol. 1 (New York: Prentice-Hall, 1962), 531.
19. Proverb: May have originated with original Persian Sufi poets.
20. Greatest discovery of our generation: Douglas McGregor, *The Human Side of Enterprise* (New York: McGraw-Hill, 2006), xliv.
21. Edison quote about fire in lab: Jack Canfield and Mark V. Hansen, *A 3rd Serving of Chicken Soup for the Soul—101 More Stories* (Deerfield Beach, FL: Health Communications, 1996), 235.
22. Roosevelt quote: Pamela Levin, *Cycles of Power: A User's Guide to the Seven Seasons of Life* (Ukiah, CA: Nourishing Company, 2007), 24.
23. History of Mary Kay Cosmetics: Mary Kay Ash and Yvonne Pendleton, *The Mary Kay Way: Timeless Principles from America's Greatest* (Hoboken, NJ: John Wiley & Sons, 2008).
24. Thoreau quote on enduring toil: J. North Conway, *The Cape Cod Canal: Breaking Through the Bared and Bended Arm* (Charleston, SC: The History Press, 2008), 74.
25. Walter Anderson quote: *Ron Karr, Lead, Sell, or Get Out of the Way: The 7 Traits of Great Sellers* (Hoboken, NJ: John Wiley & Sons, 2009), 217.
26. Quote from *Titanic* survivor: No reference found.
27. Og Mandino quote on persistence: Og Mandino, *The Greatest Salesman in the World* (Hollywood, FL: Bantam, 1983), 64.
28. Dr. Seuss quote: R. A. Wise, *Wise Quotes of Wisdom* (Bloomington, IN: AuthorHouse, 2011), 274.
29. The Little Engine that Could: Estelle Avery Sharpe, *Foundation Stones of Success* (1910), 24.
30. Anne Sullivan information: Helen Keller, *Teacher Anne Sullivan: A Tribute by the Foster-Child of Her Mind* (Westport, CT: Greenwood Press Publishers, 1985).

Guiding Constant 5

1. The old monk and the warrior: Jack Canfield and Mark Victor Hansen, *Condensed Chicken Soup for the Soul* (Deerfield Beach, FL: Health Communications, Inc., 1996), 100.
2. Dali Lama quote: Dali Lama, *My Tibet, Text by His Holiness the Fourteenth Dali Lama of Tibet* (Berkeley, CA: University of California Press, 1995), 54.
3. Victor Frankl also said, "Indeed, the major obstacle to you achieving the outcomes that you hope for in life are your thoughts." *Man's Search for Meaning* (Boston, MA: Beacon Press).
4. Dali Lama quote on changing our thoughts: http://www.dalailama.com.
5. Napoleon Hill quote on the mind: Napoleon Hill and W. Clement Stone, *Success through a Positive Attitude* (New York: Prentice-Hall, 1987), 74.
6. Napoleon Hill, "Whatever the mind can conceive and believe, it can achieve": http://www.youtube.com/watch?v=2hA-7aq6OXI.
7. Gandhi teaching that "Man always becomes what he believes himself to be": Richard L. Deats and Mary Jegen, *Mahatma Gandhi, Nonviolent Liberator: A Biography* (New York: New City Press, 2005), 108.
8. Zig Ziglar quote: Dan Spainhour, *Coach Yourself: A Motivational Guide for Coaches and Leaders* (Winston-Salem, NC: Educational Coaching and Business Communications, 2007), 174.
9. Einstein quote: Conrad P. Pritscher, *Einstein & Zen: Learning to Learn* (New York, NY: Peter Lang Publishing, 2010), 17.
10. Socrates "unexamined life" quote: Thomas C. Brickhouse and Nicholas D. Smith, *Plato's Socrates* (Oxford, UK: Oxford University Press), 201.
11. Laughter is the best medicine: http://www.umm.edu/features/laughter.htm.
12. Reference: R. Morgan Griffen, "Give Your Body a Boost—With Laughter," http://women.webmd.com/guide/give-your-body-boost-with-laughter.
13. Johns Hopkins study: Ronald A. Berk, "Student Ratings of 10 Strategies for Using Humor in College Teaching," *Journal on Excellence in College Teaching* 7, no. 3 (1996): 71–92.
14. Benefits of patience: http://ezinearticles.com/?Benefits-of-Patience&id=496228.
15. Quote, "O Lord, please give me the patience I need, and do hurry up about it.": Perry Sproat, *Please Don't Shoot Me!* (Fairfax, VA: Xulon Press), 42.
16. Sir Isaac Newton quote on patience: Troy Edwards, *A Dictionary of Thoughts: Being a Cyclopedia of Laconic Quotations* (Detroit: F. D. Dickson Co., 1908), 120.
17. Benjamin Franklin quote on patience: Roy B. Zuck, *The Speaker's Quote Book* (Grand Rapids, MI: Kregel Publications, 2009), 375.
18. Invictus: Arthur Thomas Quiller-Couch, Arthur Thomas, ed., *The Oxford Book of English Verse, 1250–1900*, 6th impression (Oxford: Clarendon Press, 1902), 1019.
19. Sri Chinmoy quote on patience and peace: www. srichinmoylibrary.com/books.
20. Mr. Potts and Washington at Valley Forge: *The Diary and Remembrances of Rev. Nathaniel Randolph Snowden, a Presbyterian Minister and a Princeton Graduate* (original manuscript at the Historical Society of Pennsylvania; Call no. PHi. Am.1561–1568).

21. Washington kneeling in prayer: http://www.ushistory.org/valleyforge/washington/prayer.html Washington in Prayer.
22. Prayer at Valley Forge: http://www.ushistory.org/valleyforge/washington/prayer.html
23. Lincoln praying for help in battle: Don E. Gehrengacher and Virginia Fehrenbacher, comp. and eds., *Recollected Words of Abraham Lincoln* (Palo Alto, CA: Stanford University Press), 406.
24. Lincoln's calm and peace at Gettysburg: William E. Barton, *The Soul of Abraham Lincoln* (University of Illinois Press, 2005), 201–202.

Guiding Constant 6

1. Tennyson quote: A. T. Tennyson and A. Roberts, *Alfred Tennyson. The Oxford Authors* (Oxford: Oxford University Press, 2000), 567.
2. Map of Puerto Monte, Chile: http://www.southernchileproperties.com/images/Map-Puerto-Montt-area-thumbnail.jpg.
3. The Golden Maxim: Harry J. Gensler, *Confucius, Formal Ethics* (London: Routledge Publishers, 1996), 97.
4. The Law of Success: http://www.matthewabaker.com/lesson16.pdf.
5. Quote on committing the Golden Rule to memory: George Karkanis, *Edward Markham: Thoughts for Meaningful Life* (Bloomington, IN: AuthorHouse, 2009), 269.
6. Story of Abram and Simri: *Poems by Clarence Cook* (1902), 6–9.
7. Quote about wishing for his brother what he wishes for himself: Jeffrey Wattles, *The Golden Rule* (Oxford: Oxford University Press, 1996), 4.
8. "All things are our relatives": http://peaceseeds.elysiumgates.com/.
9. Kennedy quote on drinking from a separate fountain: http://www.presidency.ucsb.edu/ws/index.php?pid=9271&st=&st1=#axzz1mbAoR9US.
10. Mahatma Gandhi message: Michel W. Potts, *India—West* 27, no. 13 (2002), 34.
11. Gordon B. Hinckley quote: http://www.lds.org/ensign/1991/12/do-ye-even-so-to-them?lang=eng&query=woman+chicago+airport.
12. Western Oregon sportsmanship: http://www.youtube.com/watch?v=jocw-oD2pgo; also found at http://www.usatoday.com/sports/college/2008-05-01-softball-sportsmanship_N.htm.
13. Photo of Central Washington players carrying injured Western Oregon player: http://i.usatoday.net/sports/_photos/2008/05/01/softballx.jpg.
14. Tennyson quote on newer world: Christopher B. Ricks, *Tennyson in Ulysses: Tennyson* (Berkeley, CA: University of California Press, 1989), 116.
15. Choosing civility: P. M. Forni, *The Twenty-Five Rules of Considerate Conduct* (New York: St. Martin's Press, 2002), 6.
16. Sage quote: *Tao Teh Ching*, chapter 49, Taoism. Willis Moody, *Igniting Purpose: A Spiritual Approach to Spirituality Education* (Bloomington, IN: Xilibris), 32.
17. Jewish Rabbi talking with God: http://www.story-lovers.com/listsheavenandhell.html.
18. George Washington's Rules of Civility: Frank E. Grizzard, *George Washington: A Biographical Companion* (Santa Barbara, CA: ABC-CLIO, 2002), 363.

19. Image of Good Samaritan: http://www.biblical-art.com/artwork.asp?id_artwork=24131&showmode=Full.
20. "Be the change in the world you want to see": Michael Potts, "Arun Gandhi Shares the Mahatma's Message," *India–West* 27, no. 13 (1 February 2002): A34; see also Carmella B'Hahn, "Be the Change You Wish to See: An Interview with Arun Gandhi," *Reclaiming Children and Youth* 10, no. 1 (Spring 2001): 6.
21. Napoleon Hill quote: *The Law of Success: In Sixteen Lessons* (1928): see also *Abundance Prosperity* (2006), 6; e-book.
22. Scene in police court: *"Heart Throbs in Prose and Verse Dear to the American People"—A Story Contest Initiated by the* National Magazine *in 1904* (New York: Grosset & Dunlap), 336.
23. Frankl quote: In Richard L. Daft, Patricia G. Lane, *The Leadership Experience* (Mason, OH: Thompson-Southwestern, 2008), 171.
24. Harry J. Gensler on the Golden Rule: http://www.jcu.edu/philosophy/gensler/gold-rule.htm.
25. Rae Wilson's story of serving the troops in North Platte, Nebraska: Bob Greene, *Once upon a Town: The Miracle of the North Platte Canteen* (New York: HarperCollins, 2003).

Guiding Constant 7

1. The story of the *Apollo 12* mission: http://www.designfrontier.net/articles/ Quoted here with permission.
2. Photo of *Saturn 5* lifting off: http://images.ksc.nasa.gov/photos/1969/medium/KSC-69PC-0669.jpg.
3. Photo of Lake Powell: http://thundafunda.com/3993/?level=picture&id=2632 free online pictures.
4. Satellite photo of Lake Bolta: http://infranetlab.org/blog/wp-content/uploads/2009/12/Lake_Volta-505x505.jpg.
5. Emotional bank account metaphor: Steven R. Covey, *Seven Habits of Highly Effective People—Personal Workbook* (New York: Simon and Schuster, 2004), 84.
6. Putting trust in nobility of character: Stephen J. Carroll and Patrick C. Flood, *The Persuasive Leader: Lessons from the Arts* (New York: John Wiley and Sons, 2011), 165.
7. George Washington quote on character: Morton J. Frisch and Richard G. Stevens, *American Political Thought: The Philosophic Dimension of America* (Piscataway, NJ: Transaction Publishers, 2011), 27.
8. Alfred Adler quote: Wendy Toliver, *Little Giant Encyclopedia of Inspirational Quotes* (New York: Sterling Publishing Co., 2005), 430.
9. David Armistead quote on trust: Stephen M. R. Covey, Greg Link, and Rebecca R. Merrill, *Smart Trust: Creating Prosperity, Energy, and Joy in a Low-Trust World* (New York: Free Press, 2012), 210.
10. George Macdonald quote on trust: Megan Tschannen-Moran, *The Jossey-Bass Reader on Educational Leadership* (San Francisco: John Wiley and Sons, 2006), 99.

11. George Washington quote: Roy B. Zook, *The Speaker's Quote Book* (Grand Rapids, MI: Kregel Publications, 2009), 259.
12. Solon quote: Eugene Ehrlich and Marshal De Bruhl, *The International Thesaurus of Quotations* (New York: Harper Collins, 1996), 466.
13. Maly Vue quote on trust: http://www.academicintegrity.org/fundamental_values_project/quotes_on_trust.php.
14. Henry David Thoreau quote: Henry David Thoreau and Jeffrey S. Cramer, *Walden: A Fully Annotated Edition* (London: Yale University, 2004), 10.
15. Alan Bean quote: http://rfisher.com/viewpoints_leaderdevnorgchg.htm.
16. Seth Godin blog: http://sethgodin.typepad.com/seths_blog/2007/02/apologies_ranke.html.
17. "We treat people right" quote: http://www.synergycompanies.org/index.php?option=com_content&view=article&id=112&Itemid=100.
18. Dan Rather and CBS news slip up regarding George Bush: http://www.cbsnews.com/stories/2004/09/08/60II/main641984.shtml.
19. *Huffington Post* review of Dan Rather story: http://www.huffingtonpost.com/jackson-williams/dan-rather-wins-big-round_b_242503.html.
20. Stephen M. R. Covey, Rebecca R. Merrill, and Stephen R. Covey *Trust list: Speed of Trust* (New York: Free Press, 2006), 136.
21. Ralph Waldo Emerson quote: Ralph Waldo Emerson and Barry Maxwell Andrews, *A Dream Too Wild: Emerson Meditations for Every Day of the Year* (Boston: Skinner House Books, 2004), 26.
22. "What I Believe" quote: Essays by Bertrand Russell (1925) and E. M. Forster (1938), respectively, first published in *The Nation* on July 16, 1938.
23. Christofferson on business partnership breakup story: http://www.lds.org/general-conference/2010/10/reflections-on-a-consecrated-life?lang=eng.

Guiding Constant 8

1. McCloskey quote: Ralph Keyes, *The Quote Verifier: Who Said What, Where, and When* (New York: St. Martin's Press, 2006), 233.
2. Albert Einstein quote: Eytan Bentsur, *Making Peace: A First-hand Account of the Arab-Israeli Peace Process* (Westport, CT: Praeger Publishers, 2001), 211.
3. Churchill quote: Richard Langworth, *Churchill by Himself: The Definitive Collection of Quotations* (New York: Ebury Press, Random House, 2008), 572.
4. Thomas Jefferson quote about anger and counting to one hundred: Richard A. Singer Jr., *Your Daily Walk with the Great Minds: Wisdom and Enlightenment* (Ann Arbor, MI: Loving Healing Press, 2006), 21.
5. Lincoln's attributes as a listener: William E. Doster, *Lincoln and the Episodes of the Civil War* (New York: G. P. Putnam's Sons, 1915), 17.
6. Woodrow Wilson on listening: George Manning and Kent Curtis, *The Art of Leadership* (New York: McGraw Hill, 2002), 23.
7. Dyer quote: Dan Spainhour, *Coach Yourself: A Motivational Guide for Coaches and Leaders* (Winston-Salem, NC: Education Coaching, 2007), 100.

8. Albert Einstein quote: Rosemarie Jarski , *Words from the Wise: Over 6,000 of the Smartest Things Ever Said* (New York: Skyhorse Publishing, 2007), 515.
9. Albert Einstein quote on keeping your mouth shut: Richard S. Zera, *Business Wit & Wisdom* (Washington, DC: Beard Books, 2005), 252.
10. Pat Bregman's blog: http://blogs.hbr.org/bregman/2010/06/a-ritual-to-help-you-keep-your.html.
11. Herbert Hoover quote on patience: Robert J. Dole, *Great Presidential Wit: I Wish I Was in This Book* (New York: Scribner, 2001), 106.
12. Edward H. Richards quote on the wise old owl: Terrence L Gargiulo, *Stories at Work: Using Stories to Improve Communication and Build Relationships* (Westport, CT: Praeger Publishers, 2006), 32.
13. Bergman's suggestion: Harvard Business Review Blog, http://blogs.hbr.org/bregman/2010/06/a-ritual-to-help-you-keep-your.html.
14. Stephen Levine quote: Peter H. Cole and Daisy Reese, *True Self, True Wealth: A Pathway to Prosperity* (New York: Atria Books/Simon & Schuster, 2007), 71.
15. Edward Everett "Half of the people" quote: Zig Ziglar, *Staying Up, Up, Up in a Down, Down World* (Nashville, TN: Thomas Nelson, Inc., 2000), 174.
16. Gordon B. Hinckley quote about quarreling: *Ensign,* Nov. 2007.
17. Charles W. Penrose poem: George D. Pyper, *Stories of Latter-Day Saint Hymns: Their Authors and Composers* (Salt Lake City, UT: Deseret News Press, 2004), 157.
18. Karl Menninger Lee quote on listening: Mary Cox Garner*, Hidden Souls of Words: Keys to Transformation Through the Power of Words* (New York: Select Books, 2004), 30.
19. Margo Kaufman quote: Lies Wiehl and Bruce Littlefield, *The Truth Advantage: The 7 Keys to a Happy and Fulfilling Life* (Hoboken, NJ: John Wiley & Sons, 2012).
20. Sue Patton Thoele quote: *The Art of Convening: Authentic Engagement in Meetings, Gatherings, and Conversations* (San Francisco: Barrett-Koehler Publishers, 2011), 95.
21. M. Scott Peck quote: M. Scott Peck, *The Road Less Traveled, Timeless Edition: A New Psychology of Love, Traditional Values and Spiritual Growth* (New York: Touchstone, 2012), 125.
22. Human icons from iStock photo, Stock vector, File #: 9474442.
23. Thomas Gordon story: http://www.gordontraining.com/Hearing_vs_Listening.html
24. Buck Woody quote: http://blogs.msdn.com/b/buckwoody/archive/2010/06/02/seek-first-to-understand-then-to-be-understood.aspx.
25. Baby Blues cartoon: http://www.babyblues.com/.
26. Distracting: Thomas Gordon, *Leader Effectiveness Training* (New York: Bantam Books, 1980.
27. Max DePree quote: Gill Robinson Hickman, *Leading Organizations: Perspectives for a New Era* (Thousand Oaks, CA: Sage Publications, 1998), 132.
28. Kay Lindahl quote: Kay Lindahl, *Practicing the Sacred Art of Listening, Accessed: A Guide to Enrich Your Relationships and Kindle Your Spiritual Life* (Woodstock, VT: Skylight Paths Publishing, 2003), 2.
29. The talking stick legend as told by Carol Locust: www.acaciart.com/stories/tkstick.jpg.

Guiding Constant 9

1. Helen Keller quote: David Allen, *Ready for Anything: 52 Productivity Principles for Work and Life* (New York: Simon & Schuster, 2003), 233.
2. "Fateful rendezvous": Steve Ewing and John B. Lundstrom, *Fateful Rendezvous: The Life of Butch O'Hare* (Annapolis, MD: Naval Institute Press, 1997).
3. Einstein quote on doing the best: Rosalene Glickman, *Optimal Thinking: How to Be Your Best Self* (Hoboken, NJ: John Wiley and Sons, 2002), 14.
4. Harvey McKay story: Ken Blanchard and Barbara Glanz, *The Simple Truths of Service* (Simple Truths, LLC, 2005), 41.
5. Jerry Garcia quote on being the best: Thomas J. Peters, *The Little Big Things: 163 Ways to Pursue Excellence* (New York: HarperBusiness, 2012), 443.
6. Zig Ziglar quote on duty: Zig Ziglar, *You at the Top* (Gretna, LA: Pelican Publishing, 2005), 139.
7. Helen Keller quote on good news: Eden Maxwell , *An Artist Empowered* (Fair Lawn, NJ: Eden Maxwell, 2007), 24.
8. Johnny the bagger story: Ken Blanchard and Barbara Glanz, *The Simple Truths of Service* (Simple Truths, LLC, 2005), 21.
9. Dallin H. Oaks quote: http://www.lds.org/ensign/2007/11/good-better-best?lang=eng.
10. St. Jerome quote: L. Suganthi and Anand A. Samuel, *Top Quality Management* (Prentice Hall, India), 356.
11. David Elkind on over programming our children: David Elkind, *The Hurried Child* (Cambridge, MA: Perseus Publishing, 2001), 61.
12. James Allen quote: James Allen, *Mind is the Master: The Complete James Allen Treasury—Morning and Evening Thoughts* (New York: Penguin Group, 2010), 61.
13. The Common Denominator of Success: http://www.scribd.com/doc/81446522/The-Common-Denominator-of-Success.
14. Richard Bach quote: Joyce Chapman and Bernard Gunther, *Live Your Dream: Discover and Achieve Your Life's Purpose* (Franklin Lakes, NJ: The Career Press, 2002), 17.
15. Wendy Farley quote: Wendy Farley, *The Wounding and Healing of Desire: Weaving Heaven and Earth* (Louisville, KY: Westminster John Knox Press, 2005), 16.
16. Benjamin Zander quote: Benjamin Zander and Rosamund Zander, *The Art of Possibility* (Cambridge, MA: Harvard Business School Press, 2000), 9.
17. Mario Andretti quote: Chad Bonham, *Excellence: The Heart and Soul in Sports* (Ventura, CA: Regal, 2009), 36.
18. Wayne F. Dyer quote: Dan Spainhour, Coach *Yourself: A Motivational Guide for Coaches and Leaders* (Winston-Salem, NC: Educational Coaching and Business Communications, 2007), 99.
19. Napoleon Hill quote: Napoleon Hill, *Think and Grow Rich* (Bloomington, IN: AuthorHouse, 2007), 23.
20. Kahlil Gibran quote: Judith Wright, *The One Decision: Make the Single Choice That Will Lead to a Life of More* (New York: Penguin Books, 2006).
21. Life of Dave Thomas: http://www.advfn.com/p.php?pid=financials&symbol=NYSE %3AWEN.

22. Quoting a pit boss in Las Vegas who committed to stop smoking: http://www.stevepavlina.com/articles/cultivating-burning-desire.htm.
23. Nancy Gibb and the family dinner: Nancy Gibb, "The Magic of the Family Meal," *Time,* June 12, 2006, 51–52.
24. John Wooden quote on ability: Pat Williams and James Denney, *Coach Wooden: The 7 Principles that Shaped His Life and Will* (Grand Rapids, MI: Revell, 2011), 177.
25. William James quote: Will Buckingham, Douglas Burnham, Peter J. King, Clive Hill, Marcus Weeks, and John Marenbon, *The Philosophy Book* (New York: DK Publishing, 2010), 206.
26. Win Borden quote: William Safire and Leonard Safir, *Leadership: A Treasury of Great Quotations for Those Who Aspire to Lead* (New York, NY: Galahad Books, 2001), 83.
27. Story about car salesman sending cards: Thomas J. Peters, and Robert H. Waterman Jr., *In Search of Excellence: Lessons from America's Best Run Companies* (New York: Harper & Row, 1988), 157.
28. Big O Tires advertisement: www.bigotires.com.
29. Benjamin Franklin quote: David A. Adler, *B. Franklin, Printer* (New York: Holiday House, 2001), 47.
30. Quote about Sir Robert Shirley: http://www.leics.gov.uk/index/environment/countryside/walking/walking_through_time_staunton_harold.htmhttp://www.catholiceducation.org/articles/philosophy/ph0049.htm.
31. James Joyce quote: Tim Conley, *Joyce's Mistakes: Problems of Intention, Irony and Interpretation* (Toronto, Ontario: University of Toronto Press, 2003), 3.
32. Abraham Lincoln quote on doing the best: Jim Clemmer, *Growing the Distance: Timeless Principles for Personal, Career, and Family* (TCG Press, 1999), 74.

Guiding Constant 10

1. The No. 2857 bus on which Rosa Parks was riding before she was arrested (a GM "old-look" transit bus, serial number 1132), is now a museum exhibit at the Henry Ford Museum.
2. Rosa Parks story: http://www.npr.org/templates/story/story.php?storyId=4973548.
3. Helen Keller quote on vision: Dave Ramsey, *Entre Leadership: 20 Years of Practical Business Wisdom from the Trenches* (New York: Howard Books, 2011), 25.
4. Daniel Hudson Burnham quote: *Colliers* 49 (1912): 41.
5. Kennedy quote: Nathan Olson and Brian Bascle, *John F. Kennedy: American Visionary* (North Mankato, MN: Capstone Press, 2007), 31.
6. Kennedy quote on choosing to go to the moon: A. E. Cavazos-Gaither, *Gaither's Dictionary of Scientific Quotations* (New York, NY: Springer Science and Businesss Media, 2012), 2330.
7. Cartoon: http://www.cartoonstock.com/directory/c/company_goal.asp.
8. Kennedy speech about man on the moon: http://www.presentationmagazine.com/president-kennedy-speech-man-on-the-moon-7508.htm.
9. Kennedy speech about every scientist: http://history.nasa.gov/moondec.html.
10. "It's all about me" vision statement in a cartoon: http://www.cartoonstock.com/directory/m/mission.asp.

11. Antoine de Satin-Exupery quote: Tricia Armstrong, *The Whole-Brain Solution: Thinking Tools to Help Students Observe, Make Connections, and Solve Problems* (Markham, Ontario: Pembroke Publishers, 2003), 119.
12. Invictus: Martin Gardner, ed., Best Remembered Poems (Mineola, NY: Cover Publications, 1992), 48.
13. Leonardo da Vinci quote on curiosity: http://www.leonardoda-vinci.org/biography.html or http://en.wikipedia.org/wiki/Leonardo_da_Vinci.
14. Benvenuto Cellini quote about da Vinci: Eugene Müntz, *Sirrico* (London, 2011), 142.
15. Mahatma Gandhi personal vision quote: N. R. Phatak and Bha. Ga Kunte, *Source Material for a History of the Freedom Movement in India 3, Issue 1*, 604.
16. Benjamin Franklin personal vision quote: *The Autobiography of Benjamin Franklin* (New York, NY: P. F. Collier and Sons, 1945), 69.
17. Henry Ford quote: Mary Beth Norton, Carol Sheriff, David W. Blight, *A People and a Nation: A History of the United States Since 1865* (Boston, MA: Cengage, 2009), 633.
18. Apple company vision statement: Mac McKinley, *Marketing Alignment: Breakthrough Strategies for Growth and Profitability* (Bel Air, CA: Hats Off Books, 2002), 133.
19. Avon company vision statement: John Graham and Wendy Havlick, *Mission Statements: A Guide to Corporate and Non Profit Sectors* (Oxon, UK: Routledge, 1994), 84.
20. Chevron vision statement: http://www.chevron.com/?gclid=CKKRkfXhpa4CFakbQgod2W8FRg.
21. Delta Airlines vision statement: http://www.delta.com/index.jsp?Log=1&mkcpgn=SEzzzw1a&s_kwcid=TC|8489|delta%20airlines||S|e|7967368628&clickid=5b594d83-b425-7c29-8368-00006ac8c33b&tracking_id=284x269403.
22. Facebook vision statement: https://www.facebook.com/.
23. Google vision statement: http://www.google.com/.
24. Nike vision statement: http://store.nike.com/us/en_us/?cp=USNS_KW_0611081618&l=shop,home.
25. U.S. Air Force Honor Code: www.usafa.edu/Commandant/cwc/cwch.cfm
26. Southwest Airlines vision statement: www.southwest.com/html/about-southwest/index.html.
27. Walmart vision statement: www.walmartstores.com/AboutUs/8123.aspx.
28. Kenneth H. Blanchard quote: Kenneth H. Blanchard and Sheldon Bowles, *High Five!: The Magic of Working Together* (New York: Harper-Collins Books, 2001).
29. Bur Nanus quote on having an "achievable vision": John C. Maxwell, *Developing the Leaders Around You* (Nashville, TN: Thomas Nelson, Inc., 1995), 173.
30. Ralph Waldo Emerson quote: John C. Maxwell, *Today Matters: 12 Daily Practices to Guarantee Tomorrow's Success* (Boston, MA: Hachette Book Group, 2004).

Guiding Constant 11

1. Angela Wolf story: http://www.utexas.edu/features/2005/wolf/index.html.
2. Foster quote: John C. Maxwell, *Twenty-One Indispensable Qualities of a Leader* (Nashville, TN: Thomas Nelson, 1999), 34.
3. Drucker quote: Peter Drucker, *Peter Drucker on the Profession of Management* (Cambridge, MA: Harvard Business School Publishing, 2003), 72.

4. Shackelton ad for sailors: "Leadership in Crisis: Ernest Shackelton and Epic Voyage of the Endurance," *Harvard Business Review*, June 16, 2003, 7.
5. Thomas Edison quote: Anthony St. Peter, *The Greatest Quotations of All Time* (Bloomington, IN: Xlibris Corporation, 2010), 257.
6. Goethe quote: Larry Chang, comp., *Wisdom for the Soul: Five Millennia of Prescriptions for Spiritual Healing* (Washington, DC: Gnosophia Publishers, 2006), 634.
7. Ralph Waldo Emerson quote: John C. Maxwell, *Today Matters: 12 Daily Practices to Guarantee Tomorrow's Success* (Boston, MA: Hachette Book Group, 2004).
8. Jim Collins on humility and will: Jim Collins, *Good to Great* (New York: Harper Collins Business Essentials, 2001), 17.
9. *Apollo 13* quote: Jim Lovell and Jeffrey Kluger, *Apollo 13* (New York: First Mariner Books, 1994), 95.
10. Daniel H. Burnham quote: Dana Cluff, *The Provisional City: Los Angeles Stories of Architecture and Urbanism* (Cambridge, MA: Massachusetts Institute of Technology, 2002), 4.
11. Anwar Sadat quote: Michael Collopy and Walter Cronkite, *Architects of Peace: Visions of Hope in Words and Images* (Novato, CA: New World Library, 2002), 55.
12. Peter Drucker quote: Peter F. Drucker, *The Effective Executive* (New York: Harper and Row, 1967), 23.
13. Zig Ziglar quote on potential: www.great-inspirational-quotes.com/zig-ziglar-quotes.html.
14. Tylenol and James Burke: Alan Axelrod, *Profiles in Audacity: Great Decisions and How They Were Made* (New York: Sterling Publishing, 2006), 198.
15. Lao Tzu quote: Jennifer Speake, ed., *The Oxford Dictionary of Proverbs* (India: SPI Publisher Services, 2009).
16. Peter Drucker quote: Peter F. Drucker, *The Effective Executive* (New York: Harper Collins Business Essentials, 2002), 100.
17. Hawken quote: Michelle Bernhart and Francis J. Maher, *Introduction to Management: ISO 26000 in Practice—A User Guide* (Milwaukee, WI: Quality Press), 99.
18. Van Halen and brown M&Ms: Atul Gawande, *The Checklist Manifesto: How to Get Things Right* (London: Profile Books), 80.

Guiding Constant 12

1. Four chaplains on the *Dorcester*: *Congressional Record* 144, Pat. 1 (Washington, DC: U.S. Government Printing Office, January 27–February 13, 1998), 72.
2. Photos of the four chaplains: http://3.bp.blogspot.com/-LA4BANy114k/ToreVDeibQI/AAAAAAAACKk/LxkLcOCAQTo/s1600/4+chaplains.JPG.
3. Photo of the *Dorcester*: http://www.dvrbs.com/Monuments/Camden/MMM/MM-15-2.jpg.
4. Ghandhi quote: "Lost in Statistics," *Hidustan Times*, October 5, 2009, http://www.hindustantimes.com/News-Feed/RKPachauri/Lost-in-statistics/Article1-461560.aspx.
5. Einstein quote: Wayne W. Dyer, *Real Magic: Creating Miracles in Everyday Life* (New York: Harper Collins, 2001), 38.

6. Edison quote: http://www.quoteboards.org/quotes/by-speaker/?speaker=Sterling%20W.%20Sill.
7. Mandela quote: www.un.org/en/events/mandeladay/inhiswords.shtml.
8. Peter Senge quote: Peter M. Senge, *The Fifth Discipline: The Art and Practice of the Learning Organization* (New York: Doubleday/Random House, 2006), 131.
9. Robert Collier quote on riches: http://quotationsbook.com/quote/40772/.
10. Robert Collier quote on a mental blueprint: Robert Collier, *Riches Within Your Reach* (East Setauket, NY: Robert Collier Publications, 1947).
11. Einstein quote: John J. Stachel, *Einstein from B to Z* (Boston: Center for Einstein Studies, 2002), 74.
12. Michael McMahon story: Michael McMahon, "Business and Finance," *Financial Times,* January 29, 2004.
13. David Allen on what matters most: "Being More Productive: An Interview of David Allen and Tony Schwartz, *Harvard Business Review*, May, 2011, 86.

Guiding Constant 13

1. Luke Skywalker and Yoda: Len Sandler, *Becoming an Extraordinary Manager: The 5 Essentials of Success* (New York: AMACOM Books, 2008), 132.
2. Lincoln on commitment: Teresia LaRocque, "Commitment Transforms a Promise into Reality," Erickson Business Center, 2102, accessed at erickson.edu.
3. Robert Murray quote: John Ceserani, *Big Ideas: Putting the Zest into Creativity & Innovation at Work* (Norfolk, UK: Biddles, Ltd, 2003), 48.
4. Carl Jung quote: soldierny.com.
5. Dale Carnegie quote on criticism: Dale Carnegie, *How to Win Friends and Influence People* (New York: Simon & Schuster, 1936), 28–29.
6. "A great man" quote: Roy B. Zuck, *Speaker's Quote Book* (Grand Rapids, MI: Kregel Publications, 2009), 237.
7. "To know all is to forgive all": Germaine e Staël, *Corrine*, Book 18, Chapter 5.
8. The Reverend Will Bowen war on complaining: George Lewis, *NBC TODAY Show,* 2007, http://today.msnbc.msn.com.
9. "Responsibility finds a way": Steve Springer, Kimberly Persiani-Becker, and Michael Becker, *The Organized Teacher's Guide to Building Character* (New York: McGraw-Hill, 2010), 16.
10. "The person who complains about the way the ball bounces": www.leadershipnow.com/responsibilityquotes.html.
11. M. Scott Peck quote: John C. Maxwell, *The 360 Degree Leader: Development Your Influence from Anywhere in the Organization* (Nashville, TN: Thomas Nelson, 2011), 88.
12. William James quote: William James and Henry James, *The Letters of William James: Volumes 1–2* (Boston: Little, Brown, and Company, 1920), 249.
13. Roosevelt quote: M. David Dealy and Andrew R. Thomas, *Defining the Really Great Boss* (Westport, CT: Praeger Publishers, 2004), 36.
14. Lee Iacocca quote: Esmonde Holwaty, *Unleash the Billionaire Within: Learn the Mastermind Principle* (Bloomington, IN: AuthorHouse, 2011), 348.

15. Olin Miller quote: David Cottrell and Mark Layton, *175 Ways to Get More Done in Less Time!* (Dallas, TX: Cornerstone Leadership, 2000), 6.
16. "Man must cease attributing his problems to his environment": Alexander Brown, *Personal Responsibility: Why It Matters* (London: Continuum International Publishing Group, 2009), 20.